SOLUTIONS FOR
AN ENVIRONMENT
IN PERIL

Published in cooperation with the Center for American Places, Sante Fe, New Mexico, and Harrisonburg, Virginia

SOLUTIONS *for an* ENVIRONMENT *in* PERIL

Edited by ANTHONY B. WOLBARST

THE JOHNS HOPKINS UNIVERSITY PRESS
Baltimore and London

© 2001 The Johns Hopkins University Press
All rights reserved. Published 2001
Printed in the United States of America on acid-free paper
9 8 7 6 5 4 3 2 1

The Johns Hopkins University Press
2715 North Charles Street
Baltimore, Maryland 21218-4363
www.press.jhu.edu

LIBRARY OF CONGRESS CATALOGING-IN-PUBLICATION DATA

Solutions for an environment in peril / edited by
Anthony B. Wolbarst.
    p.   cm.
  Includes index.
  ISBN 0-8018-6594-8 (acid-free paper)
  1. Environmental degradation. 2. Environmental
protection. I. Wolbarst, Anthony B.
GE140.S65 2001
363.7—dc21   00-010429

A catalog record for this book is available from the British
Library.

IN MEMORY OF
JACQUES COUSTEAU AND CARL SAGAN

When we see the rich nations become richer and the poor nations become poorer while they grow in population, the number of time bombs that are planted around us — radioactivity, overpopulation, destruction of nonrenewable resources — is such that we're inclined to yell, "Stop it!" We have to do something, we have to put tremendous pressure on our governments to stop these things. Our indignation must be told. . . . We have to yell it.
— JACQUES COUSTEAU, 1988

Perhaps there is a kind of silver lining to these global environmental problems, because they are forcing us, willy-nilly, no matter how reluctant we may be, into a new kind of thinking. . . . Out of the environmental crises of our time should come, unless we are much more foolish than I think we are, a binding up of the nations and the generations, and the end of our long childhood.
— CARL SAGAN, 1989

CONTENTS

lightened leadership. Pointing out how essential a strong, fair, balanced, and confident EPA is to the country, he suggests that the agency should be a primary force for bringing about necessary change; one area, in particular, where it should assume a greater role is environmental education.

David Brower (deceased November 5, 2000), founder of Friends of the Earth and of the Earth Island Institute, asserted that the environmental movement, and the EPA's current activities, have only slowed the rate at which things are getting worse. He proposed that the EPA should take on the broader mantle of a U.S. Environmental Conservation, Preservation, and Restoration (CPR) Agency, with a renewed sense of passion and urgency. His perspectives on protecting the environment were those of one who fought the good fight for a long time, and often won.

AGENTS OF CHANGE: THE PRIVATE SECTOR

At different times a professor of medieval English literature, cattle rancher in Montana, and president of the Wilderness Society, Jon Roush is perhaps most of all a student of human behavior in organizations. He explores several examples of conflict between conservationists and businesses and their workers who felt threatened by the prospect of environmental protection. Echoing Tip O'Neill's observation that all politics is local, he discusses the factors (such as scientific analysis and public participation) that allow community-based conservation efforts built on negotiation to work, when others do not.

It is a priority of Bill Meadows, president of the Wilderness Society, to expand efforts to conserve and protect our national parks, forests, and other wilderness areas. He points out that one million square miles — a third of our country — are public lands, owned by *us,* yet much of that land is being logged, grazed, mined, and polluted in ways that are not wholly in the public interest. One important way to improve this situation would be for political leaders and land managers to adopt Aldo Leopold's "land ethic," to which so many Americans already subscribe.

Ted Turner challenges Western civilization's domination of the earth and anything that violates norms of decency toward our fellow humans or toward nature. His list of ten voluntary initiatives, beginning with "I promise to care for Planet Earth and all living things thereon, especially my fellow human beings," provides a framework for living in greater harmony with one another, and with our ecosphere.

DRIVERS OF CHANGE: POPULATION, RESOURCES, AND SUSTAINABILITY

Senator Gaylord Nelson, founder of Earth Day, contends that forging and maintaining a sustainable society is the primary challenge for this and all generations to come. Indeed, the continuing deterioration of the environment is a greater long-term threat to people than any other peril we face. The nations of the world are all pursuing the self-destructive course of fueling their economies by drawing down our natural capital — that is to say, by degrading and depleting our resource base — and noting it only on the income side of the ledger. Instead, it is critically important to develop a guiding and controlling environmental ethic to underlie the hard decisions we have to make in creating a sustainable society.

Garrett Hardin, author of *The Tragedy of the Commons* and *Living on a Lifeboat,* asserts that in a world with finite resources and only a limited capacity to absorb ecological abuse, our growing population and expanding technologies will cause the conditions of life to worsen considerably. This perspective is contrary to that of conventional economics, he argues, which is almost entirely free of ecological insights — so the displacement of conventional economics by ecological economics is essential. Hand in glove with that must come a great increase in the level of ecological awareness among the general populace.

Over the past thirty years, largely initiated by the publication of Paul Ehrlich's *Population Bomb,* the idea of a "population explosion" has engendered much concern about possible environmental dangers lying ahead. Ben Wattenberg, political commentator and host of public television's *Think Tank,* proposes that because of rapidly declining birthrates around the world, for the first time we must consider a future with a *de*populating planet. Recent data from the United Nations reveal that fertility rates in the developed nations are near or below replacement level, and fertility in the less developed nations is in decline — the implications of which are both reassuring and alarming. In considering *any* such projections, however, it should be born in mind that they are not predictions about the future but, rather, numerical exercises based on specific assumptions about trends in fertility and mortality — trends that may change over time, for a wide variety of reasons.

AGENTS OF CHANGE: GOVERNMENT

To many who are familiar with government, William Ruckelshaus, the EPA's first administrator, serves as a symbol of integrity and en-

have to put tremendous pressure on our governments to stop these things. Our indignation must be told. . . . We have to yell it."[1]

Cousteau began expressing his indignation soon after the end of World War II, as he came to realize how badly the once-vibrant Mediterranean Sea had deteriorated. A decade later, Rachel Carson's *Silent Spring* (1961) sounded the call that awoke millions to the damage that humankind is inflicting on the earth, and roused many citizens to action. Cousteau, Carson, and the other twentieth-century warriors in defense of our planet revived a noble tradition of both working to bring about essential changes and encouraging others to help make those changes. They saw clearly that *everyone* should learn of, and become involved in, the critical struggle to preserve our one and only ecological life-support system. It is largely because of their efforts, and of those who are carrying on the work today, that much of the public is coming to understand the growing threats we face and the need to confront them honestly and effectively.

The present volume is a compilation of the thoughts of some of the most influential men and women who continue to lead this vital effort. Like the contributors to the predecessor of this volume, *Environment in Peril*, they presented seminars at the EPA on what they currently consider to be the most important environmental problems — and their possible solutions.[2] Their talks are wide-ranging, most covering several different topics, but they have been grouped here into a few clusters arranged around the unifying, and inevitable, motif of change.

INTRODUCTION

Kathryn Fuller, president of the World Wildlife Fund, touches on all the major environmental problems — global warming, toxic pollution of the air, water, and soil, loss of wildlife habitats, and reduction of biodiversity — which she views as battles that must be won. A leader of constructive environmental activism, she stresses that the public must be made aware of why we all must "tread more lightly on the earth."

1. In A. B. Wolbarst, ed., *Environment in Peril* (Washington, D.C.: Smithsonian Institution Press, 1991).

2. The presentations occurred throughout the 1990s, but the speakers edited their pieces freely in 2000, and in some cases significantly revised them, so these writings represent their current thinking.

PREFACE

For many of us in the developed countries, the turn of the century has brought renewed hopes and promises of nearly boundless opportunity. Life just seems to keep on getting better. By any standards, we enjoy far greater comfort and security than anyone a few generations ago could even have imagined. And despite the famines, the plagues, and the insane brutalities that have always been with us, and apart from the miseries brought on by inequities in our political and economic systems, people are using inexpensive energy, plentiful natural resources, and technological wizardry to make things safer, easier, and more pleasurable. No wonder that many of the more fortunate among us greeted the new millennium with celebration and great expectations.

At the same time, however, one cannot help but also feel concern about pervasive indications that the earth, and all that dwell upon it, may be heading for serious environmental troubles. There is mounting evidence that climate change, the depletion of irreplaceable materials such as clean, fresh water and rich topsoil, the transformation of vast tracts of forest into wastelands, the eradication of countless thousands of species of animals and plants (some of which might have been of extraordinary medical value to humankind), and other adverse processes are all occurring throughout the world — no longer just locally — and at an ever-accelerating pace. As many have argued, life is indeed in the balance: Now, for the first time, humans have the numbers and the industrial and agricultural presence to disrupt that balance severely, and on a global scale.

When he spoke at the EPA in 1988, Jacques Cousteau made his concerns about the future clear: "When we see the rich nations become richer and the poor nations become poorer while they grow in population, the number of time bombs that are planted around us — radioactivity, overpopulation, destruction of nonrenewable resources — is such that we're inclined to yell, 'Stop it!' We have to do something, we

INCENTIVES FOR CHANGE: ENGAGING THE
BUSINESS COMMUNITY

Thomas E. Lovejoy, a Smithsonian scientist serving as chief biodiversity adviser to the World Bank and founder of the TV program *Nature,* sees that biodiversity is constantly under attack from land development, lumbering, and so on, and argues for a halt to the onslaught on species that is doing away with a hundred of them each day. His message to the business community is to not worry about the moral and aesthetic arguments, for the moment, but rather to focus intelligently on profits: The area of overlap of biodiversity and biotechnology, if properly pursued, is a potential source of great wealth.

Amory Lovins, cofounder and co-CEO of Rocky Mountain Institute, discusses business and design opportunities that are environmentally and socially restorative while enhancing profit and competitive advantage. Powerful new technologies and design methods, emphasizing whole-system integration, can harness resources far more productively, providing much better services and products at lower costs. Such approaches can reduce or eliminate many problems of energy usage, manufacturing, transportation, water distribution, agriculture, and so forth, at a profit, and even turn some obstacles into business opportunities without creating new problems in the process.

Fred Smith, Jr., founder and president of the conservative Competitive Enterprise Institute, describes the ecological and economic benefits of expanding the role of free-market institutions — private property rights, common law liability rules and contracts — in the environmental arena, expressly to nurture and protect valuable natural resources. He discusses situations where voluntary arrangements have succeeded in preserving and even enhancing an ecological heritage: When Tanzanian African villagers came to own the nearby herds of elephants, for example, they acted effectively to protect these valuable tourist attractions (and sources of potentially legal ivory) from poachers — and the herds are actually increasing in size there.

TOOLS FOR MANAGING CHANGE: MATHEMATICAL MODELS,
RISK ANALYSIS, AND COMMUNICATION

Jerry Mahlman, director of NOAA's Geophysical Fluid Dynamics Laboratory and professor of atmospheric science at Princeton University, provides a succinct overview of the evidence (from a wide variety of measurements and from climate change modeling) that leads nearly all scientists to conclude that human activity is probably affecting the earth's climate and causing it to change far more radically and rapidly than at any time since the extinction of the dinosaurs sixty-five million years ago. This is not just an interesting academic exercise; it would appear that while some people and species may benefit from the changes, life may well become far more difficult for the vast majority of us.

As ranking minority member (and past chairman) of the U.S. Senate Environment and Public Works Committee, Senator Max Baucus has long been a wise and effective supporter of environmental causes. Focusing on the crafting of environmental legislation, he discusses a powerful prioritization tool, risk analysis/management, that can help determine the size of a given problem, its seriousness, compared to other problems, what to do about it, and how to educate the public about it.

In discussing the last of those points, professors Vincent Covello and Peter Sandman describe the principal activities of risk communication — alerting people to real hazards and reducing their fears and outrage concerning perceived, but unreal, risks. This young discipline can greatly help any environmental organization in carrying out its missions effectively, and it plays a much larger role in the messages that affect the public than most people realize.

HOPE

Jane Goodall describes her groundbreaking research on the wild chimpanzees of Gombe and her heartbreaking realization that the chimpanzees risk extinction. Her passion is to stir us to preserve as much of what remains as possible. The odds may not be exceedingly favorable, but as long as people of courage and dedication are willing to take action, as exemplified by Goodall's own life, there is still cause for hope.

The messages of the contributors to this volume differ, but there are some important common themes. Perhaps the loudest and clearest of them is that environmental degradation over the next century or so will be global in nature — caused by the activities of people in North and South America, Europe, Africa, and Asia alike, and affecting lives in *all* of those places. The consequences of rapid and significant changes in the environment, moreover, are likely to be radically disruptive, and probably harmful, to the vast majority of our descendants.

We would be wise, therefore, to expand our efforts to understand the physical, biological, and societal forces for change that underlie the environmental difficulties we face. Such an understanding is essential if we are to plan intelligently for their likely economic, social, and public health consequences. And we clearly should do more to inform and teach many others the vitally important truths that we are uncovering. Only with a much wider and deeper awareness of the seriousness of the dangers ahead can we muster the resources and the political determination to confront them and diminish their impact.

Finally, we must come to accept that these are not someone else's problems — that they are caused by, and belong to, all of us. A greenhouse gas molecule is no respecter of national or cultural boundaries, regardless of its place of origin, and once released, it stays aloft for hundreds or thousands of years. So we can help ourselves, and our children and grandchildren, only by working with others around the world, who are concerned about *their* children and grandchildren, in addressing the environmental problems we have in common. Fortunately, if we act together and with wisdom and commitment, we do have the capability, and hopefully the time, to deal effectively with them and overcome them. Addressing the EPA a decade ago, Carl Sagan expressed this idea beautifully: "Perhaps there is a kind of silver lining to these global environmental problems, because they are forcing us, willy-nilly, no matter how reluctant we may be, into a new kind of thinking. . . . Out of the environmental crises of our time should come, unless we are much more foolish than I think we are, a binding up of the nations and the generations, and the end of our long childhood."[3]

3. In A. B. Wolbarst, ed., *Environment in Peril* (Washington, D.C.: Smithsonian Institution Press, 1991).

ACKNOWLEDGMENTS

This book is based on an ongoing series of seminars hosted by the U.S. Environmental Protection Agency. Our distinguished speakers are asked to convey to the management and staff of the EPA the most important messages that we should hear on general issues having to do with the environment and public health. The addresses they have delivered, in response, represent a variety of significant, thought-provoking, and responsible viewpoints and demand our most careful consideration. Although the presentations occurred throughout the 1990s, the speakers freely edited their pieces in 2000 and in some cases significantly revised them, so these writings represent their current thinking.

We at the EPA wish to express our deepest appreciation to our speakers. Receiving no honoraria or even travel support, they have taken precious time out of their busy schedules to prepare, present, and update their talks. Their reward, perhaps, is the knowledge that the two volumes *Environment In Peril* and *Solutions for an Environment in Peril,* may help spur on people everywhere in their efforts to create and maintain a world that is environmentally safe, habitable, and pleasing for us all.

The operation of the seminar series and the preparation of the book have involved the energy and ideas of many individuals. Our thanks to Steven Richard of the Arena Stage and George F. Thompson and Randall B. Jones of the Center for American Places, to Carol Ehrlich and Linda Forlifer, and to Jack Anderson, Paul Bubbosh, Kathy Hogan, Dana Murphy, Glen Nathan, Renelle Rae, Clare Shea, Nena Shaw, John Smegal, Brian Taylor, and others at the EPA and in the offices of the speakers who helped to make it all work smoothly.

Part I　　　INTRODUCTION

Chapter 1   THE CLIMATE FOR
ENVIRONMENTALISM

Principles for the New Millennium

KATHRYN S.   I believe very strongly that the United States has an
FULLER   enormous opportunity to provide global leadership
                on environmental issues in the decades ahead. If we
succeed in meeting our domestic challenges concerning the environment
while also looking for ways to contribute in the broader global arena,
this country can become exemplary in environmental affairs.

The United States has long been a beacon of political freedom and
economic strength for countless people around the world. We became
aware of the pollution consequent to our affluence long before many
other nations, moreover, and took action before them. Today, we can be
at the forefront of the next generation of environmental progress by
learning how to prevent pollution rather than containerizing it and ship-
ping it somewhere else, and by applying technology to use our natural
resources far more productively.

Both the challenges and opportunities I see are on a global scale.
These really are tremendously heady times for those of us involved in
conservation. Opinion polls show that the U.S. public is overwhelmingly
committed to environmental action, even to the point of favoring higher
taxes and accepting other economic costs for environmental protection.

The U.S. public is acting on those convictions. I see that in the growth
of World Wildlife Fund, as well as in diverse environmental organizations around the country. We had about 170,000 members in 1985; now,
at the beginning of the millennium, it is more than a million. This continuing expansion is a reflection of the enormous concern felt by the
American public in all corners of this country. Remarkably, our rate of
growth here in the United States is dwarfed by the growth of some of our
affiliates in Europe and other parts of the world.

Businesses have responded to consumer demands for dolphin-safe
tuna, recyclable containers, and a host of other green products. Political
leaders have become engaged as well. Financial resources committed to

some aspects of environmental protection are expanding, even during a period when other resource allocations are being cut.

But we still have enormous challenges to face. First, while we have made great progress over the past few decades in many areas, we have been staying in place in others — or even losing ground — as the pace of change has accelerated around the world. While each new American car is cleaner than any model on the road twenty years ago, for example, the number of cars and the total miles people drive are overwhelming our goals for pollution control. Seen in that light, the Clean Air Act Amendments do not reflect total success.

We seem perpetually unable to get on top of urban ozone problems, acid precipitation, or airborne toxic chemicals — problems that extend beyond local or even regional boundaries. These, of course, are not problems just in the United States. I was in Thailand a while ago and was astonished at the traffic heading into the city from the airport. The sheer volume would stun anybody, even someone who lived in Los Angeles. With jobs scarce in the countryside, people are pouring into Bangkok looking for work. The head of our project office there said that estimates indicate that if all the cars in Bangkok were placed end to end, they would exceed the length of road surface.

With strong economic growth has come steady encroachment on critical habitats. Half of our own country's national endowment of wetlands has been lost, and half a million acres of what remains are being consumed each year. In developing nations, wholesale destruction of tropical rain forests is occurring on a truly horrifying scale that could only be dimly imagined in 1970. The tropical forest continues to be cut and burned at an annual rate of 1 percent — an acre per second.

We are just beginning to contend with global problems that were unknown when environmentalism took its first steps. Certainly, the prospect of global warming and climate change ranks at the top of these issues. So does the rapid dispersion of man-made chemicals throughout the ecosphere, with unknown effects. What all this means is that the current interest in and enthusiasm for things environmental are not motivated solely by a sense of satisfaction over what we have accomplished. Instead, we recognize that we have won some battles but are still losing the war. We are driven by the magnitude and urgency of the challenges we face.

We acknowledge the unarguable significance of human population numbers to any successful efforts to sustain the ecological health of the planet and to improve the well-being of the people and other living things that inhabit it. Clearly, if the number of people continues to increase at current rates, all the parks and local jobs we create will not make much of a difference. But the population question, I think, cannot be addressed solely head-on either. We need to consider the economic side of the issue — helping to improve the economic conditions of people in order to deal with the matter of our growing numbers.

This leads to my second point. It is essential that we show progress, for a number of reasons. We cannot afford another decade or two of action that falls short of our goals. In a tropical forest, to cite E. O. Wilson of Harvard, deforestation costs us four thousand to six thousand species a year, an extinction rate that is ten thousand times greater than the naturally occurring background extinction rate prior to the appearance of human beings. Likewise, in assessing the prospects for climate change, the UN's International Panel on Climate Change (IPCC) projected in 1995 that increasing amounts of man-made greenhouse gases in the atmosphere will most likely cause a 1–3.5° Celsius (2–6° Fahrenheit) climb in Earth's average surface temperature over the next fifty to one hundred years [even higher increases are projected in the 2001 report — editor]. This would result in disruptions unprecedented in human history. The increase may (or may not) be less than the estimated 5° increase in temperature that has occurred since the peak of the last Ice Age, but it would take effect much more rapidly.

In this country, failure to control the emission of greenhouse gases would mean allowing conditions that cause ill health, shorten lives, and impose annual costs estimated at tens of billions of dollars to persist, if not worsen considerably. The political imperative to succeed is also strong. We would do well, I think, to remember that public opinion is a fragile and fickle commodity. Our citizens will want a tangible return on their environmental investments, in terms of cleaner, healthier air and water. If government measures to deal with toxic substances, one of the public's deepest environmental concerns, cannot do the job, people will want to know why, and at that point, opposing interests will attempt to shape the debate.

The broader message from all this is that if environmental programs do not deliver the goods, support could certainly weaken, as it has for so many other government initiatives when what had been achieved fell notably short of what was promised. Of course, if we have a recession, then all bets are off. As a nation, we find ourselves unable to pay for all the things we want, even after a long period of vigorous economic growth. The terms of the debate will be very different, and probably much less pleasant, if the available resources dramatically shrink.

Our environmental priorities are important. But our nation has other pressing priorities as well: education, drugs, healthcare, and so on. If anything jeopardizes the American sense of prosperity and peace, those priorities could shove the environmental agenda aside. In managing my organization, I am delighted to see new resources pouring in so that we can do more, in more places, and pursue our own set of priorities. But I am not banking on having those resources available, or growing at the current rate, forever.

To these not very cheerful comments, let me add a third: we have not, so far, really managed to define what we mean by "environment." Now, that may sound trivial, but I do not think it is. Is our concern for the environment driven by opposition to pollution and fear that chemicals harm human health? Or is it grounded in the American tradition of conservation and concern for natural places and open spaces? Or is it motivated by an interest in using resources more efficiently? Or is it prompted by some ethical sense that it is not right for humans to tread so heavily on their environment?

Of course, "environment" implies some or all of those things, but we have not yet been able to sort out the different elements completely. For that reason, we cannot very well define what environmental policy ought to be, nor can we judge how effective it is. And it certainly weakens our case when we appeal to the public for necessary environmentally sound changes in behavior that can occur only on an individual basis. Even now, although people profess support for environmentalism in record numbers, their actions are often at odds with what they profess.

At a time of rising concern about toxic substances, Americans have made pesticide and herbicide treatment for their lawns a growth industry, as if government regulations alone address every aspect of preventing toxic pollution. Anyone who buys a car is free to choose an energy-efficient model, yet all the trends in recent years run in the opposite direction. For all the genuine enthusiasm for recycled products, we have a long way to go if we wish to change consumer behavior, to make it easier for people to make those choices.

We are also vulnerable to fuzzy definitions of what environmentalism really is. We are prey for any politician who thinks that he or she can claim to be "green" just by wearing a down vest and spouting rhetoric.

For all these reasons, environmental professionals need to have a sense of direction so we can set goals that the public can understand and endorse. The challenges we face are enormously serious and complex, and the current interest in the environment is an opportunity we really cannot afford to squander. In my organization, we feel that we have arrived at an intellectually constructive set of principles to guide our actions. First, though, a bit of background. The Conservation Foundation was established nearly five decades ago and has built a solid reputation for independent policy analysis on many important issues: groundwater protection, wetlands conservation, nonpoint sources of water pollution, policy for national parks, risk assessment, integrated management of pollutants, and so forth. World Wildlife Fund-U.S. was created in 1961. From the outset, it has focused on protecting endangered species and their habitats, as well as other scientifically valuable habitats, principally through field programs in Latin America, Africa, and Asia. The two organizations merged in 1990. Our programs create parks and reserves, train local managers, build capabilities, and support economic development practices that are compatible with maintaining the natural resource base.

Sketched in this way, the EPA and World Wildlife Fund seem quite different — on the one hand, a policy research shop focusing mostly on domestic pollution and conservation issues, and, on the other, a nature preservation group focusing on direct delivery of field services outside the United States. But, in fact, as the world has changed and our view of it as well, these two approaches have begun to converge, in a concerted way.

Here is an illustration of that. My ultimate destination on the trip that got me stuck in traffic in Bangkok was Bhutan, truly a remarkable place. Two-thirds of it is still forested, reflecting the protection, inherent in the Buddhist ethic, of what is still nearly impenetrable Himalayan frontier in many places. Yet when I followed the footsteps of the not more than a thousand tourists a year who trek in the Himalayas in Bhutan, I found trails littered with discarded juice packs — the same sort that we find at the supermarket and put in children's lunch boxes. So we see that the effects of our innovation in the United States are a problem in a Bhutanese setting where, already, people are discovering that they need to prevent pollution and deal with recycling. More broadly, World Wildlife Fund has been remarkably successful in establishing parks and reserves for many critical habitats in the tropical rain forests of Latin America. But not far outside these parks and reserves are economies that increasingly produce toxic waste, airborne pollution, and a growing demand for electricity — all consequences we associate with industrialized societies, and all of them oblivious to park boundaries drawn on a map. In many instances, the specific victories we have won in protecting a rare ecosystem can be quickly undone by these new threats. And so to protect nature, we want to bring broader public policy skills to bear on pollution and other problems of thoughtless growth.

Conversely, the health of nature has much to tell us about pollution and human health. When World Wildlife Fund and the Conservation Foundation undertook a comprehensive study of the Great Lakes ecosystem, we found some very disturbing things. For example, Lake Superior, the least industrialized of all the lakes, has serious problems from toxic contaminants blown in from cities and farms that are hundreds, sometimes a thousand, miles away. The Great Lakes fish, bird, and other species exhibit gross developmental defects, raising very serious and legitimate concerns about human effects from exposure to the same substances. In other words, we are learning that the quality of natural systems and the quality of human life, the conservation and pollution strains of environmentalism, if you will, are far more intimately related than we ever knew. If theories about global warming and climate change are borne out, of course, we will learn to our dismay that these relationships are even more extensive than we ever imagined.

World Wildlife Fund consists of a network of organizations — twenty-seven of them worldwide — sharing a common mission. That common purpose is to save the abundance and diversity of plant and animal life on Earth by conserving the most important harbors of biodiversity, changing global patterns of resource use that threaten biodiversity, and stopping and reversing the decline of key threatened species.

Now, that is a big mission — trying to save life on Earth — but I think that these are goals that should drive the EPA's work, too. We are dealing, after all, not just with nature, or with the human species in isolation, but with nature and humankind as they influence each other. We watch and listen to nature, in search of new crop species and valuable medicines, and also to detect warnings that the air and water have become unfit or that a chemical is toxic. In moving to clean the air with scrubbers, we do not want to run the risk of poisoning the land. In trying to isolate waste in landfills, we have to monitor and safeguard the water. We interact continuously with nature, within and across environmental media. Our programs and policies must be designed broadly enough so that they take this interaction into account and thereby ultimately focus on preventing pollution.

But, for all the visible ill effects we associate with economic growth, environmental protection depends on raising standards of living around the world. Whatever the benefits to nature, human health, and the economy from cleaning up or preventing pollution, there are up-front costs as well—the costs of building more efficient factories, retrofitting existing ones, producing and purchasing cleaner cars, designing refrigerators that operate without chlorofluorocarbons (CFCs), and so on. A vigorous economy helps businesses and consumers pay for those investments and speeds up the vital process of replacing our existing capital stock with newer, more benign processes and equipment. As we begin to price natural resources more realistically, rising incomes and productivity should help pay for the technology that will let us be far more sparing in their use. Our policies must favor this sort of investment, and we must strive to remove the obstacles that retard the modernization of our industrial infrastructure.

The message is even clearer, and more compelling, in Eastern Europe. What we saw as the Iron Curtain receded was really no less than an environmental hellhole—a huge zone of acid blast in East Germany, Poland, and Czechoslovakia, with poisoned croplands and sterile rivers, and people forced to stay indoors and underground to escape being choked by the toxic air. Here, the answer is, unmistakably, capital investment and economic reform to replace outdated, environmentally disastrous production systems on a national scale. These are people who can benefit from emulating our successes here in the United States—and understanding our failures as well.

In the developing world, too, rising incomes are part of the solution. We work hard to stem the fires in the Amazon and Indonesia and to reverse the misguided policies that encourage the continued destruction of the forests—the subsidies and tax incentives that prompt corporations to clear land for uneconomic farms and cattle ranches in Brazil, for example. Much of the destruction is caused by desperately poor people who are struggling to find enough food each day and build a rudimentary shelter for their families. Driven by hunger, and often out of ignorance as well, they do not realize that the soil will be exhausted in a season or two and that they are wasting priceless resources. These are people with nothing like our education and technical skills, and they have everything to gain from our sharing what we have learned here.

What does that mean? It means helping to provide technical information and resources to these people on how to create small, local sawmills, roads so that they can reach markets, banks so they can get credit for seed and fertilizer—in short, basic education and the means to put it into practice. Those are the kinds of changes that will transform people from the miners of a resource into its stewards.

This brings me to another message, one that is a core principle for my organization: the importance of acting locally, with sensitivity to the needs and abilities of diverse people and different cultures. It was in the Chitwan National Park in Nepal that I first confronted, personally, the dilemma faced by people living in and around nature reserves. It is an extraordinary place in the lowlands just above India, a subtropical forested area that supports a variety of spectacular wildlife — among them rhinos, tigers, and sloth bears, all of which are endangered as a result of human hunting as well as habitat loss. At the same time, these dangerous wildlife species present serious risks to the lives of the villagers, who come into the park to cut thatch for roofs and fuel. Their dilemma is not one you can resolve simply by declaring a national policy to protect wildlife and then enacting legislation to enforce it.

In the same way, while we at World Wildlife Fund have led a vigorous effort to ban the international trade in ivory, we also recognized that declaring elephants a protected species and prohibiting the ivory trade is not, in and of itself, an answer to the problem. The people who live next to, around, and among elephants, which are enormously destructive animals, need viable opportunities to feed themselves, whether through environmentally sound tourism or environmentally controlled hunting schemes.

In short, we have to find ways to make wildlife conservation and natural resource conservation produce direct economic benefits for local people. This is a battle that must be won on a local level, village by village, a thousand times over. Throughout the Amazon, permanent progress will be achieved in the same way. A colleague at World Wildlife Fund who oversees the projects we design to look for innovative ways to conserve wildlife, and at the same time to meet the economic needs of local people, says that the problems are enormous, but they will not be solved by enormous projects.

That advice could apply to our approach in Eastern Europe, too. For the industrial pollution problems there, the American control technologies, regulatory approaches, and standards may not be wholly appropriate. We need to be sure that we offer our expertise and assistance, but that we let local processes and choices play out as well.

Here at home, too, we are beginning to become more sensitive to regional differences and attitudes. Building bridges across cultures and cooperation among people will matter a great deal as we come to depend increasingly on the environmental effects of state and local decisions on transportation, utilities, and land use. Those decisions will have a tremendous impact on lowering energy consumption, reducing the generation of air and water pollutants, and habitat preservation — from the most local of issues to our attempts to deal with climate change on a global scale.

Nowhere in our mission at World Wildlife Fund do we focus on a specific country or region. We believe that these principles apply worldwide, and we seek to act on the highest priority problems and the highest priority areas where we have, or can create, the opportunity and capability to make a difference. So I would urge the EPA to think very broadly about the scope of its mission. Much of the agency's work is necessarily within U.S. borders. The EPA is charged with protecting and enhancing environmental quality in the United States. On the one hand, the local strategies it devises to prevent pollution and increase the efficiency with which we use energy and other natural resources can begin to resonate worldwide. On the other, if the EPA is charged with devising a cost-effective strategy to reduce the release of greenhouse gases, then, dollar for dollar, you might find the best return on investment in Romania or the Amazon, rather than in the coal-burning power plants along the Ohio River.

This point brings me back to what I said before: the United States, through what is accomplished at the EPA, is in a remarkable position to establish environmental models for other countries and to influence behavior worldwide. Doing so obviously depends on a realistic assessment of this country's enormous resources and knowledge and, in addition, on a commitment to a vision of what we can and should do. For World Wildlife Fund, our goals are clear: Protect biological diversity, promote sustainable development, and prevent pollution. In attempting to meet those goals, we intend to address the relationship between nature and humankind in a broad way, not by artificially isolating one from the other. In doing so, we serve as advocates for the sensitive, sustainable use of resources. Among the developing nations, that is the pathway out of the ignorance and poverty that press them into destroying the natural resources they depend on. Among industrial countries, that kind of economic activity pays for environmental quality and new processes that make use of natural resources far more productively.

While we are eager to craft environmentally sound national policies and to reverse those that are destructive, we are also sensitive to local differences. We believe in making a difference on the ground — in the villages and communities where people live and work. We see pressing needs worldwide. In the years ahead, many of these strategies, I think, can apply to the EPA's work — seeing the environment whole and encouraging effective action, not only in Washington but throughout our country and around the globe. Those are among the EPA's very greatest challenges.

Environmentalism has begun to come of age in America and around the world. It is up to us to bring environmental sensitivity and knowledge to maturity throughout our society. If the EPA, in particular, can succeed in its role, and I think it can, then the agency has a superb opportunity to deliver on one of the most far-reaching, urgent responsibilities ever assigned to a group of people in public service. And that is the surest way to win public support for the environmental policies and practices that we have the urgent responsibility to create together.

Part II   DRIVERS OF CHANGE

*Population, Resources, and
Sustainability*

Chapter 2   ENVIRONMENT, POPULATION,

SUSTAINABLE DEVELOPMENT

Where Do We Go from Here?

GAYLORD A.
NELSON

As a society, we expend a great deal of time and energy exploring and debating weighty issues like war and peace, economics, crime on the streets, poverty, human rights, education, religion, international relations, healthcare, jobs, and many more, as we should: These are important matters, and they deserve our constant attention.

Having acknowledged that, however, I would like to focus on something far more important than these issues, which capture the front page in the press and command the daily attention of Congress and the public. There is a growing recognition and understanding that human activity on the planet is dangerously compromising the world resource base, that we are, in fact, seriously degrading those ecosystems that sustain all species — including us. The reality is that no war, revolution, or peril of any kind measures up in importance to the threat of continued environmental deterioration.

At this point in history, no nation has managed, either by design or accident, to evolve into a sustainable society, which can be described as one that meets the needs of the present without compromising the ability of future generations to meet their own needs. We are all pursuing a self-destructive course of fueling our economies by consuming our capital — that is to say, by degrading and depleting our resource base — and counting it on the income side of the ledger. That, obviously, is not a sustainable situation over the long term.

Forging and maintaining a sustainable society is *the* critical challenge for this and all generations to come. In responding to that challenge, population will be one of the key factors in determining whether we succeed or fail. By almost any measure, the population of the world exceeds the carrying capacity of the planet. That constitutes a peril.

What is not yet generally recognized is that along with most of the rest of the world, the United States is also overpopulated and in the process of consuming capital resources at an ever-increasing rate to satisfy current consumption demands. The reality is that while the population is booming here and around the world, the resource base that sustains the economy is rapidly dwindling. It is not just a problem in faraway lands; it is an urgent problem here at home right now.

Fortunately, we are finally coming to understand that the wealth of the nation resides, in fact, in its air, water, soil, forests, minerals, rivers, lakes, oceans, scenic beauty, wildlife habitats, and biodiversity. Take this resource base away and all that is left is a wasteland. The question at hand is this — will we use this understanding to preserve a friendly habitat for plants and animals in the world of nature? Or will we fail to overcome one of the major political obstacles to environmental progress, the mistaken belief that protecting the environment threatens jobs? We frequently hear political and business leaders, economists, and others who should know better vacuously asserting that they "are for the environment if it doesn't cost jobs." That discloses a failure to understand that jobs *are* inextricably tied to the environment and totally dependent upon it.

I have a friend whose guiding theology for all political matters is the editorial page of the *Wall Street Journal*. He could never quite understand that there is a direct and beneficial connection between a healthy environment and a prosperous economy until I described the connection in the jargon of his business world. I said to him, "Look at it this way and the connection becomes obvious. It is this: The economy is a wholly owned subsidiary of the environment. All economic activity is dependent upon that environment with its underlying resource base. When the environment is finally forced to file for bankruptcy under Chapter 11 because its resource base has been polluted, degraded, dissipated, and irretrievably compromised, then the economy goes into bankruptcy along with it, because the economy is just a subset within the ecological system." Then my friend got it.

When experts are asked to list the most critical environmental problems, they are practically unanimous in ranking exponential population growth at the top of the list. This is so because it is clear that every addition beyond some optimum level adversely affects the quality of life and the sustainability of the resource base. In my view, however, the absence of a guiding and controlling environmental ethic in our culture is at least as important a factor as population growth. Such an ethic is evolving, but until we become a society truly guided by such an ethic, we will not make those hard decisions necessary to forge a sustainable society.

In a dramatic and sobering joint statement in 1992, the United States

National Academy of Sciences and the Royal Society of London, two of the world's leading scientific bodies, addressed the state of the planet in the following words: "If current predictions of population growth prove accurate and patterns of human activity on the planet remain unchanged, science and technology may not be able to prevent either irreversible degradation of the environment or continued poverty for much of the world. . . . The future of our planet is in the balance. Sustainable development can be achieved, but only if irreversible degradation of the environment can be halted in time. The next 30 years may be crucial."

Is there any other single issue even a fraction as important as this? Yet, the leaders of both political parties went through the last campaign in near silence about sustainability and the disastrous consequences of continued exponential population growth.

The first step in the process of addressing the urgent population question is to institute a national dialogue. Important issues involving emotionally laden political controversy, as population matters do, can only come to resolution after a national dialogue and a political consensus of some kind.

In his book *The Diversity of Life,* which appeared in 1992, two-time Pulitzer Prize winner E. O. Wilson of Harvard says:

> The time has come to speak more openly of a population policy. By this I mean not just capping the growth when the population hits the wall, as in India and China, but a policy based on a rational solution of this problem: what, in the judgment of its informed citizenry, is the optimal population. . . . The goal of an optimal population will require addressing, for the first time, the full range of processes that lock together the economy and the environment, the national interest and the global commons, the welfare of the present generation with that of future generations. The matter should be aired not only in think tanks but in public debate. (P. 329)

Wilson's admonition that it is time to speak "more openly of a population policy" is right on target, as it would have been over a half century earlier in 1940 when our nation's population registered at a comparatively modest 132 million. Each decade, Wilson's admonition becomes more urgent. Since 1940, the U.S. population has roughly doubled and, at the current rate, will double again to a total of about 520 million two or three decades past midcentury — some seventy or eighty years from now.

In 1972, the President's Commission on Population Growth and the

American Future, headed by John D. Rockefeller III, published an important five-volume report. The bottom-line conclusion was that the commission could not identify a single value in American life that would be enhanced by any further population growth. In addition, the report recommended that we move vigorously to stabilize our population, then 200 million, as rapidly as possible. Seventy million more people and nearly thirty years later, we have yet to begin a serious discussion of the critical issues raised by the commission. The reason is obvious enough. Stabilizing our population will require a significant reduction in the immigration rate. That, it seems, is sufficiently controversial to bar an open discussion of continued population growth.

If the Congress, the president, the press, and the public cannot engage in a rational discussion of the most meaningful challenges we face as a society, what does that say? Does not that tell us our system has contrived somehow to become irrelevant to the major issues of our time? How else can we explain the political frenzy that seems, every election campaign, to revolve around matters of relatively minor importance such as flag burning, prayer in the schools, and congressional term limits, while the seminal issues of our time, population and sustainability, are met only with silence. If the Founding Fathers had been so myopic in their vision of the future and so cravenly skittish about controversy, there would have been no Constitution and no United States.

In the debate over population, the country seems to divide roughly into three groups: those who are alarmed by the prospect of continued exponential population growth, those who are alarmed that the first group is alarmed, and those who could care less about any of the alarms. In fact, exponential population growth is something to be alarmed about. While an annual population growth rate of 1 or 2 percent looks small, over the long term its effects are dramatic, indeed. A 1 percent annual growth rate will double the population in 70 years; a 2 percent rate will double it in 35 years; a 3 percent rate will double it in 23 plus years. The current U.S. growth rate is 1.1 percent per year. At that rate, the U.S. population will double in 63 years.

When anatomically modern human beings first walked the earth, some one hundred thousand to fifty thousand years ago, give or take a bit, there were perhaps several hundred thousand of us, according to Carl Haub of the Population Reference Bureau in Washington, D.C. With the first development of agriculture and fixed communities some ten thousand years ago, the number had grown to five to ten million. At the time of Christ, there were several hundred million people, and it was

TABLE 2.1 *Growth of Human Population over Time*

Year	World Population
−50,000	a few hundred thousand
−10,000	5–10 million
0	a few hundred million
1800	1 billion
1930	2 billion
1960	3 billion
1975	4 billion
1987	5 billion
1999	6 billion

Source: Population Division, United Nations, *World Population Prospects: The 1998 Revision* (New York: United Nations, 1999).

Note: Pre-1825 numbers from personal communication with Carl Haub of the Population Reference Bureau, Washington, D.C.

not until 1825, still early in the Industrial Revolution, that we hit the one billion mark. But the next billion took only a century, and the most recent increment of a billion, which we proudly noted in 1999, required but a dozen years.

Those who are alarmed about world population are strangely complacent about the U.S. population. They think population is a problem in China, India, Africa, and elsewhere, but not in the United States. The facts tell a different story. Arguably, the optimal population level for the United States was reached before we entered World War II, when it was about half of its current value of 270 million. Clearly, that growth has compromised the quality of our environment.

It is obvious that once an optimal population level is reached, all additions tend to have a negative quality-of-life impact on the environment. These effects include impingement on freedom of movement and action caused by population pressures and further aggravated by the necessary intervention of government controls and regulations; overcrowding in our streets, parks, and open spaces; loss of scenic beauty and wildlife habitat; pollution of our rivers, lakes, ocean estuaries, and air — as well as noise pollution and much more. Those treasured freedoms, opportunities, privileges, and enjoyments, which have been assumed to be a part of our environmental inheritance, will continue to be compromised or lost as population pressures increase.

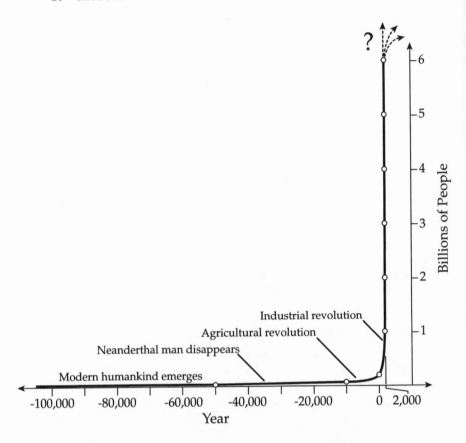

What would be the consequences of a further doubling of the current U.S. population? The ramifications are almost endless. Many aspects of our lives will suffer significant erosion of quality. Indeed, I can think of no aspect that will be enhanced.

With twice as many people by 2075 or so, it will probably be necessary to roughly double the total U.S. infrastructure accumulated over two hundred years in a little more than sixty years. Here are a few examples:

— There will be twice as many cars, trucks, planes, airports, parking lots, streets and freeways, and traffic jams. Indeed, highway miles traveled annually has more than doubled since 1970 and the number of vehicles has risen by 90 percent. With double the population by the mid- or late twenty-first century, what will our highways look like then?

— There will be twice as many houses and apartment buildings.
— Twice as many grade schools, high schools, trade schools, and colleges.
— Twice as many hospitals.
— Twice as many prisons.
— In short, twice as much of everything, except open spaces.

Consider what effect this has already had on wildlife habitats. Population growth has already destroyed half of the nation's wetlands and a major portion of habitats for birds and other animals. With twice the current population, will we have left any wilderness areas, remote and quiet places, and habitats for songbirds, waterfowl, and other wild creatures? Certainly, not very many. What will happen to the last of our great natural areas, the national parks, national forests, wildlife refuges, and wilderness areas, which are already experiencing serious degradation from population pressures?

The numbers are staggering. Annual national park visits, for example, have ballooned since 1950, from thirty million to almost three hundred million — a tenfold increase in just half a century. The park system is already in a sorry state of decline and deterioration from people pressure and commercialization. What will this remarkable natural heritage be like, and look like, when visits double or triple in the next couple of decades? Our great national parks will be little more than overcrowded theme parks inhabited by tame "wild" animals. The last of our great natural areas will be gone. There is something terribly wrong with a society that remains complacent while this kind of irrational destruction erodes its life-sustaining resource base.

Will megacities twice the size of New York, Miami, Chicago, Detroit, and Los Angeles be more manageable, more livable and safer? The answer is obvious. Some are already borderline ungovernable. The question is this: Do we have the foresight clearly to perceive the long-term implications of continued exponential population growth soon enough to address that issue effectively within our own borders? At the rates of urbanization seen over the past few decades, the urbanized area of the United States will double by about 2050, from 155,000 square miles to about 312,000. Much of it will be prime farmland we can ill afford to lose. This is an area larger than Wisconsin, Iowa, Illinois, Indiana, Ohio, and Michigan combined. If we permit that to happen, the loss of this much land to urbanization will have huge negative consequences without any offsetting benefits. Population stabilization at the earliest possible date is key to successfully addressing this issue, and nothing short of stabilization will do it.

Incidentally, it is important to note that mainstream economists have long dominated economic thought with comfortable assurances that there is no foreseeable limit to economic expansion — and that exponential population growth is an asset, not a liability. Thus, it is little wonder that the economics profession, except for a small number of resource economists, has made itself irrelevant to the central issue of our time. The extent of their irrelevance was aptly captured by Amory Lovins when he said, "Economists are those people who lie awake nights worrying about whether what actually works in the real world could conceivably work in theory."

We are dealing with a social, ecological, and economic challenge unlike any in our previous history. It is a challenge that begs for the kind of dedicated, inspirational leadership that Franklin Roosevelt and Winston Churchill provided in their single-minded pursuit of victory in World War II. And this current challenge is far more serious than the military threat was to the democratic West then. Nations can recover from lost wars — witness Germany and Japan — but there is no recovery from a destroyed ecosystem.

But perhaps the opportunity for a gradual but complete break with our destructive environmental history and a new beginning is at hand. Reaching a general understanding that sustainability is the ultimate issue will finally bring us face-to-face with the political challenge of forging a sustainable society during the next few decades. It is a challenge we can meet if we have the leadership and the political will to do so. Indeed, none of the so-called sacrifices required to forge a sustainable society would be considered unduly burdensome by our grandparents. We have evolved willy-nilly into a frenzied, consumer-oriented society, and in the process we are dissipating our sustaining resource base.

As I contemplate this throwaway society, I am reminded of a comment by Socrates, who was put to death in 399 B.C. He was asked why he bothered to visit the open market regularly, when he never seemed to buy anything. He replied that he did so because he was always amazed by how many things were for sale that he did not need.

The bottom line is this — a sustainable society, at some bare subsistence level, will ultimately evolve even if we as a society simply do nothing. Unfortunately, at that stage what we end up debating will be the roster of possible earth-friendly solutions to severe scarcities.

Planning for sustainability will be enormously complicated and controversial, far beyond anything ever before attempted. Debate and controversy are vital to the process of developing public understanding and support for making the hard decisions and the right decisions. If we fail to make the necessary decisions, nature will make them for us and all future generations. But there is no real reason we would fail, provided the public does its part and the government assumes responsibility for enlightened leadership.

With so many problems that we face in this world — the political and the leadership issues, the education issues, and so forth — people sometimes ask me if I am fundamentally optimistic or pessimistic about it all. I describe myself as either pessimistically optimistic or optimistically pessimistic. If I did not think we could or would do anything to help ourselves, I would just pick up my fly rod and head out to the trout stream. But I do see significant change — though nothing happens as fast as we would like. Once you reach a conclusion that something must be done, you want to have it done right now. We have to muster the understanding, the consent, the active support of 270 million people. We have to get the leadership focused on the important issues. But it is happening.

On the first Earth Day, April 22, 1970, there was only one full-time environmental writer on any newspaper in America that I knew about, and that was Gladwin Hill of the *New York Times*. Now, almost every metropolitan paper has science and environmental reporters and editorial writers. There were no environmental departments or institutes on any campus in America, except the University of Wisconsin, in 1970. Now, every college I speak at has one. There were no general-circulation environmental magazines in the United States in 1970. There were no regular environmental programs on TV. Now, I can find one every night. There were few, if any, law schools that taught environmental law. Now, every law school that I know of teaches environmental law. Most important of all, few grade schools or high schools provided any environmental education. Now, there are thousands of schools and colleges involved in environmental education. Nurturing a generation imbued with a guiding environmental ethic is the key to the future.

That generation will very soon come of age. A generation guided by such an ethic will have the foresight and courage to make the hard decisions necessary to forge a sustainable society.

Chapter 3 PROTECTION, YES.
BUT AGAINST WHOM?
FOR WHOM?

GARRETT   I would like to discuss some of the great generalities
HARDIN   about environmental protection that lie at the foun-
          dation of what we are all trying to accomplish.
Foundations are often neglected because we are so busy working on the
upper stories, correcting the previous inconsistencies. Many of the objec-
tions we encounter (as well as the support that we fail to get) arise
because we have not considered the implications of our assumptions.

For example, environmental reforms are often impeded by tacit assumptions about the meaning of *property*. Most people assume that this
is a simple idea, that property is a thing, the way specific gravity is a
"thing." But, of course, it is not at all; "property" is an interpretation of
the relationships between people. My friend Dan McKinley once pro-
tested that "private property includes the smokestack, but not what
comes out of it." And that is the problem. To be ecologically acceptable,
the concept of property must weld privilege and responsibility together.
He who benefits from the products must accept responsibility for the by-
products. This is a shocking idea for people brought up on a simpler view
of "private property."

Ecologists are trying to teach people what can only be called "total
economics." Card-carrying economists do not like this interpretation.
They think of economics as one of the great academic disciplines, with
ecology as no more than a problematic one. In contrast, ecologists focus
on the relationships between peoples and many other elements of "the
real world." From that perspective, economics is just one subdivision
of ecology. This attitude does not get us any Nobel Prizes, of course, or
even attract many friends from the competing discipline. Our excuse:
society must learn to deal with all aspects of the humanity-environment
interchange.

The most basic fact in human ecology is this: We human beings create
nothing. We merely take the atoms the earth gives us and, using the sun's
energy (sometimes in fossilized form), *reorganize* them into arrange-

ments that are better suited to our purposes. For example, we cite figures on "the yearly production of petroleum." Question: How many barrels of petroleum did human beings produce last year? The correct answer is zero. We extracted the petroleum from the earth and burned it, deriving energy thereby. We certainly did not truly produce any oil. All we do is transfer commodities from the account called "nature" to the account called "human society."

Legions of influential people casually identified as "well educated" live by persuasive superstitions. In the early 1990s, Malcolm S. Forbes, Jr., the editor-in-chief of *Forbes* magazine, wrote: "Overpopulation is all nonsense. Since Malthus' time, the Earth's population has increased six-fold and the standard of living has become infinitely higher." So here is a man who is certainly "educated," yet he gloriously supports the superstition that perpetual growth is possible in a severely limited world.

Evidently there is more than one kind of education. I think it helps to distinguish three kinds of competence produced by education. I will refer to the variety as three kinds of intellectual filters. The oldest is literacy, which can be defined as competence with words, whether the result is expressed in speech or in print. In the 1950s someone coined the term "numeracy" to stand for a second kind of filter, which is coupled with a facility in using numbers and quantitative reasoning. Speaking broadly, we may say that, as a class, scientists are more numerate than the typical novelist or poet. Journalists, who should be both literate and numerate, are often weak in the second area.

Beginning about 1960, with the sensitization of the public to the importance of ecology and environmentalism, it became apparent that there needed to be a third intellectual filter, which was soon called "ecolacy." This orientation implies sensitivity to "And then what?" types of questions, and to the ability to see and predict subtle and delayed interactions of many influences.

Over time, for example, a herbicide may have an important side effect on herbivores, thereby diminishing its value to humans; an insecticide may kill more than just harmful insects. Bactericides may select for inheritable resistance not only among useful microorganisms but also among the harmful ones. So widespread are these effects that, as a working hypothesis, we now say that each blank-icide selects for its own defeat as a controller of the unwanted blank. Not meliorism, but rather pejoration is the new expectation in the Era of Ecology.

The ecolate view is not welcome to timid minds. Even if you come up with a true answer, you may have a hard time persuading others that you are on the right track. But we have to try. Literacy, numeracy, ecolacy: we need all three abilities.

We moderns are following in the footsteps of the old Romans who habitually asked, "Cui bono? Cui malo?" Who is benefited (by a new measure), and who is harmed? Though the word "society" is grammatically singular, the reality is very plural indeed: many people, many vested interests. Whenever we propose changing a system of reward and control, we must try to predict who will be harmed, and who helped, by the change. Most pressing is the need to foresee how those who are harmed will respond to the change. We must not forget that we cannot just throw away unwanted things. In whose backyard might they land? What is he or she then likely to do about it? Such questions must be ever in the forefront of the environmentalist's mind.

Numbers influence results; situation ethics acknowledges this. The relative blindness of traditional ethics to real-world situations creates ever new problems for environmentalists. As long ago as the fourth century A.D. one of the Fathers of the Christian church, Tertullian, implied as much in a passage that has shocked many traditionalists over the centuries: "The scourges of pestilence, famine, wars, and earthquakes have come to be regarded as a blessing to overcrowded nations, since they serve to prune away the luxuriant growth of the human race."

A standard reaction to that statement is that the writer must really have hated human beings, since he saw some good in death. But let us take a second look. Note, first, that Tertullian implies that this was not a new thought in the world: he says that the negative factors (disease, etc.) "have come to be regarded" as benefits, in part. He did not originate the thought; he merely reported it. The second thing to notice is the agricultural image that shaped Tertullian's words. He says that pestilences can be regarded as blessings because "they serve to prune away the luxuriant growth of the human race." That is both a numerate and an ecolate contention, since it implies the reality of limits and carrying capacity. And "pruning" is an eminently agricultural figure of speech: a city dweller would be unlikely to use such language. These days most Americans are born and raised in cities; for that reason they seldom think in the rural images implied by the concepts of carrying capacity, overpopulation, and pruning.

It is amusing to observe the results of citified thinking when a long-time urban resident moves to more spacious suburbs and decides to have a garden. He is almost sure to plant seeds too close together, being poor at imagining the future as biological expansiveness threatens the inflexible limits of the environment. As his crowded plants get bigger, he has trouble bringing himself to thin them out: long exposure to the propaganda resident in the phrase "the sanctity of life" has stunted his imagination. Citified persons need to muster courage to reject the "civilized" images they were brought up on as they liquidate the excess members of the population of plants for the sake of a fraction that can survive into the future in a state of vigorous health. Ours is now a thoroughly citified world. To save civilization, we must educate its citified denizens to understand the language of agriculture and the environment. People must become ecolate in their thinking.

By virtue of the content of their specialty, economists should be among the principal supporters of ecolate thinking. Unfortunately, the accidents of history have made them powerful opponents of the concept. Through and through, their theory assumes limitless supplies. This has led to the amazing assumption that if a society wants more of a good thing, it has only to raise the price of it and supplies will increase without limit. Julian Simon and Herman Kahn stated in 1984 that "the term carrying capacity has by now no useful meaning." It is true that when we are dealing with the earth's carrying capacity for human beings, there is considerable wiggle room for variations in the standard of living assumed; but wiggling at what cost?

One of the peculiarities of modern economics is that though the indexes of elementary texts sometimes include the entry "diseconomies of scale"—the important observation that in many situations, beyond a point things may get worse as size or numbers increase—the subject is not treated extensively in most of them. But the positive economies of scale are always dwelt upon at length. One can only conclude that both sales personnel in business firms and economics professors in colleges know that optimism pays.

In the opinion of human ecologists, the bottom line of economic and political organization is this: With unfettered growth, diseconomies of scale rule. Consider democracy, for example. As the number of participants grows, a reasonable facsimile of true democracy is still possible— up to about 100–150 souls, according to the centuries-old experiments of the Hutterites, an earnest religious group in the northwestern United States. Beyond that point, the greater the population, the less the democracy, and eventually it must be abandoned and replaced by some sort of representative government. But were we to achieve the idealists' dream of "One World," our schoolbooks would no doubt crow about a global democracy of ten billion people. "Democracy" is a sacred word, and sacred words cannot be easily replaced by the truth.

More generally, many aspects of the quality of human life are negatively related to the number of people living in the community, once it exceeds a certain size. If every family now living on Earth is to have two automobiles, the number of families living on nature's bounty will have to be markedly reduced. The question that begins with "How many people . . ." is meaningless if it is not preceded by the question, "What kind of life . . ." Widespread agreement on the second question will be hard to achieve; once it is introduced, the pejorative word "elitism" is likely to dominate the discussion.

Reaching a community-wide agreement on the size of the population to strive for involves not only scientific questions but also arbitrary decisions. Unfortunately, the word "arbitrary" is understood differently in science and law. In the law the word is used with obvious distaste. By contrast, scientists frankly defend the word and its related practices, particularly in the field of statistics, where an arbitrary standard of significance has to be agreed upon. If you want to make one in twenty the limit for nonsignificant deviation from pure chance, fine. If you choose one in one hundred, also fine. But in every contested case some arbitrary decision has to be made. (Actually, John Q. Citizen makes such decisions every day, but he may not be aware of this fact.) If you cringe at "arbitrary," you might try to coin a new word.

The ecologist's basic question, "And then what?" runs all through human affairs. Different stages in the development of a nation may evoke different answers. For example, in this country, there was a time when Kit Carson, traveling across the prairies, would shoot a buffalo, cut out the tongue for eating, and leave the rest of the carcass to rot. "What a waste!" we say now, but the lonely horseman had no refrigerator with him; and for him to interrupt his journey to build a fire (with what fuel?) and smoke-dry the extra carcass would involve wastes of other sorts. "Waste" is defined by circumstances.

The ecologist's "And then what?" needs to be applied to one of the most ancient of the commandments in the Bible: "Be fruitful and multiply." The rabbi who wrote this was living in a village, and it was a village version of morality that he was calling for. In a world of many separate villages, tribes, and ethnic groups, vigorous reproductive competition arises naturally. (If you do not believe that, read the Old Testament.) Other things being equal, fast multipliers win out over slow.

Circumstances have changed now, but most ethnic groups continue to follow the biblical advice just cited. We are thus laying the ground for the great tragedy that would follow from transgressing the carrying capacity of the earth, unless we somehow find the wisdom and ability to come to grips with the situation. There may not be much time, but we do not have too many other choices.

As you can see, ecological analysis is not for the faint of heart.

Chapter 4   IS THE POPULATION
EXPLOSION OVER?

BEN J.
WATTENBERG

For at least thirty years, one root notion has shaped much of modern thought: that the human species is running out of control and has to be controlled. "The enemy is us," said Pogo. The issue of population growth has been a premier case in point because it touches on so many other aspects of public policy, from pollution to pensions, from sex to security.

In *The Population Bomb*, his best-selling book of 1968, Paul Ehrlich wrote that "the cancer of population growth must be cut out . . . [or] we will breed ourselves into oblivion." He appeared on the Johnny Carson show twenty-five times to sell the idea. Lester Brown's *29th Day* compared people to geometrically multiplying water lilies, out of control. A famous study by the Club of Rome, later renounced, described how rapacious humans would soon "run out of resources." A later book, *The Population Explosion* by Paul and Anne Ehrlich, proposed doubling the price of gasoline and limiting "personal freedom" in choosing family size because "the world can't afford more Americans . . . any more stuff in the world should not go to the likes of us . . . rich nations will now have to pay for their greed."

Extreme? Surely but perhaps less so than imagined. A mainstream political leader wrote a blurb for the Ehrlichs' book: "The time for action is due and past due. The Ehrlichs have written the prescription," said then-Sen. Albert Gore, Jr. This, thirty years after global fertility rates had begun to decline. A 1992 CNN documentary matter-of-factly described global chaos to come "as the planet's population grows exponentially." Well, Al Gore and Ted Turner's CNN had become mainstream greenies. What else would you expect?

But what do we talk about today? One hot topic is global warming, an allegedly dangerous situation tightly linked to soaring human population deep into the next century. It is just the sort of thing that several generations of schoolchildren have been taught. In the present century, however, population will likely level off and then shrink, quite possibly substantially. Repeat: shrink.

In early November 1997, for the first time ever, the United Nations Population Division convened expert demographers to consider de-population. That discussion represents a step, both symbolic and real, in a near-Copernican shift in the way our species looks at itself. Now, Copernicus is a very big gun to deploy in this sort of argument. In 1543 the Polish astronomer posited that Earth moved around the sun, not the other way around. People were put in their place — a new place.

That is happening again. Never have birthrates fallen so far, so fast, so low, for so long, all around the world. The potential implications — environmental, economic, geopolitical, and personal — are monumental, for good, for ill, probably for both.

What is happening can be best seen in *World Population Prospects: The 1996 Revisions,* a remarkable reference book published by the United Nations, from which most data used here are drawn. From 1950 to 1955, the global Total Fertility Rate (TFR) — roughly speaking, the average number of children born per woman, per lifetime — was *five.* That rate was explosively above the replacement rate, the 2.1 children per woman needed to keep a population stable over time by replacing their two parents, who will eventually die. For about fifteen years the rate stayed five-ish. But by 1975–80, the rate had fallen to *four* children per woman. In the 1990–95 period, the rate had dropped to *three.* By mid-1997, it was estimated at 2.8, and sinking.

Five children per woman. Then four. Then three. Then fewer than three. Demographers were caught with their projections up. Suddenly, more than 600 million statistical people were "missing." They will never be born.

But what about women in those teeming Less Developed Countries (LDCs), those swarming places where the population bomb was al-legedly ticking? The fuse is sputtering. The LDC fertility rate in the 1965–70 period was six. Now it is about three, and falling more quickly than anything previously seen in demographic history.

Those are broad numbers. Consider some specific countries. Italy, a Catholic country, has a fertility rate of 1.2 children per woman, the lowest rate in the world — and the lowest rate in the history of the world absent famines, plagues, wars, or economic catastrophes. Europe may become an ever-smaller picture postcard continent of pretty old castles and old churches tended by old people with old ideas. Or it may become

World TFR

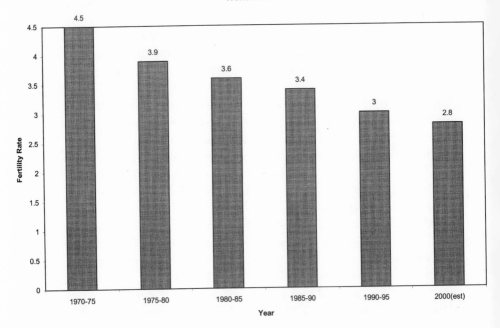

a much more pluralist place with ever-greater proportions of Africans and Muslims, a prospect regarded with horror by the vast majority of European voters.

India has a rate lower than American rates in the 1950s. The rate in Bangladesh has fallen from 6.2 to 3.4 — in just ten years. The Japanese rate has plunged to 1.4 children per woman, which if maintained would cut the Japanese population in half by the middle of the twenty-first century. In Russia, also 1.4. In Muslim Tunisia over three decades, the rate has fallen from 7.2 to 2.9. Rates are higher but still way down in Iran and Syria. Fertility rates in many (not all) sub-Saharan African nations, including Kenya, which was once regarded as the premier demographic horror show, are plunging. Mexico has moved 80 percent of the way to replacement level. European birthrates of the 1980s, already at recordbreaking low levels, fell another 20 percent in the 1990s, to about 1.5 children per woman.

American rates, much higher than Europe's, have nonetheless been below replacement for twenty-five straight years. There was an uptick in the late 1980s, but rates have fallen for five of the last six years,

TFR in Less Developed Regions

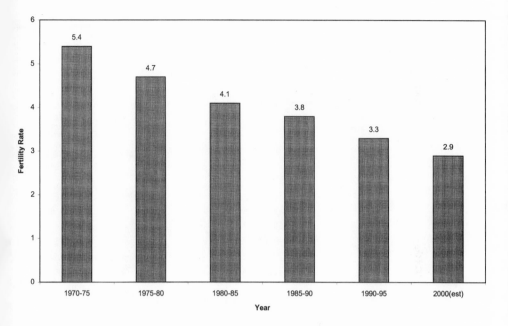

and the National Center for Health Statistics reports decreasing rates, which "continue the generally downward trend observed since early 1991."

This sounds strange. After all, we have gone through a half century of the greatest population growth in history, and such growth has not quite ended, as we shall see. The words "population explosion," appropriately, became commonplace.

What is happening is that two powerful trends — the population explosion and the baby bust — are now at war. They can coexist, but only for awhile. Mounting evidence makes it clear which trend will prevail: the baby bust.

The population explosion is a long-distance runner. From 1750 to 1950, the population of the world increased from 1 billion to 2.5 billion. From 1950 to 2000, it has increased to 6 billion. Remarkable. But the baby bust is also a marathon player. In 1790, American women bore an average of 7.7 children. Benjamin Franklin saw children "swarming across the countryside like locusts." But for two centuries, with a bump during the baby boom, American fertility has fallen steadily. Between

TFR in More Developed Regions

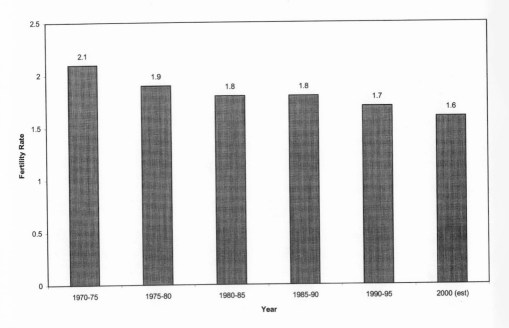

Year

1972 and 1997 the fertility rate averaged 1.9, with the lowest rates accruing to Jewish women and black women with college degrees.

An explosion and a bust? It sounds contradictory. But the number of potential mothers today was set two and three decades ago, when they were born and when birthrates were much higher. And the rates in most LDCs, while falling rapidly, are still mostly above replacement. Life expectancy has been climbing. These factors create "population momentum," which automatically yields more people — for awhile. Soon, however, reflecting the recent sharp reduction in fertility, the number of potential mothers will fall. Fertility will likely drop below replacement level in many LDCs. It already has in nineteen such countries, including Cuba, China, Thailand, and, momentarily, Brazil. The momentum turns the other way, and the baby bust smothers the population explosion.

That is already in the deck. The right questions about the bust now: How deep? How long? To what level? Good or bad? What, if anything, should we try to do about it? How will it change our view of ourselves? There are disagreements, as well there should be when dealing with such an important indicator of the future.

The UN "medium variant" projection shows a global population of

United States Total Fertility Rate

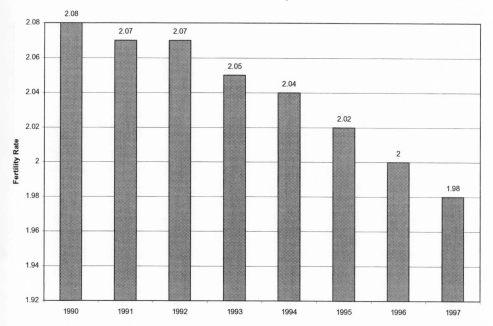

9.4 billion in 2050. Because of its "medium" designation, this Mama Bear projection is cited most often. But its central assumption is questionable, that all nations will move to a TFR of about 2.1 children per woman by 2050. Based on the current situation, this scenario seems implausible. Indeed, the experts met at the United Nations in 1997 to change the assumptions in the medium variant projections — downward.

There is an existing alternative UN "low variant" projection. It does not yield a population anywhere near 9.4 billion; it comes in at 7.7 billion people in 2050 and *shrinking*. By how much? By a lot, and relatively quickly: down to about 6 billion in 2100 and 4.3 billion in 2150. A bust, like an explosion, moves in a geometric progression. The central assumption in the existing "low" version is that the global TFR will drop to 1.6 children per woman. Unlike the 2.1 figure, that is not an abstract construct. It is the current rate in the developed nations. The assumption is that as nations modernize they will behave like modern nations.

When the United Nations revises its medium variant downward, it will not go that far, certainly not in one jump. But even splitting the difference would yield a global TFR of about 1.85 children per woman by 2050. Call it the "new medium" projection. Global population would

TABLE 4.1   *United Nations World Population Estimates (in billions)*

	2000	2010	2015	2020	2025	2030	2040	2050
Medium variant	6.1	6.9	7.3	7.7	8.0	8.4	8.9	9.4
Low variant	6.1	6.7	7.0	7.3	7.5	7.6	7.7	7.7

then top out at about 8.5 billion people and start declining. Demographer Samuel Preston, director of the University of Pennsylvania School of Population Studies, and other leading demographers think that is near the range of what is most likely to happen.

How valid are these sorts of demographic calculations? Far from perfect, and sometimes contentious, but far better than a simplistic, straight-line-to-the-future projection. After all, medium-range demographic projections deal with females who have already been born. A baby born today will be twenty in 2021. Knowing what the potential pool of mothers will be — far smaller than previously — forms a solid basis for projections.

But what about the unpredicted baby boom? Birthrates soared unexpectedly from 1945 to 1965. Could this happen again? Yes. But that boom followed two unusual circumstances that had artificially depressed fertility: a harsh economic depression and a blistering world war. In part, the boomer kids made up for kids not born earlier.

Projection making has long been a demographic staple. But now there is a big difference. In earlier times demographers drew neat charts that showed rates going down to the 2.1 replacement level and staying there. But young men and women, deciding to conceive children or not, are not thinking about an invisible line called "replacement." Instead, they are thinking about a good life for themselves, in quite new circumstances. Their recent collective actions have sliced through the invisible line of 2.1 like a laser through grits.

The United Nations also issues a "high variant." It uses the same pool of mothers as do the medium and the low variants, but it assumes that the rate in modern countries will go up from 1.6 children per woman, not just to 2.1, but to 2.6.

Four scenarios: the current high, medium, low, and a forthcoming "new medium." Only the latter two are consistent with the potent global trend that has been in motion for a quarter of a century.

What caused the birth dearth? "The demographic transition" did, a somewhat mystical process that Paul Demeny, editor of *Population and Development Review,* describes as the move "from high fertility and high mortality to low fertility and low mortality, with lots of complicated and contradictory things going on in the middle." Among the factors pushing the transition: urbanization, more education for women, legal abortion, higher incomes, unemployment yielding lower incomes, greater acceptance of homosexuality, new aspirations for women, better contraception (including "morning-after pills," now with new Food and Drug Administration guidelines), later marriage, more difficulty in conception at older ages, more divorce and separation, and, critically, lower infant mortality rates. In 1900, the global infant mortality rate was 290 deaths per 1,000 births. By the early 1950s, it was 156. Today the number is 57 — and 9 in the more developed countries. When parents know their children will survive, fertility rates plummet.

These "modernization" trends are continuing, along with some new ones. For example, the black American fertility rate is now at about the national average; black teenage birthrates have declined by 20 percent since 1991.

Choice plays a critical role in these declines. But as pointed out by Garrett Hardin in "The Tragedy of the Commons," a decision can be wise from a personal perspective but perhaps not so wise collectively. One of the principal problems faced by Europeans is how to pay for old people. If we do not reproduce, then Social Security, Medicare, and similar programs will have funding problems. The European demographers all agree that their society is unsustainable with these birthrates. Our Social Security systems are Ponzi schemes, but only insofar as life is a Ponzi scheme. You have kids, you take care of your kids; they have kids and take care of you and their kids, and so on.

Demographic transition theory explains, or at least describes, why high rates come down. But there is no theory (yet) that explains why, when, or how low fertility rates go back up. Therefore what? When people have fewer babies and live longer, the median age of society climbs. Today the global median age is about twenty-five. By 2050 it will be about forty-two — prompting a "grayby boom." By having relatively few children, middle-aged people today are eroding the population base that should pay for their pensions in their old age. In 1955, there were nine Americans of working age to support each Social Security recipient. Today there are three. By 2030, the number is expected to be two.

Where will the money come from? No one knows. Perhaps from funds not spent supporting children who are never born. Perhaps from (politically difficult) tax increases or benefit cuts. Perhaps from immigration or higher fertility. Perhaps from the partial privatization of Social Security or from long-term economic growth more robust than the 1.3 percent per year rate now factored into Social Security projections.

For the environment, the prospect of fewer people than expected should be good news. The specter of a population explosion has been the Archimedean lever of environmental thinking: more people cause more pollution; more people use more resources; more affluent people do both. Environmentalists and population activists, long at the forefront of providing family-planning services, can appropriately claim much credit for the brighter outlook. But they do not go unrebutted: others argue that it is not mostly family planning but mostly modernism, urbanization, education, and wealth driven by market economics that have done much of the job.

The good news may, however, make it more difficult to sell bad news. The demographic models used in global-warming calculations are based on projections keyed to a population of 11.5 billion people. Inevitably, these numbers will have to be revised downward. When the models start showing 8, 7, or 6 billion, the threat is reduced. Warning: Even as we get fewer people than were expected, we should remember they can still make a big mess. The case for exaggeration has been diminished. The case for environmental realism remains powerful.

Consider geopolitics. In 1950, roughly 28 percent of the world's population lived in "the West," the modern nations of Europe, North America, and Japan. Today 18 percent do, and in 2050, it will be more like 11 percent. So what? Arguably, a large population is a necessary but not sufficient condition for global power and influence. India is not now a global power of the first magnitude. Belgium never will be.

The West has been the driving force of civilization for centuries. Will it be so when its share of the total population is only 11 percent? Perhaps as less developed countries modernize, they will assimilate Western views and values. Perhaps the twenty-first will be another "American century." Perhaps not, alas.

Changing demographics offer a split vision of the economic future. Existing businesses tend to do better when their potential customer base grows. For awhile there will be plenty of extra customers coming on stream no matter what projection is used. Two billion more, even under the low scenario, is a lot of people. Moreover, much of the population in the developing nations is now moving upscale, providing additional numbers to the global consumer economy.

A robust domestic market is very important. Try building new houses in a depopulating country. In the past forty years in America, the population grew by 59 percent. That escalator of consumer demand will not continue; the American population in the next forty years will likely grow about half as fast, with most growth coming in the next twenty years. After that, expect very slow growth, at most.

Could a declining population be good for an economy? The country that had the longest sustained growth in population is also the country that became the most affluent, influential, and powerful—the United States. There is an old Indian proverb, "Every baby is born with one mouth and two hands," meaning that people are producers as well as consumers. There are no finite numbers of jobs, however; in areas of America where the population is declining, people are doing worse. The famine in Africa has been political in origin, not demographic; there is no lack of grain in the world. Many of these countries are self-supporting. Julian Simon believed that more people are better. Now some of his views are a bit extreme—he believed we could go on forever—but he was a very smart man. He argued that there is only one natural resource: the intellect of man. What made coal, oil, and uranium into resources? The intellect of man. That is not only a renewable resource but an expanding one, because of education and population growth.

Certainly there are areas where the distribution of resources causes problems. In my judgment, however, it is not the number of people that is the problem, it is what they do. But ask yourself this question: If we have created a society where many more millions of people can get in an RV and go see the Grand Canyon (although the crowding may somehow diminish the benefit to those who used to see the canyon when it was less crowded), is society, as a whole, necessarily worse off?

In the post–World War II period, the population went up from 2.5 to 6.0 billion. We live longer, healthier lives. We have less pollution, better homes, and more exposure to wilderness—and you can go on and on. What is making that standard of living increase despite a more than doubling of the population? Technology. Industry. Where do you think those new drugs come from?

Eventually demography blends into psychology. There is likely to be much extra personal sadness ahead. There will be missing children and missing grandchildren. Demographer Nick Eberstadt of Harvard and the American Enterprise Institute looks ahead and writes that, "for many people, 'family' would be understood as a unit that does not include any biological contemporaries or peers" and that we may live in "a world in which the only biological relatives for many people — perhaps most people — will be their ancestors." Lots of people without brothers or sisters, uncles, aunts, or cousins, children or grandchildren — lonelier people.

A lonelier world? Isn't it lonely enough now? Some observers say friends and colleagues will become "like family." Do not count on that if you end up in a nursing home. Young DINKs (double income, no kids) may be cute; OLINKs (old, low income, no kids) may be tragic. Clergymen say the saddest funerals are those where the deceased has no offspring. Manhattan is said to be a borough dominated by live-alone singles. Young men say that it is so hard find women; young women say the reverse and worry about the ticking biological clock. Adoption is excruciatingly difficult. People well into their sixties, looking for grandchildren, are asking, "Where's the beef?"

Jews wondering about survival in America. Blacks looking for role models but finding that existing role models do not come close to replacing their number. Women saying they could never imagine the intense love engendered by having a baby in their life. Young people, everywhere, saying that they cannot afford to have two children, in the most affluent moment in world history. "Pronatalism," like the new $500 tax credit, gets mixed reviews. We worry about family values and family erosion, which are moot until there is family formation.

Troubling. If you follow a baby bust spiraling inexorably and geometrically downward, there will be no people left. But we do not need to worry about that because we learned something. Those demographers at the United Nations were not talking about a world where people cannot control their destiny. Quite the opposite: we are in control, and we are changing how we see ourselves and our world. Destiny is not inexorable. We can shape it. We are doing it now.

Part III   AGENTS OF CHANGE

Government

Chapter 5   ETHICS AND SOCIAL
              REGULATION IN AMERICA

WILLIAM D.   In 1970, when the U.S. Environmental Protection
RUCKELSHAUS   Agency first opened its doors, the initial rush of en-
               thusiasm for it was really astonishing. In the first
forty-five days of our existence, we received 220,000 applications for
jobs from everywhere in the United States. People were responding to the
first wave of environmentalism that came along in the late '60s and had
been building throughout that decade. The EPA was a governmental
response, finally, to the public demand that something be done about our
deteriorating environment. In thinking back on those days and how
exciting everything was, how much promise and expectation there was
for the EPA, it certainly evokes in those of us who were here at the time a
very strong emotion about the agency — about its mission and its people.

There is conflict in the very heart of the work that the EPA does. It is
involved in so many controversial decisions that it is impossible not to
anger people occasionally, and it is very common to get a sense that
things are not going perfectly. I think it is necessary for the agency to
recognize the nature of the trouble that exists today for institutions of
this kind, and to think about what we must do to adjust to the changes
that are largely responsible for some of these problems.

Certainly, our country needs a strong, intelligent, balanced, fair, cou-
rageous, confident, and trusted EPA. I have chosen those words carefully,
because given the kinds of issues the EPA deals with, it is terribly important that the American people feel confident that this is a federal agency
that looks out for their interests, making sure that their health and environment are protected. If the agency is strong, intelligent, fair, and
confident, it will be trusted. And providing sound reasons for trusting the
agency is probably the single most important thing that the EPA can do
to ensure its continued effectiveness.

The erosion of trust in government institutions should compel the
attention of everybody in the agency. You cannot just sit back and think,
"Well, that is an inevitable part of what is involved in working in a place

like the EPA. Some people get angry every time we make a decision. It goes with the territory." To a certain extent, that is true. But when the public reaction is considerably more intense than that, the controversy may lead to a serious erosion of essential trust, and it becomes important to understand why the reaction happened. More generally, it is increasingly important to know that adjustments will have to be made to accommodate the changes occurring in society, so as to keep the agency effective and strong in the implementation of its programs. It was Edmund Burke who observed that a state without the means of change is without the means of its own conservation.

In April 1973, I left the EPA suddenly to move to the FBI, in the midst of the Watergate crisis. Coming back in 1983, ten years after that event, I was acutely aware of how markedly the EPA and its mission had already changed. The gross kinds of pollution — the sort that led to the creation of the EPA in the first place back in 1970 — the "smell, touch, and feel" kinds of pollution, were well on their way to being brought under social control. They had not vanished; pollution is the kind of problem that you have to work at everlastingly or it begins to get worse again. But by 1983, the early pollution problems were greatly reduced. There was much more focus on public health, and less on the environment, as people then understood it.

I think the balance in emphasis is largely dictated by public opinion. It depends on which problems have the public's attention at any one time. At first, it was gross pollution of rivers, lakes, and urban air. In the latter part of the '70s and in the '80s, toxic substances, such as found at Love Canal, got the public focused on issues involving public health. More recently, with the awareness of acid rain and the ozone hole and global warming, more attention has begun to be paid to ecological kinds of issues, and more resources and attention are devoted to them. In a free society, that is all right, within limits. It seems to me that if the public is concerned about something, they need to be able to believe their government is responding effectively to it. The more trusted the EPA is, the more opportunities we have to make our own decisions and thereby avoid wild swings back and forth, in terms of the allocation of resources to one problem versus another.

As to what the proper balance should be, it is hard to say. Measuring the importance of the rain forest or fisheries or the planet itself, or of global warming versus living near a Superfund site, is very difficult to do. We need to address all of those problems, with some kind of priority system. We need to recognize that we have limited resources. To the extent that we can increase the agency's flexibility to allocate available resources to the biggest problems first, we are going to be better off.

We had a much greater knowledge about the effects of chemicals and other substances on human health and the environment in 1983, when I returned, than we did when we started out (and, of course, that knowledge base has grown tremendously since then). But we do not have enough information to say with certainty what should be done in the case of every substance or every chemical humans are exposed to. Given the potential for synergistic effects when chemicals are combined with one another, we are not likely to have that kind of knowledge, not within my lifetime. It certainly does not mean that we do not or should not act; we just acknowledge that there are gaps in our knowledge that are not likely to be closed any time soon.

Likewise, our ability to detect or to measure smaller and smaller amounts of pollutants increased dramatically between 1973 and 1983. There came a much greater awareness and knowledge of our past mistakes and a desire to do something about them. The environmental laws introduced around 1983 reflected new public concerns and new realities. The Resource Conservation and Recovery Act (RCRA) was not on the books in 1973 — nor was the Safe Drinking Water Act, or Superfund. The public was, if anything, more agitated in 1983 than they had been when the EPA got started.

Acid rain was a very politically charged issue, probably the most difficult environmental problem I ever faced, for one simple reason: the source of the pollution was remote from its impact. The people who would normally pay for its abatement, at the source, received no benefit. They resisted very strongly the notion of paying for anything. Conversely, for the people at the point of impact, there was no cost entailed in saying, "Take care of that problem, all of you living in Ohio or Indiana or wherever the pollution is coming from." It was a prescription for political gridlock, which is in fact what occurred while I was here.

Currently, we have all kinds of difficult problems. And one of the most challenging is linked only indirectly with the physical deterioration of the environment — namely, how to deal with potentially alienated members of the public. How do we get them to understand better the nature of the issues that we are trying to wrestle with and the ways in which they might affect them? And where warranted, how do we encourage them to buy into solutions that, at the outset at least, they are not willing to accept. The approach now is pretty much the same as it was when I was last here at the agency. That is, the public has demanded a bigger piece of the action and more involvement in the decisions of all kinds that affect their lives. The politicians have responded by giving people greatly expanded access to the courts and to the administrative process, so that they can influence those decisions.

Whether or not that is how it should be is really a different subject. It is the way it is. We are not very good at moving from a point where we meet public demands with political responses to a point where we meet them administratively. How do we allow the public a bigger say in what goes on, while doing so in a way that gives them the strong sense that they have been a real part of the process? That is very tricky, but I think it is the kind of problem that the EPA has to deal with effectively.

At first, we thought it was generally necessary to draft regulations that were prescriptive. The idea was to try to ensure that any time people or companies stepped over the line, they would stand a good chance of getting caught and becoming subject to enforcement. I used to think about that approach a lot when we first started the EPA. But there is no way we would ever be able to sue everyone in the country who violated a regulation, no matter how much we lawyers might think that would be a good thing to do.

How does our society get the hypothetical plant manager to stop trying to bar the door to keep the regulator out and, instead, to go back and examine the plant to see what he can do to make the industrial processes cleaner? If we could cause him to do that, we would abate much more environmental degradation than we could with a million environmental regulations or laws. We should try to create the right kinds of incentives, which would motivate that person to turn around and look inside.

In industry, fundamentally, those incentives are economic. We can depend to a certain extent on the goodwill of some in industry to protect the environment, but we cannot depend on it for everyone. And it is simply unrealistic to depend on that goodwill alone when the costs for abatement get so high that they render a factory uncompetitive. So we need a system that makes it clear to the operator of the plant that there are economic benefits from improving the environment. Some provisions, like tax incentives and disincentives and various other mechanisms meant to trigger that economic response for environmental improvement, have great promise. I also think we must not give command-and-control too bad a name. We have made a lot of progress over the past few decades using just such techniques. But we can make a lot more progress if we can figure out how to get the incentives right.

When I went to Browning Ferris Industries, for example, we operated about 110 landfills around the country. The clear priority for the operator of each one was to ensure that he reached his monthly profit goals. Each understood the regulatory compliance responsibilities in a fairly fundamental way, but that was not anyone's highest priority. Now, for all the people who work on those sites, a portion of their incentive pay is based on their compliance record. Believe me, that got the operators' attention.

I have become convinced of the wisdom of Edmund Burke's remarks about how important it is for institutions, whether public or private, to anticipate successfully and adapt to change. That will have more to do with their remaining viable than any other single factor. Failure to adapt probably does not mean extinction, but it certainly can result in second-rate status, loss of influence, and the inability to affect the future or accomplish one's mission.

In the private sector, the price of failing to change and adapt to change is devastating, and quite quantifiable. You get a report card every day in the stock market: investors tell you how well they think you are doing. The quantification of revenues, profits, and market share is an unavoidable index of success or failure and is out there for everyone to see.

The commercial landscape is littered with examples of large, preeminent institutions that failed to anticipate and adapt to change. Think of some of the giant American corporations that no longer exist. In recent years, some lost their market focus and stopped listening to their customers. These companies failed to see or, worse, ignored signals of change in the country and their industry, and their response was often too late. What defines those drastic plunges from leadership is the unwillingness or inability to recognize change and to understand the opportunity that change creates.

Commitment to the known is more comfortable, and certainly easier, than the often unsettling and uncertain embracing of change. I make this obvious point for several reasons. The EPA has had to change over the years. To sustain all of the attributes I noted before, such as "strong" and "confident" and "trustworthy," we simply need to get better at doing it. The evidence of the need to adapt to change at the EPA has been mounting for awhile, and let me note here that this statement has nothing to do with partisanship. From everything I can tell, Carol Browner is a capable, able woman, doing the best job she can to manage this agency. But the drumbeat from the usual "support groups" goes on — whether it is that weekly phenomenon, the editorial page of the *Wall Street Journal* whipping itself into an anti-EPA frenzy, or from the environmentalists, industry, Congress, the OMB, and, on occasion, the White House.

One understanding that came home to me with tremendous force when I returned to the EPA was that the agency really has no natural constituency. When we started out back in 1970, I believed that ours consisted of the public and environmental groups. I am not even sure of that anymore. To continue to attract members and support for their organizations and their causes, environmental groups sometimes feel the need to stake out positions that are at variance with those of the EPA; an inevitable antagonistic relationship builds up between these groups and the agency charged with the responsibility of implementing the laws that have come into existence as a result of their demands. Not having a natural constituency makes it even more difficult for the agency to maintain the requisite level of trust among the general public, which is still the closest thing to a natural constituency that the EPA has.

The sense that the EPA is at risk is real. The atmosphere surrounding its work is more politicized and contentious than it has been in the past. I think both political parties have made it so. And I believe the statutory base that we put in place largely in the '70s needs serious adjustment. It needs to change so as to reflect the new realities. Many of the laws, as currently written, can best be understood as expressions of the lack of trust between the legislative branch and any administration. This has been fundamentally true since the beginning of the EPA.

When I was first here, I used to trot up to the Senate Environment and Public Works Committee and testify before Senator Muskie, who was then the leading opponent of the incumbent president, Richard Nixon. This situation did not exactly make for a deep well of trust between the agency and that committee, and many of the laws that emerged were very prescriptive, in terms of standards and deadlines, with minimal operational discretion for the agency. The standards and requirements attached to the deadlines were often unrealistic. They set up something like a cycle of inevitable failure for the agency that, in turn, led to more acrimony, more recrimination, and more accusations in testimony on the Hill — more mistrust. We are still trapped in this spiral.

The agency would be better off with a larger, generic multimedia statute (i.e., covering air, water, and land), with a lot more flexibility built into it to move resources back and forth among the programs. That would help control pollution in the most effective and cost-effective way. It is very hard to do that now, with separate statutes, separate committees in Congress, and separate program areas within the EPA (even though there are initiatives within the agency to coordinate the efforts of these programs across all media). It seems to me that dealing with the impact of pollution across all media — so that it can be interdicted at the proper point, not just moved from one medium to the next, with victory declared at every step along the way — is a much preferable approach.

What must happen to make that kind of change occur? Congress and the administration certainly have to respond to public opinion. That is where the EPA came from in the first place — from public demand. I was fortunate enough to serve as administrator of this agency under two Republican presidents, Nixon and Reagan. I think it is fair to say that neither one was a charter member of the Sierra Club during his political career, and yet neither found it possible, politically, to withstand the pressure of public demand that something more be done about the environment.

In addition to a responsibility to respond to its constituents, Congress also has an obligation to heed the advice of those who administer the laws they pass. Equally important, the EPA needs to recognize that one of its key roles is that of an educator. If there is a need for better mechanisms to achieve the goals that are established for the agency, then Congress and the public need to be educated about the nature of the existing mechanisms and the kinds of changes that need to be made to give the agency a chance of success.

Let me give you an example: Superfund. It is certainly one of the most complex, controversial laws that the EPA administers. As best I can tell, no one is happy with Superfund. I worked with a group called the National Commission on Superfund. The commission represented a broad cross-section of public and private entities, including presidents of some of the major environmental organizations in the country and CEOs of many corporations. There were also representatives from foundations and community activist groups. If all these groups could agree that Superfund is not working very well, it seemed possible that we could reach a consensus about how to do a better job in achieving the original objectives of the Superfund law. Our task was complicated by the fact that many of the groups represented on the commission (including both the environmental and the industry groups) were lobbying for change. But it is remarkable to me how similar, rather than dissimilar, the perspectives were on what is wrong and what is required to make Superfund work properly.

I mention this to bring home my point about the agency's troubles. At one of the Superfund commission's meetings in New Orleans, we got together for several hours with residents of communities around Superfund sites, all of whom were minorities. We asked them to tell us about their experience with the program. Many had had a site in their neighborhood for more than ten years. These people were passionate, emotional, angry—among the most alienated Americans I have seen since the Vietnam War. They all blamed the EPA for their troubles. They felt trapped in circumstances that were totally beyond their control. They felt that their property values had been destroyed and their health adversely affected. Many believed their loved ones—children, husbands, wives, and relatives—had been killed by exposure to these sites. Aside from whether they were right or wrong, that is what they believed. Many EPA staff have had the same experience: sitting for hours listening to people vent their anger and seeing it all directed at the agency. What I went through made me very concerned about the EPA. The conviction of these people could not be any more fundamental or firm, that their health problems result from exposure to a Superfund site. For them to believe that the agency, created specifically to help solve these kinds of problems, is itself the problem indicates that something is clearly wrong.

We need to do something about the Superfund law itself. The agency, therefore, must see its role as one of an agent of change if it wants to respond effectively to the problems associated with Superfund. I realize that it is in the very nature of government bureaucracy, in fact, in human nature, to become invested in the laws one is charged with administering. But I think it is essential that everyone working at the EPA step back from their day-to-day responsibilities, examine the statutory base of the agency critically, and call for improvements when necessary. In fact, I think the EPA has a responsibility to itself as an institution to inform Congress when current laws are not working. Very simply, the Superfund law does not work, and the EPA must ask for Congress's help in adjusting it.

The EPA has already taken some important steps to focus attention on these issues. Almost everyone who has occupied the administrator's chair has asked Congress to allow more flexibility in dealing with our environmental problems. The landmark agency report, *Unfinished Business,* confirmed that many of the laws that the EPA administers do not allow the agency to address first the most important priorities, the highest risks, by allocating its necessarily limited resources to the highest environmental and public health priorities.

Those who criticize the EPA must remember that the agency is trying very hard to implement complex, difficult, and prescriptive laws that are often passed based on the flimsiest of data in an atmosphere charged with emotion and politics. What the agency needs is honest oversight by Congress, designed to elucidate the problems in the statutes they have passed. It needs guidance on what must be done to fix them, in an atmosphere of cooperation that builds the public's trust, which the EPA critically depends on — not in one of recrimination and suspicion.

Whatever "clean air" and "clean water" actually mean to the American people, they mean something that reaches way down deep inside. The people have demonstrated that fact over and over again. For many years, these feelings have been among the most powerful social forces in this country. It is up to the government, Congress as well as the EPA, to harness that concern, that energy, and apply it toward an effective and efficient mechanism for achieving progress. It is especially important that we accomplish this, because the rest of the world looks to our country, and how it deals with the environment, as a model. We have set the standard in the past, and in many respects we are still far ahead of most other countries.

I am well aware that the problems that remain for us in the developed world, particularly in this country, pale in significance when contrasted with those of the 80 percent of the world that falls below our poverty line. The creation of a sustainable world under such circumstances is a tremendously important challenge.

Some people argue that the primary factor underlying the most intransigent and threatening of the global environmental problems, including the extreme poverty that encompasses much of the world, is the incredible growth in world population. The rapid increase in population is clearly a major factor in much environmental degradation — in the ecological stresses on the whole planet. And it was the conclusion of every member of the UN World Commission on Environment and Development that unless we are able to marry environmental protection and economic growth so as to attain sustainable development, there is simply no way we are going to control population.

We can moralize about it, we can wring our hands about it, we can do everything we want to about it, pointing out the relationship between population growth and environmental problems. But the evidence is overwhelming: it is only when the wealth in a society approaches a certain level that its population begins to stabilize. So unless we are able to meet the minimum, legitimate material aspirations of far more people in the world than we are doing now, there will not be the kinds of population control necessary to take us to some form of equilibrium between the numbers of people in the world and the ability of the planet to safely carry that number.

It seems to me that the challenge of creating a sustainable world demands from the EPA — indeed, from everyone who is aware and concerned about the crucial and growing environmental issues that we together face — a concentration of all of our abilities, and a serious willingness to embrace the opportunities that change presents.

Chapter 6 U.S. ENVIRONMENTAL
CONSERVATION,
PRESERVATION, AND
RESTORATION AGENCY

DAVID R.   One of the early administrators at the Environmen-
BROWER   tal Protection Agency, Russell Train, once said of
me, "Thank God for David Brower — he makes it so
easy for the rest of us to be reasonable." I have always been quite fond of
that quote, and I have not gotten any more reasonable as I have matured.
In fact, I have decided to assign a new charge to the EPA — to become
the U.S. Environmental Conservation, Preservation, and Restoration
Agency. Protection alone is no longer enough. As my friend California
state senator Tom Hayden has said, "All I have been able to do in my
career is to slow the rate at which things get worse." That is all I have
been able to do, too, and that is also true of the EPA. Indeed, it is in
global CPR — conservation, preservation, and restoration — that our future lies.

Conservation, as I define it, means "Let's use our resources ratio-
nally." This has to start with the recognition that our most valuable
natural resources are not raw materials but rather the earth's living ecosystems, the natural capital which provide flows of valuable and irreplaceable natural services like climate stabilization, crop pollination,
and soil creation, to name just a few. We will not have true capitalism or
conservation until the marketplace recognizes how precious this kind of
natural capital is.

Next, I would replace the Protection in EPA with Preservation, to
emphasize that we need to protect the things we cannot replace, particularly endangered species and ecosystems. Preservation, following
Aldo Leopold's thinking (never a bad idea), means saving all the pieces
from a planet we have taken apart.

Finally, Restoration of natural and human systems is something quite
distinct. Restoring natural systems requires a bit of ego, and perhaps we
should bring some humility as well, because nature can do a much better
job than we can. But we can help in jump-starting natural healing pro-

cesses. In contrast, restoring and redesigning human systems is certainly something we can handle, since we created them.

One does not have to be in Washington, D.C., for more than a few hours to spot a few human institutions that could use some restoration and redesign, especially with regard to how they think about the planet and our future on it. For starters, Alan Greenspan should have the word "green" stricken from his name until the Federal Reserve and its devotees stop praying at the Temple of Blind Economic Growth and put the right kind of green into their thinking. I like to say that I am not blindly opposed to growth, just opposed to blind growth. With the way our cleverness and our vast numbers are overwhelming the earth's ecosystems, we need to consider all growth guilty until proved innocent. My favorite biblical prophet, Isaiah, was on to this problem about twenty-seven hundred years ago when he wrote (Isaiah 5:8): "Woe unto them that join house to house, that lay field to field, till there be no place, that they may be placed alone in the midst of the earth!" Wilderness buffs, take note. Developers of sprawl, take heed!

One of the delights of reaching your late eighties is that you can look back over quite an extent of time. In nearly ninety years, only a few things have happened that are not old news to most people. But remember that the population of the earth has tripled. The population of California has gone up by a factor of sixteen, which is absolutely ridiculous. Since World War II, the world as a whole has used up four times as much resources as in all previous human history combined.

In our great central valley of California, where once there were six thousand miles of salmon streams, now we have two hundred. In 1912, when I was born, we had 75 percent of our original redwoods; now we are down to 4 percent. We had a sardine fishery; that is gone too. We had two Yosemite valleys in Yosemite National Park, but San Francisco got one of them and proceeded to flood it. All that is within my lifetime. On the Columbia River, there was only one small dam when I was born; now, they have rather more than that and a lot fewer salmon.

That is an eighty-year period; maybe twenty is a more useful number for younger people (which for me is most of them). In the last twenty years, enough new man-made deserts have been created to equal all the cropland in China. In the same period, we destroyed arable land equal to all the cropland in India. Our fertile soil has been lost by many means: inundation, paving it over, development, accelerating erosion by wind and water, and the application of chemicals in places where we do not really know the consequences, but think we do. Simultaneously, the world lost enough forest to completely cover the United States from the Mississippi to the Atlantic seaboard, north to south.

Destroying forests, fertile land, rivers, and fisheries to exponentially increase our wealth and population is bad news for our children, but it is far worse for the other species that used to call these areas home. Harvard ecologist E. O. Wilson gives us these figures on species: the number of plant and animal species on Earth that we have identified is about 1.4 million, but the actual number of species on Earth is between 10 million and 100 million. Assuming the 10 million figure, we are losing 100 species a day, at the present rate. Evolution never did that.

The point is that these are actions that cannot be repeated, since the natural capital to do it simply does not exist. We have already spent that capital; yet we go on with our planning everywhere as if we had not spent it, as if it still existed.

The advocates for the North American Free Trade Agreement (NAFTA) and the creation of the World Trade Organization (WTO) promised that the treaties would step up world trade by $4 trillion a year. The UN report *Our Common Future* made the argument that ending poverty on Earth would require growing the world's economy by a factor of five to ten times. But there is not one word in any of this about what would be used in terms of natural capital to support the new growth.

When I was arguing for the National Environmental Policy Act (NEPA) before Congress, it occurred to me that what we needed was the equivalent of an Office of Management and Budget, which controls dollars, to be equally concerned about controlling natural capital. How much natural capital do we have? Put another way, what is the earth worth? One group of economists from the University of Maryland came up with a number: each year humans receive from the earth's natural capital an average of $33 trillion in natural goods and services (income), which stacks up favorably with the global Gross National Product (GNP). Just wait until some clever economist tries to calculate the earth's replacement value. We have only one Earth, for which there is no spare. Yet no one on Wall Street or in the corporate world wants to factor this into their decisions.

Redesigning what we have foolishly called capitalism to put our most important capital on the balance sheet should be the new charge for the Environmental Protection Agency. And it is so big a charge, so important a charge, that I have a very important suggestion to make. We are not getting much national or global security out of that strangely shaped building across the river, the Pentagon. I do not want federal money to stop flowing to the Pentagon, but I would like the military people moved over to EPA headquarters, and the EPA people sent over to the much more spacious Pentagon, with the full complement of a Pentagon staff, so that they can do the most important job on earth: CPR for the earth's conservation, preservation, and restoration. It is these C, P, and R jobs that are all-important.

No one has yet expressed the meaning of CPR to global security better than our UN ambassador Adlai Stevenson did in his final speech before the United Nations in July 1965: "We travel together, passengers on a little space ship, dependent upon its vulnerable reserves of air and soil, committed for our safety to its security and peace, preserved from annihilation only by the care, the work, and, I will say, the love we give our fragile craft. We cannot maintain it half fortunate, half miserable, half confident, half despairing, half slave to the ancient enemies of mankind, half free in a liberation of resources undreamed of until this day. No craft, no crew, can travel safely with such vast contradictions. On their resolution depends the survival of us all."

Adlai's beautiful words were dire enough, and he had not even caught onto the population problem yet. I encouraged Paul Ehrlich to write *The Population Bomb* several years after Adlai's speech, and we then had to ask, how many "crew" can our "fragile craft" handle sustainably? Canadian author David Suzuki asked E. O. Wilson that same question and reported to me that his answer was that if everyone had the same appetite for resources as people in the United States and Japan, then the number would be 200 million. I had never heard a figure that low, so I called and asked him if he really said it, and he said no, but it sounds reasonable. Suzuki insists he did, but either way, the point is that in terms of the demographic drain on this planet, the United States is number one, regardless of the specific size of our population.

Interestingly, in births and deaths, the U.S. population is approximately stable; our growth is due primarily to immigration. Now, this has become a very touchy subject, but I do not believe that we can ignore it. After all, the original Americans treated the land quite well but were undone by *their* bad immigration policy. People had lived on this continent for at least ten thousand years and hardly damaged it at all, but in the last five hundred years a collection of rowdy immigrants whose culture taught them that they must multiply and subdue the earth have left it nearly unrecognizable. Today, American environmentalists are in the awkward position of saying that the earth cannot afford any more Americans, so the newer immigrants are suddenly scrutinized. But the immigrants themselves are not the problem; what the earth cannot handle is the culture of overconsumption that they are likely to add to in America.

We should be learning more from the cultures of the world that have learned to live with fewer possessions but no less joy, like the indigenous peoples we have become so good at eliminating — either with our guns or by luring away their young people with Coca-Cola and McDonald's. The American system must have been foreseen by Isaiah: "Thou hast multiplied the nation, and not increased the joy" (Isa. 9:3). The average American consumes forty times as much resources annually as a person in India, but are we forty times happier?

There is no question that in many of these countries, healthcare and education must be dramatically improved. In some countries in Africa, the average family size is 8.5, and this has been shown to be correlated with a lack of education and empowerment of women. Birthrates are down in the industrialized world, but we have to admit to our enormous overconsumption here any time we talk to people in the third world about their numbers, or we will not even be heard. We need to strive for negative population growth in our country while reducing our consumption. The sooner we can start back downhill, the sooner we will reach something that is sustainable; our current population absolutely is not. We are at least ten times beyond what can be sustained. We are living off the relentless mining of our natural capital, not off any income that can renew itself.

The planet may appear to offer plenty of raw material — rocks, oceans, and so on. But we have to think about the "law of the minimum." It does not matter how much water we have if we run out of air. It does not matter how much air we have if we run out of the part of the air that is oxygen. It does not matter how much oxygen we have if the earth loses its natural sun screen and we are left without the ozone layer to stop ultraviolet radiation. It does not matter how much ozone we have if we run out of judgment. And maybe that is what we are going to run out of first.

There is a considerable amount of evidence to that effect, on a global scale, as we watch what is happening now, as the population gets bigger and bigger while the resources get fewer and fewer. Civilization seems to be fragmenting before us as human tribes seek to decimate each other in various kinds of conflicts. Several experts I know believe that the next world war will be fought over the world's dwindling fresh water supplies. This is a dismal future, the future Adlai Stevenson was warning us about, and we simply have to change it.

So I am assigning to the EPA the job of changing that future. National and global security will depend on what this agency does; no other agency is up to it. The EPA is not even as old as Friends of the Earth, so it will have to get ready to think big, and that is what I intend to try to help the agency do.

But all we have done so far is to say, "We can't do it now; it costs too much; it might mean higher taxes. So let's forget it, and let the kids pick up the tab." That is what we are doing, and Lester Brown commented on it in his book *Building a Sustainable Society:* "We do not inherit the earth from our fathers, we borrow it from our children." Some have attributed this quote to me, and apparently I did say it in an interview in *Mother Earth News* awhile back. I was very concerned at that time about the fact that we are not just borrowing from our children; we are stealing from them. There is no chance to ever pay back the things we have used up that cannot be replaced. If you have neither the intent nor the ability to pay something back, that is very close to stealing.

This is part of my idea for the U.S. Environmental CPR Agency. We are not getting very far in our efforts to pay something back, to heal the earth. There are a good many organizations that have been working on restoration; we do not have to invent anything new. We could learn a lot from Franklin Roosevelt's administration, with its National Recovery Administration. There was also the Civil Conservation Corps — the CCC. All of this was put in place to pull us out of the Great Depression.

Now we face a much bigger challenge because things have deteriorated at a very rapid rate. It is a much bigger challenge at this point to get Earth out of its "environmental depression." A lot of new thinking will be needed for this effort; I will not pretend that I can do any of that thinking for the EPA. But let me recall some of the things history shows us. The CCC did a great deal of good work. It deployed many young people who otherwise would have been doing nothing to develop trails and build roads. Unfortunately, some of what they constructed was not very good. There was essentially no restoration, because there was not much consideration given to restoring things back then. But that is what we need now, in spades.

Some people equate restoring with mitigation and an excuse for further misdevelopment, but I say we can avoid that. If someone offers to drain and develop a wetland and says they will compensate by building a new wetland somewhere else, I would respond, "Well, build that other wetland first, and make it so good that it can serve as the site where you want your development." That is an extension of what I used to say during the Grand Canyon battle: I don't mind how many dams you put in the Grand Canyon, provided you build a separate and equal Grand Canyon somewhere else first. And this gets to the first mistake in restoration, which is trying to restore something that was never there to begin with. Our attempts at artificial wetlands cannot match the complexity of a natural wetland, and sending rabbits to Australia and the mongoose to Hawaii were outright disasters. Our guidebook for what *will* work in restoration is dependent on the success of our efforts at preservation. If we preserve wilderness, we can answer the question, What did the ecosystems do in this region before we came along?

If people are still concerned about the cost of this effort, first, consider what it will cost if we *do not* restore the earth, which leads us back to the strange question, What is the earth worth? We can start with an easier question, What is a tree worth? I went to Vermont Mountain School on one occasion to speak to the students. A student there told me that, according to one calculation, a typical tree provides $196,250 worth of ecological benefits in the form of oxygen, air clearing, soil fertility, erosion control, and wildlife habitat. Sold as timber, the same tree is worth only about $590. Has anyone really thought very much about what a tree does in its one century to five centuries to a thousand years of service to humanity? It holds soil in place, generates oxygen, locks up carbon, helps to regulate water flow, and keeps the air clear. If you tried to do for cash what a forest does for nothing, you would have to spend a great deal of money. That is what this calculation tells us. Right now, half of all the trees we cut down are used to make pulp, and half of that goes into landfills as paper.

But back to the question of what the earth is worth. You can begin to get an idea of what something is worth if you try to estimate the cost of restoring it. So one of the things that restoration will do is help us put a value on the earth. One good case of restoration happened in our state of California, when Jerry Brown was governor and Huey Johnson was his resources secretary. Huey came up with an idea that he called "Investing for Prosperity." He proposed more than thirty projects to restore natural resources including wetlands, salmon streams, forests, and soil fertility. First he went to corporations, and he asked IBM to be his lobbyist. He got the Southern Pacific railroad to help too. He talked to the Bank of America and other corporations, as well as the League of Women Voters and organized labor. He got their enthusiastic support. Then he went back to get the environmental organizations, who had initially laughed at his bold proposal, on board. Finally, he got $125 million a year from the California legislature, which was otherwise cutting back on spending. This was covered primarily by money the state received from industries that exploit nonrenewable resources, principally fossil fuels. His programs got under way, and they succeeded, and they are still saving California money and resources today.

This is the kind of major rethinking we need right now in the area of investing. Too many people on Wall Street and in Silicon Valley are merely speculating with their money. When are we going to start investing in a sustainable future, investing for lasting prosperity? All we see in the newspapers and on the TV news is more about the growing economy (or panic when it is not growing fast enough) and the GNP. But the GNP does not measure prosperity or anything of real importance. If you need to be rushed to the hospital, or if the Bureau of Reclamation decides to drown a national treasure like Glen Canyon, the GNP goes up. This makes no sense, yet the concept of the GNP influences everybody who is unwilling to consider the value of the earth or what we are costing future generations. I have been part of a group called Redefining Progress. They have developed new indicators of progress and success, because what we have been doing so far, which we thought of as progress and success, is not that at all. So these old measures are in reality counterindicators. What we need to know is this: What is happening to the resource inventory? What is happening to the air? The water? Our health?

The EPA will need to enlist a lot of help with their new charge, and I will do what I can personally. I am just unreasonable enough that, as I visit the various federal agencies, I am telling all of them to add this basic mantra — conservation, preservation, and restoration — to their particular missions. It is just as important as breathing. We need to enlist all the cultures, all the creeds, all the countries, all the classes; we need to make work on this problem part of everybody's job description.

We need people of all ages. I certainly want to keep busy as long as I am around. At some point, I will announce a new organization, Retirees for Posterity. All of my contemporaries should be working on something besides counting their ailments and their entitlements. There is a lot of good work they can do, for the earth and for the future. If you reach that age, do not retire, because retiring is fatal. Avoid it. As Theodore Roosevelt said, "It's better to wear out than to rust out."

Among other thoughts on aging, I like the bumper stickers that say, "You are never too old to have a happy childhood," and I am doing precisely that. And then there is this: "When you are over the hill, you pick up speed." Ansel Adams had a very good one: "If you are going to get old, get as old as you can get." As George Burns once said, "Shoot for 100, because very few people die after 100." This is the point: we need to motivate all the older people who are just sitting around the house, clipping coupons. I can tell them that at eighty-eight it is fun if you stay active and involved, and it is not fun if you do not.

We need all the people we can find to take this charge, whoever they are. And I include all the sexes. I come from San Francisco, where we count ten of them. The point here is to jettison prejudice, as fast as we can, for the sake of our common home. An old friend once said, "You can't reason prejudice out of a person, because it didn't get in that way." But try your best.

What can we do, once we have enlisted everyone we can find, to start rebuilding the life support system on which we all depend? Above all: respect the biosphere; celebrate it. Remember that the boundaries are very thin — you cannot go far up and survive; you cannot go very far down, either, and it is not a very big planet in surface area. And it is all that there is. It is the only biosphere we know of, and it is unique in all the universe, as far as we know. And yet we persist in treating it unkindly.

If you consider the earth as the size of a grapefruit, then all the water on earth — 99 percent of it is salt water — will be the size of a maraschino cherry. If the atmosphere were converted to liquid, for comparison, it would be about the size of a kiwi seed. The soil and the fresh water would be about the size of a poppy seed, and you would have to magnify the earth's natural sun screen, the ozone barrier, at its sea-level density, by fifty thousand times to see it at all. That is the biosphere; all of us are responsible for it. The EPA had better make sure that we all know how to take care of it.

It is time for the EPA and everyone else to get over simply studying environmental problems and get into widespread action to solve them. I like what Holly White said in *The Organization Man,* that we need to do some "retroactive planning." We should do now what we know, viscerally, is right, and find the data to support our assumptions later. You might call that intuition. I think that we have to depend heavily on intuition, because I do not think that it is possible to reason our way out of our current predicament.

If you need science, use The Natural Step, a set of four system conditions based on broad scientific consensus about what is and, mostly, what is not sustainable human activity, given what we *do* know about the earth. My abbreviated version of the four principles goes like this: do not take things out of the earth that we cannot handle (oil, uranium, heavy metal, etc.); do not put things on the earth that *it* cannot handle (PCBs and other man-made toxins); respect the diversity and abundance of natural ecosystems (the economy cannot live for long without them); and give equity a chance (it is not sustainable to have three hundred billionaires with as much money as the bottom three billion people). This is not a set of rules that we can follow right away, but rather a compass to guide us in taking action now.

A book I have praised in my speeches is *The Ecology of Commerce* (1993), by Paul Hawken, who brought The Natural Step to the United States from Sweden. The book includes the example of the 3M company, which made an extra $500 million in profits over a fifteen-year period through decreasing waste and pollution. Ray Anderson, the CEO of Interface (a carpet and interiors company), read Hawken's book and decided that he could and should do even better. After only a few years, by redesigning their operations and facilities (using The Natural Step as a compass) to reduce emissions, waste, and toxic components, Interface experienced a $200 million growth in income with no increase in re- source use. This is starting to sound sustainable! But Interface is not done yet; they want their business to actually restore the earth. Interface and other ecologically intelligent businesses are featured in Hawken's latest book (written with Amory and Hunter Lovins), *Natural Capital- ism: Creating the Next Industrial Revolution* (1999). The new book gives us examples, far beyond even what 3M has done, of what they call "radical resource productivity." They started with "Factor Four" com- panies, twice as productive with half the resources, but now the goal is Factor Ten and beyond. We can do this! Hawken and the Lovinses show that companies that do not redesign themselves to conserve, preserve, and restore natural capital will soon be at a serious competitive disad- vantage and will not last long in the twenty-first century.

This is the question to take to the rest of the Fortune 500: Have you done anything recently about redesigning your processes in light of what is happening to the earth? I think if they start thinking that way, we are going to include some measure of ecological conscience in corporate behavior, and possibly even in the behavior of the people investing in those corporations.

When I travel around and speak, I often ask people how many of them would be willing to commit at least one year of their lives to working on saving the earth. They could serve as volunteers or for pay — as teachers, organizers, lawyers, lenders, or whatever. Two-thirds of all the hands go up, everywhere I talk. I have asked the same thing of doctors and healthcare specialists in Denver; of producers and writers in Hollywood; and, of course, students, whom I visit a lot. Then I ask the question another way, because I did not see all the hands raised: How many people in the audience would be unwilling to commit at least a year out of the next ten years? Rarely do I see a hand up. So there is unanimity on this issue. So I say, since we are all for it, we should do it. All we need to do is to get organized, give people their assignments, and go at it. If we fail to do it, we will not be here much longer, because the rate at which things are deteriorating is accelerating. In the face of all this, we need to hang on to hope more than ever. Lord Snow said, "Despair is a sin." Even better, and I forget who first said it: "Action is the antidote to despair." If you are in despair, you are probably not in action.

Nevertheless, I suppose I have not cheered anyone up, and I have not made people laugh as much as I would have liked to, but these are some thoughts on problems that I hope we will all confront. In the end, what this task requires is commitment, and until you commit yourself fully, there is always a chance to give up or fail. My friend and fellow mountaineer William Murray said it best: "The moment one definitely commits oneself, then Providence moves too. All sorts of things occur to help one that would never otherwise have occurred."

We are asking for some dreams here. Just take the first steps. As Goethe said, "Whatever you can do, or dream you can, begin it; boldness has genius, power, and magic in it." You have magic within you; you only need to let it out.

Part IV   AGENTS OF CHANGE

The Private Sector

Chapter 7   COMMUNITY-BASED
CONSERVATION

JON ROUSH   We are witnessing a fundamental change in the relationship between the federal government and local
governments. Three trends, in particular, are very
important: (1) The locus of critical action is shifting from federal decisions to state and local decisions; (2) increasingly, strategies are emphasizing private action and deemphasizing public action; (3) the focus of
attention is changing from piecemeal conservation to whole systems.

The Environmental Protection Agency acknowledged these trends
in its 1994 Strategic Plan: "EPA must collaborate with other Federal,
Tribal, State, and local agencies, as well as private partners, to reverse
those trends and achieve the ultimate goal of healthy, sustainable ecosystems." The plan also promises that the agency "will enlist the support
of a spectrum of participants in priority setting and decision-making
processes." That is the right course, but a difficult one.

It would be easier were it not for the pressure of history. Many
scholars mark the beginning of the modern conservation movement with
the fight to save the Hetch Hetchy Valley in Yosemite. The Tuolumne
River flows out of Yosemite Park and through the Hetch Hetchy Valley.
"Hetch Hetchy" is the Indian name for green meadows; the meadows
were green and beautiful. After leaving those meadows, the river flows
through the Central Valley and into the San Francisco Bay. In the 1880s
and 1890s, San Francisco got its drinking water from a private company,
the Spring Valley Water company, which was charging high rates for
poor service. The city elected a new mayor, a reformer, James E. Taylor,
who intended to do something to change that. In 1901, he persuaded
Congress to pass a bill allowing community water to be taken from
national parks "for domestic, public, or other beneficial use," and the
city of San Francisco immediately applied to the Department of the
Interior for water rights from the river. Theodore Roosevelt's secretary
of the Interior, Manning Ethan Hitchcock, denied the application. He
thought that national parks were "a poor place for a public works proj-

ect." In contrast, another member of the Roosevelt administration, also a great name in conservation, Gifford Pinchot, argued that the Hetch Hetchy could be developed without any aesthetic harm.

That brought John Muir out of the woods. Muir was another giant of the period and one of the great publicists of conservation. He wrote a letter to his friend Teddy Roosevelt, describing the prior proposals to develop dams in the Hetch Hetchy Valley. All of those projects, he said, "show forth the pride — the sort of confidence that comes of a good sound irrefragable ignorance." The battle was joined, and it raged through three administrations and in the national press until 1913, when President Wilson finally signed a bill authorizing the dam.

The Hetch Hetchy battle was a galvanizing moment in the history of conservation. It was the first environmental issue to attract the attention of the national press, and it marked the first time that the disparate parties working on conservation issues came together in an effective national network. By the time the issue was resolved, the Sierra Club had transformed itself into the major national force it is today.

In addition, Hetch Hetchy inspired rhetoric from which activists like me still borrow. It was truly a classic environmental issue. It had everything. It had the archetypical conflict between voices for absolute preservation, led by Muir, and those who argued for multiple use, led by Pinchot. It pitted conservationists against developers or, again in Muir's words, "developers, mischief-makers, and robbers of every degree from Satan to Senators trying to make everything 'dollarable.' " It hastened an emerging divide between professionals — in this case, the city's engineers and consultants — and citizen activists. Like many issues that still divide us today, it pitted the interests of a local economy against national interests in the conservation of public lands. Throughout most of the twentieth century, all these polarities were apparent in most environmental fights. They have become so familiar to us that it almost seems as if they have the inevitability of nature, like the division between Earth and sky.

Now consider another story, with similar issues but a different outcome. This one starts about a century after the opening salvos of the battle of Hetch Hetchy. The U.S. Fish and Wildlife Service circulated a petition to list the Louisiana black bear as a threatened species. In Louisiana, Mississippi, and East Texas, the black bear was in trouble, partly because its habitat was disintegrating. Ninety percent of the black bears' habitats were on private land, most of which was commercial timberland. Many communities in the region were dependent on that timber for their income. People in the region, and especially those in the timber industry, feared that listing the bear as a threatened species would hurt the local economy. But the issue was not so simple, because the bears served as an indicator species for the hardwood bottomland ecosystems in the southern watercourse. If the bear was in trouble, one could assume that other elements of the ecosystem were suffering also. Conservation of the bears would help many other species.

Environmentalists were determined to protect the bear, but land-owners were equally determined to protect their rights. The situation was ripe for another classic environmental showdown, but this time the parties at issue declined to follow the script. In 1990, a group of eighteen people representing industry, federal and state agencies, landowners, and conservation groups started to hold meetings. Acting on their own initiative, they named themselves the Black Bear Conservation Committee (BBCC), and they established some important ground rules. Committee members agreed to respect each other and to set aside, as much as possible, their personal agendas. Whenever possible, they would let scientific data and the scientific theory provide the criteria by which their decisions were made.

Meanwhile, biologists in the U.S. Fish and Wildlife Service determined that the black bear could survive along with careful commercial logging, as long as more habitat was not lost. The BBCC agreed to some preliminary measures to protect the bears, and those measures allowed the Fish and Wildlife Service to delay listing the species, to give them some time to work things out. The Louisiana black bear was finally listed as threatened, but with the provision that any unintentional killing as a result of normal logging operations was exempt.

Since then, the BBCC has enlarged its membership and has continued to work on behalf of the black bear in issues involving habitat, management, and education. For example, they produced a management handbook for landowners, and they launched a public education campaign to persuade people in the region, especially landowners, that the black bear is an economic asset. The Endangered Species Act requires that the Fish and Wildlife Service draft a recovery plan for the bear. At this time, the BBCC is completing a restoration plan that will be the core of that draft recovery plan.

So we have two models for resolving issues that pertain to natural resource management: the Hetch Hetchy model and the BBCC model. In the Hetch Hetchy model, combatants dig in, refuse to negotiate, and slug it out in courts, legislatures, or executive offices until somebody with sufficient authority to do so makes a decision. Then, once a decision is made, it is over, case closed. There are clear winners and losers. In the BBCC model, in contrast, citizens do not just influence the process — to a larger extent, they *are* the process. The model specifies a commitment to inclusiveness. People look for a solution that lets everyone win. The goal is to protect both the environment and jobs — to address both national and local concerns. To that end, participants agree to be guided by the best available science and not get embroiled in one-upmanship.

The BBCC is an example of a movement that has produced thousands of local voluntary community-based conservation initiatives. Let me give you a few other examples. My home state of Montana has a huge Superfund site, the polluted Clark's Fork River, but pollution is not the only problem in the Clark's Fork. There is another very high-stakes issue: irrigation versus fish. Some twenty years ago, Montana voters authorized the state to reserve water in high-quality trout rivers. In terms of statute, this is a new type of water right. The state could not take water out of the rivers but instead was legally required to keep it in them, to protect their biological integrity. Yet unfortunately for the trout, these new water rights can be invoked *only after all preexisting rights for irrigation have been exercised.* So in a low-water season, when the trout really need the water, it is possible that all the water could be taken from the rivers for irrigation, with none left for the fish.

The result was a clash between two icons equally venerated in Montana: trout and cows. One possible solution would be to allow the state to lease water rights from farmers and ranchers. That seems like a sensible free-market solution, but at first, the state's agriculturists opposed it. It would force them to acknowledge that the use of water for wildlife preservation and protection was indeed a beneficial use of water. In a state where over three-fourths of the water is used for farming and ranching, they feared that such an admission would mean the end of agriculture as they knew it.

In 1989, a diverse group of citizens concerned about the Clark's Fork formed the Clark's Fork Basin Committee. After a year of meetings, they agreed to ask the state legislature for a four-year truce. During this four years, irrigators would agree that no new water rights would be granted in the upper Clark's Fork Basin. And the environmentalists in the state would agree not to petition for any in-stream flow regulations. They would use that four-year window to draft a consensual Basin Management Plan. In 1991, the legislature agreed.

The voluntary committee evolved into an official commission appointed by the governor. It created six new voluntary committees, one for each of the six watersheds in the basin. They worked assiduously, and in 1995, the state legislature adopted all their recommendations. Then, the legislature went further. For the first time, it passed an act allowing the experimental leasing of water rights to protect wildlife. The work of the Clark's Fork Committee had persuaded agriculturalists across the state that their opponents, the conservationists, might actually have a good idea.

In small ways and large, people are inventing their own versions of the BBCC and the Clark's Fork Committee. In Miami, the Miami River Neighborhood Restoration Association and other citizens and agencies are working to restore the Miami River works in the city's Little Havana District. In Portland, Oregon, many different groups have joined forces to restore the Columbia River watershed. The Trust for Public Land, the Urban League, and the local parks department are converting vacant industrial parkland into parks alongside the river.

In the watershed of Oregon's Applegate River, private landowners own only 30 percent of the land. The U.S. Forest Service and the U.S. Bureau of Land Management control the other 70 percent. Only twelve thousand people inhabit the region. There are no incorporated towns. Several years ago, some sixty residents got together to look for ways to save the Applegate natural resources and, at the same time, to save its economy. They included members of the Sierra Club, the Audubon Society, the Wilderness Society, community groups, the farm bureau, loggers, and officials of the Forest Service and the BLM. Their objective was to restore the watershed through a cooperative community effort.

I could cite many more examples of this sort of collaboration. They reveal a broad diversity of strategies and goals, but some underlying similarities as well. Community-based conservation is typically a local phenomenon. People who live close to problems are frequently more ingenious in finding appropriate solutions. Community-based conservation is also inclusive. It seeks to involve all stakeholders — sometimes everyone in the community — in defining issues and solutions. Because it stresses accountability, decisions are made in the public arena by government agencies, elected officials, business executives, and everyone else who will be accountable for those decisions. Most important, the emphasis is not on winning, but rather on gaining a consensus. People are encouraged to put aside the question, Will the decision give me everything I want? and instead ask themselves, Can I live with it?

So this is the new politics of conservation, in which technical expertise is essential but is not the final arbiter in decisions. The new model places more control over the essential decisions in the hands of the people who will be affected by them. But it can work only if people see themselves as representing ethical interests and principles, not political interests. That is how the new model works, but the important question remains: Is this new model better?

It all depends. It has many attractive features. It addresses a range of interconnected issues, rather than taking a narrow, project-by-project focus. It generates buy-in from the people who have to implement the decisions. By tapping into people's unpredictable creativity, the model also encourages innovation. It draws upon the knowledge of people who are close to the problem and therefore have relevant local experience. And it also builds trust, so that the people are better prepared to work together again on the next problem that comes along.

The model, in fact, has so much power that it is quickly emerging as the new orthodoxy. The report of the President's Council on Sustainable Development devotes an entire chapter to strengthening communities.[1] That chapter opens with a passage that could serve as the credo of the new politics of conservation: "Creating a better future depends in part on a knowledge that involvement of citizens [is essential] and on a decision-making process that embraces and encourages different perspectives of those affected by government policies." Steps toward a more sustainable future include developing community-driven strategic planning and collaborative regional planning, improving communities and building designs, and creating strong, diversified local economies while simultaneously increasing jobs and other economic opportunities.

One key reason that the collaborative approach is gaining adherents is that participants in it feel empowered. Empowerment is a powerful motivator, but it also produces a "halo effect." Feeling good about these processes, even wanting them to work, encourages people to overlook shortcomings.

These processes can reduce conflict, but do they produce good decisions? The answer to that question depends partly on what one is trying to achieve. If one's goal is to help communities work well, the results are usually very positive. If the goal is to promote sustainable systems, the results are more uncertain. Ecological systems have their own measures

---

1. The President's Council on Sustainable Development, *Sustainable America: A New Consensus for the Future* (Washington, D.C.: U.S. Government Printing Office, 1996), chap. 4.

of proof that may have little to do with community consensus and may even contradict it. Conceivably, a decision-making process could be perfectly democratic, participatory, and equitable, and still lead to decisions that hurt nature. I recall the character in *Huckleberry Finn* who said, "Ain't we got all the fools in town on our side, and ain't that a big enough majority in any town?" Besides, too often the decision processes are not really participatory or equitable. The community model does not work when it is overpowered by conventional politics. Conventional politics favors those with money, perceived expertise, or superior organizing ability. Those political advantages may subvert the community's long-term interest in sustainability.

It is important, too, to be clear about what it is we mean by a "community." The word has many meanings. Most often it refers to a community of people living in a place with defined boundaries, such as a city. Conventionally, they are called "communities of place." But there are kinds of communities other than community of place. There are, for instance, communities of value, wherein people are held together by common values. Such a group can be structured (for example, a religious community) or it can be informal, like the fans of country music. But shared values are an essential ingredient in any healthy community, and differences in values tend to lead to conflict. Communities of place usually include conflicting communities of value. If you value someone's right to have an abortion and I value the sanctity of life at conception, our disagreement can threaten the fabric of community. Analogous conflicts of values divide communities on environmental issues. People can live in the same town but disagree violently about the value of old-growth forests.

Often, communities of place do not act like "communities" in most senses of the word. I used to live near a town of about a hundred people. From the outside, it looked like a Norman Rockwell kind of place. Yet, in that town the decision to sit down and have a public cup of coffee with somebody could have unexpected political consequences. People have lived there for generations, and they tend to carry grudges almost that long.

In such communities, the pressure toward conformity is strong. If your house is on fire or you are stuck in the snow, everybody will drop everything to help you. Yet if you have a difference of opinion about something important — for example, whether there should be more or less grazing on U.S. Forest Service land — then you can quickly come to understand the other (political) meaning of community. If we expect such communities to become more active and play a constructive role in community-based conservation, the local people may need some outside help, but help of the most judicious sort. In an atmosphere of conflict, one person's helper can be another person's enemy. When natural resources issues are left to local decisionmakers, and those issues involve national interests, outsiders will make their influence felt, complicating an already complicated situation.

When communities of value become politically organized, then communities of interest emerge. A "community of interest" is a group of people held together by the noble goal of getting the better of some other group of people — for example, loggers versus environmentalists. Therein lies the problem. Communities of interest can simply choose not to participate in consensus-driven community-based conservation. A single interest group intent on winning can slam the door on any community-based conservation effort.

That happened in 1995, when Congress passed the so-called Salvage Timber Rider, an amendment to the Budget Efficiency Act. The Efficiency Act was described as a deficit-reduction measure that stopped Congress from spending money that had previously been authorized. The Salvage Timber Rider allowed the Forest Service to expedite the sale of salvage timber, which is usually defined as timber that is dead or nearly dead. The new Salvage Timber Rider redefined salvage timber much more broadly, with a definition justified not by science but by the politics of short-term profits. More important, the rider exempted these salvage sales from any citizens' review under the Endangered Species Act, NEPA, or the Clean Water Act, the relevant environmental laws that were in effect. That allowed the Forest Service to reclassify sales that would not, under other circumstances, comply with the law.

The consequences of this legislation, beyond ecological destruction, were horrendous for community-based conservation. Once the Salvage Rider was passed, some fledgling community groups disintegrated, simply because there was no longer an incentive for some of the parties to come to the table.

Whenever I meet somebody with expertise or experience in community-based conservation, I ask what he or she thinks are the key elements in community-based conservation. Based on what I have heard, and on my own thinking over the years, I have developed a short list. I think these are the essentials.

The first is a preexisting spirit of community. Areas that are experiencing rapid growth tend to have difficulties with community-based conservation because there are so many newcomers with little or no psychological investment in place. In contrast, in the Clark's Fork River example, a shared commitment to a river has allowed people to set aside their differences and work together.

The second necessary condition is a local awareness of the need for a rule or agreement. The crisis in the local economy, a polluted river, even an inspiring vision can provide the motivation for the rule. Whatever it is, though, it must be sufficiently urgent to spur people to collaborate and engage in hard work. Often, the perceived need is to make some effective response to the threat of federal action. That is why, for so much of community-based action, endangered species become the weapons both sides deploy.

Third, people need adequate technical support. They may need capability for geographic information systems or help with techniques for visualizing the species of value. They may need professional facilitators and scientists and technicians. Many communities do not have these capacities locally; if that is so, they should be able to turn to state or federal agencies for such help. Technical support also can take the form of state or federal standards, which can provide a sense of guidance.

Fourth, people need good information. Most of us do not understand the workings of our local economic or ecological systems. For effective community-based conservation, there must be an education process to provide good information. Education is helpful for another reason, too: when everyone focuses on the same facts, they tend to reach an agreement. Community-based conservation often requires exactly the kind of information that, until recently, was supplied by the National Biological Service. People also need help in analyzing the economic flows in their areas. This sort of assistance is provided through the Community Development Workshops that are sponsored by the Commerce Department.

Fifth, communities need an institutional framework for action. The framework can be supplied by facilitating public agencies or private organizations, as well as the appropriate laws and social customs. These institutions give the legal and moral authority sufficient to bring people together and enforce decisions. When we destroy our watersheds, it often happens because these institutional frameworks simply are not there.

Sixth, every community exists within larger communities, larger polities, larger jurisdictions, up to and including states, and the federal government. Frequently those larger communities are engaged in environmental actions that include the smaller community. Community-based conservation requires that these two or more entities work together.

Seventh, community-based conservation needs money. The process involved often requires paid facilitators or technology and data gathering; the solutions may require capital investment in facilities or land acquisition. Federal grants may be the only available source that is feasible for this purpose.

Finally—and most important—the key prerequisite is leadership. Someone in the community must generate the idea for effective action, gather the people, and keep them together when the going gets tough. People outside the community can also play important roles, but only local or regional leaders will have the credibility, the influence, and the knowledge to pull a community together for conservation. A community can have all the right political, economic, and technological tools in place but still exhaust its natural resources. Unless community leaders step forward, nothing positive will happen.

When these elements are in place, communities have a better chance of sticking it out through a protracted battle over some conservation-related issue than outsiders do. There are many instances where community-based conservation has been going on for decades—for instance, through local land trusts. Another example is the EPA's innovative work in the Chesapeake Bay some twenty years ago. The community efforts that grew up in response to that work are, in many cases, still there and still very, very strong. If the community sees the conservation of its environment as a part of its local identity, that perception is not going to change very quickly.

For the new politics of conservation, success is going to depend on educating people in the skills and the art of citizenship. Should the federal government contribute to that education? I am convinced that it should. Community-based conservation promises some powerful corrections to the shortcomings of the old politics of command and control, but it is not a perfect substitute. It does not always work. When it does, success is often partly the result of a strong partnership between the community and the federal government.

Most global problems are at least in part community problems. Overpopulation—the root of most environmental problems—is happening globally at an alarming rate, but its solutions will have to be community based. People's decisions about reproduction are socially and ethically as well as biologically bound, and the social and ethical decisions are based largely on what the community feels is the right thing to do. For resources that we share nationally, such as air and water, we need national standards. Yet we need standards that measure outputs, without micromanaging procedures for meeting those standards. In that way, we can allow for local innovation and appropriate adjustments for local conditions.

Still, in the current shift toward localism, we must think twice before weakening federal agencies. Doing so could be disastrous for community-based conservation. We must constantly search for a dynamic balance between national goals and standards and locally appropriate strategies for meeting those goals.

The gap between national and local agendas sometimes seems unbridgeable. The problem is one of scale: local communities have a local focus. Ecological systems (watersheds, for example) often include much larger territories, and the common good often involves many more people. We need mediating institutions. They would be systems expansive enough to reflect large-scale needs, resources, and constraints, but small enough to be responsive to local needs, to interpret larger goals in terms relevant to local capabilities. They should have the resources and credibility to represent all communities in their territory in even larger, federal arenas, and they should have the political, economic, and social familiarity to inform and guide local decisions appropriately. In most cases, the institutions best prepared for those roles are found in state governments.

Of course, every state has a complex set of environmental and natural-resource agencies, and many of them have explicit responsibilities for helping implement federal laws and regulations. Usually, however, they have responsibility for specific elements or issues — fish and wildlife, air pollution, and so forth. Only a few states coordinate such agencies in comprehensive programs to support local decisionmakers with relevant information and to help disparate communities work together. With a quarter century of statewide land-use planning, Oregon has developed some useful models. More recently, Maryland has developed a statewide geographic information system that captures diverse data, integrates it, and makes it comprehensible to local officials and activists. We need to replicate such programs and create new ones, in every state.

Community-based conservation is a winning political strategy. More than that, it is a powerful strategy for conserving natural systems and honoring natural processes. When it works, it is also an engine of hope, reminding us of the resilient strengths of democracy. We must accept, however, that it is not a panacea, nor does it provide an easy road. Like most important efforts, community-based conservation will take time, energy, and commitment. We will make mistakes, but we can learn from our mistakes and build on our successes.

Whatever happens, the new model will not work without the pressure of latent federal action and without the help of federal information, expertise, and money. For the EPA and other federal agencies, the ground rules may be changing, but the need for federal help and attention remains.

Chapter 8   HOW TO SAVE THE WORLD . . . OR AT LEAST OUR CORNER OF IT

WILLIAM H. MEADOWS   At the age of fifty-five, Ed Garvey made a life-changing decision. For many years, Garvey had hiked and studied the Appalachian Trail; it was what he loved to do. But by 1970, the long-term health and survival of the trail was threatened by encroaching development. So he decided to act on his love for this place. He lobbied members of Congress and top officials from various land management agencies. He wrote countless letters, testified at innumerable hearings, and inspired others to join the fight. He persevered, and with perseverance came success.

In 1978, Congress passed a bill to protect the trail, and, in recognition of his efforts, President Jimmy Carter gave Garvey a citation in 1980. But his work was far from over. He continued to push for complete implementation of this law. Thirty years after making his fateful decision, his dream of protection for the entire trail is nearly complete.

Ed Garvey seems to be a quiet, unassuming sort of person. But when it comes to saving the corner of the world he loves, he is a passionate fighter. The world needs more Ed Garveys, more people with passion for special places.

The Wilderness Society would not exist if it were not for a handful of people who, like Ed Garvey, cared passionately about America's wild places. In launching the society in 1935, our founders declared, "All we desire to save from invasion is that extremely minor fraction of outdoor America which yet remains free from mechanical sights and sounds and smells." Perhaps surprisingly, this sentiment came from a group of men who were predominantly scientists. We do not always think of scientists as being passionate, but each of the society's founders was committed to the idea that wilderness needs protecting from those who seem unable to value land by any measure other than its ability to "produce goods." The founders also believed that people could change the world for the better. In calling for others to join the new Wilderness Society, Bob Marshall, a forester with the Forest Service, cautioned the timid to think twice. "We want no straddlers," he said. Instead, he summoned only those "spirited people who will fight for the freedom of wilderness."

Early on, the conservation movement concentrated on saving our "national jewels," and there were notable successes, including the Everglades and Dinosaur National Park. But the boom years following World War II proved that something more was needed. The national forests were becoming enormous factories for the production of timber. The Bureau of Land Management greatly accelerated grazing and mining programs throughout the three hundred million acres of public lands under its control. The National Wildlife Refuge System had become a target for farming, oil drilling, and other kinds of development. The National Park Service launched a program called Mission 66, vowing to expand roads and tourist facilities in the parks to vastly higher levels by 1966.

Against this disheartening backdrop, one man came up with a visionary response. The Wilderness Society's executive director, Howard Zahniser, drafted a bill enabling Congress to set aside America's special places as wilderness. These would be designated areas in the national forests, national parks, national wildlife refuges, and Bureau of Land Management lands that would be kept permanently undisturbed by any human enterprise. That meant no roads, no development for economic purposes, no structures, no vehicles, and no significant impacts of any kind. Zahniser understood what was at stake when he wrote into his bill, "A wilderness, in contrast with those areas where man and his own works dominate the landscape, is hereby recognized as an area where the earth and its community of life are untrammeled by man, where man himself is a visitor who does not remain."

The bill was introduced in 1957. Before all was said and done, Zahniser had rewritten the bill sixty-six times and testified, or had testimony presented, before no fewer than eighteen public hearings in ten states, as three separate sessions of Congress deliberated on it. He testified for the last time on April 27, 1964. A week later he died, but he was present in memory when the Wilderness Act became law in September of 1964. Although he was not there to witness it, Howard Zahniser's passion had changed America for the better. At its inception, the act designated some 9 million acres as wilderness. Some of the treasures protected under the act are New Mexico's Superstition Wilderness, California's Ansel Adams Wilderness, Idaho's Selway-Bitterroot, Minnesota's Boundary Waters, North Carolina's Linville Gorge, and New Hampshire's Great Gulf. Over the last three decades, the Wilderness System has expanded to 105 million acres, thanks to years of diligent and dedicated work by wilderness advocates.

Yet, as successful as the Wilderness Act has been, it is not sufficient. The sad truth is that as beneficial as many of our environmental laws have been, such as the Clean Water Act and the Endangered Species Act, they are not enough. America has been at the forefront of land protection, but our natural heritage, especially our biological diversity, is at great risk. Unsustainable development of all kinds has severely fragmented and disconnected our wild lands. Ecology teaches us that wild lands must be both protected and connected if we want healthy landscapes and biological diversity.

Again the nation has reached a point where a new vision is needed if we are to succeed in preserving some of the country's natural heritage. That vision is of a nationwide network of wild lands, designed to protect permanently America's forests, deserts, prairies, rivers, coastal areas, wildlife, and biodiversity.

The network is based upon the notion that wildness exists in many different forms, in many different places. It exists across the landscape along a continuum. At one end is wilderness, which encompasses those places on the landscape that are most wild. At the other end is the highly developed. In between are lands of varying wildness, some of which can be considered wild only within the context of the surrounding landscape. For example, while not true wilderness, the Santa Monica Mountains situated in the midst of urban Los Angeles contain a great deal of wildness. Coyotes, rattlesnakes, and abundant wildflowers are just a few of the reasons why their mountain parks come to mind for many people in southern California when the word "wilderness" is mentioned.

In some places the network will physically connect the nation's largest wilderness areas with important open spaces in cities and suburbs. The linkages will be through protected public lands at the federal, state, and local levels, which in turn will be connected with wild lands found within farms, ranches, and other working landscapes. Ultimately, these "working" wild lands will be connected to local parks and forests through rivers, greenways, and other corridors. In other places, where physical connections are not feasible, the linkages will be through wildlife habitat areas, such as those of migratory birds. In addition, they will be through the emotional and cultural connections people have with distant places.

At the heart of the network is America's wilderness system. Although the nation has set aside more than one hundred million acres of our federal lands as wilderness, the system must, at minimum, be doubled in size. Many important wild places remain unprotected. Spend a day in the vast stretches of the Arctic Wildlife Refuge or the redrock canyonlands of southern Utah, or even among the small patches of remote forests still left in the Appalachian Mountains, and you will be convinced of their need for protection.

Yet it is the network's capacity to include smaller, relatively wild places at the community, county, and state levels — along with the larger wilderness areas — that makes it a powerful tool for connecting people. The experience most Americans have of "wilderness" is of these smaller places, yet they share much common ground with the most ardent big wilderness advocates. For many, it is a shared belief that wild things have a right to exist in their own space and time, without our defining, framing, or limiting them. This is the very essence of wildness — nature operating under its own rules, free of human controls. In recognizing this right and in choosing to protect wild places, we simultaneously acknowledge the deep emotional and spiritual needs we have for healthy and wild landscapes.

After covering the horrors of war in Bosnia, a journalist returned to her childhood home to recuperate from a combination of physical and emotional ailments. Her painful path to recovery, as recounted in a magazine article, literally takes place in a park near her house. Daily walks through the mature forest provide her with solitude, experiences, and insights that help her regain an emotional footing. It is a story that speaks directly to the restorative and redemptive powers of wild places — and to the emotional needs we have for those places.

It is this deeper, more profound connection to place that gives rise to the commitment and courage demonstrated time and time again by citizens from Maine to Alaska, from Florida to California. Each group works to protect a special place, one they grew up with as children or perhaps grew to love later as adults. To each of us in our own way, these are sacred places that grace our lives with beauty and wonder and offer us a way to experience solitude and connection simultaneously. These are wild places that help make our lives whole.

The benefits of this network will be plentiful. First, it will help protect our drinking water by maintaining the ecological integrity of watersheds. Second, by serving as filtering agents the forests of the network will clean our air. Third, it will help ensure that doctors searching for new lifesaving drugs will have available to them a full range of animal and plant species for new discoveries. Fourth, it will guarantee people, regardless of where they live, access to places for outdoor recreation and a way to stay physically fit. Finally, because people have a spiritual and emotional need for nature, it will help promote our mental health as well.

Yet, as significant as all these issues are, perhaps the most important reason to establish the network is the ethical responsibility we have to protect the land and the life it sustains. Wilderness Society founder Aldo Leopold called it a "land ethic." In his classic work, *A Sand County Almanac,* he wrote, "[A] land ethic changes the role of Homo sapiens from conqueror of the land-community to plain member and citizen of it. It implies respect for his fellow-members, and also respect for the community as such."

There is already abundant evidence of this nation's willingness to embrace a new American land ethic, even if we do not know it by that name. It is present in our children's insistence that we recycle, in our willingness to ride-share or take public transportation to work, and in our commitment to make our air and water cleaner tomorrow than they are today. It is reflected in the efforts under way all across the country to protect wild lands, watersheds, river corridors, and other such places. We see it in the backlash against sprawl and the ever-mounting concern over quality-of-life issues.

At the same time, important changes are already under way in the Forest Service, which manages 192 million acres of national forests and grasslands. Chief Michael Dombeck acknowledged this sentiment in an extraordinary open letter to Forest Service employees dated July 1, 1998: "Values such as wilderness and roadless areas, clean water, protection of rare species, old growth forests, naturalness — these are the reasons most Americans cherish their public lands. . . . First and foremost, we must be loyal to our agency's land ethic. In fifty years, we will not be remembered for the resources we developed; we will be thanked for those we maintained and restored for future generations."

If only our elected leaders embraced this ethic, we would not be continuously fighting to strengthen the rules to clean up our air, because the need to do so would be self-evident. If more land managers believed in the American land ethic, there would be no debate about logging old-growth forests or punching roads into remote roadless areas. They would understand intuitively that the destruction of these wild lands threatens the overall health of our national landscape.

Important change does not come easily, nor, at times, without great turmoil. It took a bloody war to end slavery in this country, and another hundred years of struggle before the nation recognized both the legal and the moral imperative of protecting everyone's civil rights. Today, few people would deny that we are a stronger nation for it.

"I have no illusions," wrote Aldo Leopold, "about the speed or accuracy with which an ecological conscience can become functional. We should not worry too much about anything except the direction in which we travel. The direction is clear, and the first step is to throw your weight around on matters of right and wrong in land-use. Cease being intimidated by the argument that a right action is impossible."

But in working to build a network of wild lands and establish a new American land ethic, there is strength, optimism, and hope. It is the hope that Vaclav Havel, the poet and former president of Czechoslovakia, meant when he wrote that "the deepest and most important form of hope, and the only true source of the breathtaking dimension of the human spirit, is the hope which gives us the strength to live and continually to try new things."

Establishing a nationwide network of wild lands is a majestic goal with far-reaching implications for all generations to come. Like the space program that put America on the moon, or the interstate highway system that transformed our lives, it requires an unwavering national pledge, forged on the common understanding that a protected network of wild lands will make us a better and stronger nation. In the same way that those earlier endeavors gave us a sense of national purpose and community with our fellow Americans, so too can the building of the network. It allows urban and rural, rich and poor, black and white, to join together in a common goal that benefits us all. And in the end, we will leave to the future a legacy of which we can all be proud, and wild lands for which our children and grandchildren will be most grateful.

Chapter 9   WHAT IS TO BE DONE ABOUT THE ENVIRONMENT?

TED
TURNER

My biggest concerns are as a private citizen, not as the vice-chairman of AOL Time Warner Inc. However, I have been able to influence our networks to do a good deal of television programming on the environment, to try to help us build a reasonable future for humanity and for the planet.

There are many people like me. Remember the character in the movie *Network* — the news announcer — who is overwhelmed by frustration. He opens a window, sticks his head out, and screams, "I'm mad as hell, and I'm not going to take it anymore." It's disturbing what this nation and the world are doing to the environment.

What is needed is a whole sea change in the way we think. My generation was raised to believe that you should have as many children as you want, if you can afford to feed them and educate them, and so forth. We were raised to think that cutting down the forest for shopping centers and subdivisions was progress. It meant more consumers, more business; it was good for the GNP. We thought automobiles were wonderful and that making them provided employment. No one ever worried about emissions problems. And a big house, with every kind of electrical gadget possible and central air conditioning, was good too. Refrigerators seemed innocuous; nobody had ever heard of the ozone layer or CFCs or aerosol cans. Refrigerators were wonderful things. Then, over the next thirty years of my life, I learned that everything we had been taught when growing up — nearly all of it — was wrong.

The real problem is how to change many, many minds in the same way — so that people come to see that a lifestyle we have always taken for granted as being desirable may, in fact, be highly destructive to the ecology and may pose a severe threat to the well-being of our children and grandchildren.

Sometimes the problem feels insurmountable. Jacques Cousteau spoke with me about it when he was filming a seven-hour program we aired on the current status of the Amazon. We were talking about nuclear weapons, because the cold war was at its height at the time, and he did not think there was any way to get rid of them. I asked him if there was any hope for us. He replied, "Certainly, there's hope. But even if there weren't, and even if I knew for certain that humanity wasn't going to make it, then what else could I do but try?" So if I were on the *Titanic*, I would be running around yelling, "Stop, stop! There's an iceberg ahead!"

In one generation, what people had accepted as truth over the last several thousand years has gone out the window. Just a hundred years ago, we thought that Christianity, Western civilization, and industrialization could together provide an answer to everything. We thought that the indigenous American people, the Indians in the rain forest, the Native Americans here in the states, the Stone Age people who had lived for tens of thousands of years in balance with nature, were all bizarre and primitive. Now we have learned that maintaining such a balance is the only way humans can live and sustain themselves for extended periods of time.

It is very difficult for human beings to accept change. Look at the former Soviet Union and how hard it has been for them to change from a totalitarian socialist state to a freer market and a freer system. They have had terrible problems with the transition. It may be even harder for all of us to change our attitudes about how to live in balance with nature. But even though we seem to have difficulty with change, we are the species that has had the least trouble making it. We have transformed ourselves completely in the last 10,000 or so years from life as hunter-gatherers to life in a modern industrial world — which itself is only 250 years old.

Changes do not have to be grand affairs. Let me give you an example of a small change, but one for the better. For many reasons, I got rid of the cattle on my ranch and replaced them with bison. First, bison is sold for meat. It has half the cholesterol and half the fat of beef. Next, cattle do not belong in North America. They were imported from Europe and are better suited for more clement weather. Consequently, they are not very good at digging down in the snow, nor do they know how to feed efficiently in the winter. Bison, by contrast, were originally from this ecosystem and have no trouble at all foraging in winter. Bison also have much thicker coats in the winter, and their metabolism slows down, so they do not have to eat as much as beef cattle, which have much thinner coats and need more energy from food to keep their bodies warm enough to make it through the winter. For these reasons, raising bison is a more energy-efficient and a less labor-intensive alternative to raising cattle.

It is all a matter of perspective. Look at how little time modern humankind has had to get our act together, and consider how much we have had to learn in such a short period of time and all the changes we have had to make. While some might say our situation is one that is cause for total despair, we could just as easily say there is every reason for feeling encouraged.

What we must change is our relationship with the earth and with each other. We must have peace; we must have respect for each other and mutual understanding. We have to learn to live together and settle our differences peacefully, or there really *is* no hope. We have to gain control of the constant growth in human numbers, which is the root cause of so many of our environmental problems; we have to encourage people not to have more than two children in the developed world, and maybe not more than one in the developing world.

Let me offer my own set of precepts, or Ten Voluntary Initiatives, which I myself try to live by. It would help us to maintain a balance with nature if we all did this, or something like it.

I pledge that I will do, or at least seriously try to do, these things:

1. I promise to care for Planet Earth and all living things thereon, especially my fellow human beings.
2. I promise to treat all persons everywhere with dignity, respect, and friendliness.
3. I promise to have no more than one or two children.
4. I promise to use my best efforts to help save what is left of our natural world in its undisturbed state and to restore degraded areas.
5. I promise to use as little of our nonrenewable resources as possible.
6. I promise to minimize my use of toxic chemicals, pesticides, and other poisons and to encourage others to do the same.
7. I promise to contribute to those less fortunate to help them become self-sufficient and enjoy the benefits of a decent life, including clean air and water, adequate food, healthcare, housing, education, and individual rights.
8. I reject the use of force, in particular military force, and I support the United Nations's arbitration of international disputes.

9. I support the total elimination of all nuclear, chemical, and biological weapons and ultimately the elimination of *all* weapons of mass destruction.

10. I support the United Nations and its efforts to improve the conditions of the planet.

Without these initiatives, there will never be peace among nations or between humanity and the environment, since people who are starving and uneducated will persist in encroaching on one another and the environment.

I have walked every continent of the planet and been out into the hinterlands. This firsthand view of how the world is being destroyed at an unprecedented rate is frightening. It is happening in the United States, too. If we cannot stop it here, we cannot stop it anywhere.

Remember, though, that every problem is really nothing more than a solution in disguise. We cannot get discouraged. We have to go out every day and do what we can. The war to save the planet cannot be won in one great battle. As Ken Burns said in his massive documentary on the subject, "The Civil War was not fought in one, two, four, five, eight battles; it was fought in over a thousand battles, in a thousand places." Just so, the environmental war to save humanity and the planet will be fought in a million places and a million battles in the two hundred countries of the planet. And all of us will be involved in them.

In my travels, a number of indications of changed thinking about the environment have been noticed. One of the best was in 1985, with Alexander Yakovlev, Gorbachev's number two man. In his office, he was talking about Lake Baikal, in Siberia, the deepest lake in the world. He was in charge of the media, the environment, and the educational system. Talk about a powerful position! We do not have anything like that in the United States. He said that several Soviet scientists came into his office with two jars of water, one of which had a couple of minnows in it and just a bit of water. The minnows were swimming around the bottom. And the scientists said, "Mr. Yakovlev, this is how we want to show the effects of pollution in Lake Baikal." Then they poured some water from Lake Baikal, from the area of the lake where plants put out emissions, into the jar. Then they all watched as the two minnows just turned over and died. Yakovlev said, "That worked." And he added that as a result, Russia began trying to clean up Lake Baikal.

Is enough being done? Of course not. But there are many countries that are ahead of us in, say, cleaning up acid rain. Canada, for instance, has always been pushing us to get involved with it.

We are the world's greatest polluters, and we are also the wealthiest large nation on Earth. We can afford things for conservation that many other countries cannot. What an extraordinary opportunity we have to lead by example, working vigorously to make the world a better place to pass on to our descendants!

Part V   INCENTIVES FOR CHANGE

Engaging the Business Community

Chapter 10 CONFRONTING BIOTIC
IMPOVERISHMENT

THOMAS E. It is imperative that when people consider environ-
LOVEJOY mental problems, they do so largely from a biological perspective — in particular, they should main-
tain an active, vigilant concern for biological diversity. There are a
number of reasons for this, in that biological diversity means many
things at the same time. But first and foremost: if we continue to blindly
cut away large bits and pieces from our ecosystem, from the global
network of interdependent living things that makes our planet habitable,
we will impoverish our existence in multiple ways and even create new
problems that are hard or impossible to see in advance.

Biological diversity refers to the existence of the millions of species of
animals and plants (and other kinds of living things) that differ from one
another greatly, in some cases, or very subtly, in others. It also refers to
diversity at the genetic level within species, as well as to the diversity of
ecosystems and landscapes. And it is a set of natural resources upon
which we ourselves depend in various ways. Among other things, it
performs countless public services for us — it provides us with food, puri-
fies our drinking water, and even helps to stabilize the weather.

But with several thousands of species in a forest, say, are all of them
really needed for the management of its watershed? Surely, at any given
moment, there must be many of them that are not performing any particularly essential functions. But such a one-time snapshot of what is
actually a highly dynamic ecosystem would be greatly misleading. A
slight change in conditions might easily tip the scales in favor of one of
those "irrelevant" species, which then would begin to perform a very
important role.

Unfortunately we still have only a poor understanding of how ecosystems work, but some of what we have found is truly astounding. A
dramatic example involves a species of yeast in eastern Pennsylvania that
normally is very rare in the aquatic ecosystem. It has a peculiar metabolic
pathway: it skips over some important biochemical steps, so that its

metabolism is not highly efficient, and it is outcompeted most of the time by the other organisms in the ecosystem. But the steps that are skipped include some that are highly sensitive to mercury poisoning. So when mercury pollution—natural or unnatural—occurs, suddenly the balance is tipped in favor of the yeast. Other species are adversely affected, but this particular yeast has no trouble reducing the mercury compounds to elemental mercury, a liquid metal, which it concentrates in its internal organs and then deposits on rocks. So, as the major mercury survivor around, the yeast undergoes a population explosion and, in this case, cleans up the environment. But that then puts it back at a disadvantage, and it once again becomes rare. So ecosystem function and its relation to biological diversity can be quite complex.

In addition, biological diversity provides us with a set of indicators— probably the most sensitive indicators we have to most kinds of environmental stress. The decline of the peregrine falcon was a signal that DDT was accumulating to toxic levels in the ecosystems of North America. There are endless examples of that sort. This should not be surprising, because each species represents a unique set of solutions to a unique set of biological problems and is therefore especially sensitive to a particular set of environmental changes. The fact that frogs are vanishing in many parts of the world is sending some kind of signal. The cause may be multifactorial or there may be just a single problem, but whatever the cause, it is important to discover it. So as the EPA and other environmental groups carry out their monitoring activities, keeping a watch over biological diversity will play a central role.

Any particular kind of ecosystem has a characteristic level of biological diversity or species number, however you choose to measure it. Consider what happens when a pasture is stressed through the heavy use of fertilizer. The number of species decreases, and the biological diversity declines. With the removal of the stressor, exactly the opposite happens—biological diversity increases and approaches something close to whatever dynamic equilibrium the ecosystem had originally.

One particularly important kind of biological stress is that applied by global warming and the other aspects of climate change. The rates of temperature change projected from the most sophisticated mathematical models are ten to one hundred times more rapid than species seem to have historically been subjected to in normal swings of the climate. Furthermore, this is all happening in a landscape that has been highly modified, in which biological diversity is increasingly trapped in small, isolated reserves. So even if species could move fast enough to keep up with new and changing conditions, they would still confront tremendous obstacle courses just to follow their requisite climatic conditions. As Michael Robinson, one of the authors included in *Environment in Peril,* likes to say, "A species would normally move, but Philadelphia may be in the way."

For an article in the *Washington Post* on the future promise of biological diversity, I began with a biochemical reaction called the polymerase chain reaction once described at a meeting of the President's Council of Advisors in Science and Technology. That certainly sounds very scientific and abstruse, but this reaction actually plays an important role in everyday life. Nowadays, when a person is coming down with a cold or possibly strep throat, the doctor can find out what organism has caused it in two or three hours; it is no longer necessary to wait two or three days to culture a throat swab to get the results. The polymerase chain reaction makes it possible to take just a small sample of chromosomes from the bacteria, or whatever type of organism it may be, and multiply it hundreds and even thousands of times in a very short while, quickly producing a large enough amount to do the relevant testing. The procedure employed to trigger this reaction involves successive pulses of heat, which cause the two strands of each chromosome to unravel, followed by replication, followed by additional heating and unraveling, and so on.

When this reaction was first conceived, however, there was a serious stumbling block. The enzyme that catalyzed the replication itself denatured when the heat was applied. So after each round of unraveling, more of the enzyme had to be added, which was very clumsy, time-consuming, and expensive — hardly a chain reaction. Here is where biological diversity comes in. Might there be, someone reasoned, somewhere among the millions of species in the world, some kinds that live in extremely hot environments and that have developed heat-resistant enzymes? Indeed, in the hot springs of Yellowstone there lives an organism called *Thermus aquaticus,* which is highly resistant to denaturing by heat. The enzyme from this Yellowstone slime bacterium is now widely used in diagnostic medicine. Forensic medicine uses it, too, as does biotechnology. Billions, if not tens of billions, of dollars of the GNP are generated by an enzyme derived from something that you would normally clean up with scouring powder. This is the sort of power inherent in the biological world as we enter the age of biotechnology. I firmly believe that the intersection of biotechnology and biological diversity, if properly pursued (although there are problems and pitfalls in it), can be an extremely fruitful new source of wealth.

From the perspective of that potential wealth (among others), it would obviously be smart to worry about what is happening to the global stock of species. Extinction rates at present are running possibly ten thousand times faster than in prior eras, and we are losing many life forms that science does not even know about, or knows only by name.

Clearly, that translates into a mandate for a global exercise in biological inventory. This effort should begin here at home, in North America. But instead of taking advantage of the opportunity inherent in our biological diversity, the National Biological Survey dwindled away in the early part of the twentieth century.

A UN conference held in June of 1992 included a general agreement that, as part of Agenda 21, every nation should actively inventory its own biological resources. In this country, there is astonishingly little legislation on biological diversity. All we have is the Endangered Species Act, which was designed only as a safety net for species just about to fall over the edge into extinction. There is no legislation in place that, in any comprehensive way, promotes and underwrites a basic biological inventory and/or monitoring, as well as conservation plans. The consequence is that we fall back on the Endangered Species Act far too often. As long as that is the situation, again and again some "insignificant" species will be held up in a simplistic way by opponents and perhaps even by the media as an impediment to "progress" and to all the good things that presumably flow from it.

It is crucial to realize that the solution is not to alter the Endangered Species Act in any major way. The answer, rather, is to have more conservation, not less, and more laws on biological diversity, not fewer, on the books. Staying ahead of the game now avoids many unnecessary conflicts later.

Subsequent to 1992, a new National Biological Survey was created at the Interior Department, ultimately becoming the Biological Research Division of the U.S. Geological Survey. As part of that, a National Biodiversity Information Infrastructure (NBII) is being built to assist in more intelligent decisionmaking.

Issues of endangered species and problems related to biological diversity in nations with temperate climates are dwarfed by those in the tropical countries, where countless millions of species flourish. There, on the mere 7 percent of the dryland surface of the earth that is occupied by tropical rain forests, live half or more of all plant and animal species. This estimate is rough, precisely because there is such an enormous inventory job yet to be done. I personally think that it is an embarrassment to modern science that there are astronomers who study movement of the tectonic plates on Jupiter, and molecular biologists who are completely unraveling and interpreting the entire message contained in the DNA of a human, and yet we are unable to state within an order of magnitude how many fellow species share this planet with us.

In any event, one of the most daunting problems for maintaining biological richness in the tropical nations and their forests is that, by and large, the people there get precious little financial return from protecting their natural resources. The unfortunate story of natural-resource management and use in the tropics is that much of the money from it has historically gone into the pockets of the industrialized nations. That works as a serious disincentive for those countries that wish to protect their tropical forests.

Anyone who has listened to lectures about tropical forests, for example, has inevitably heard about the rosy periwinkle, found in Madagascar, and how it contains certain compounds that are very important in the treatment of Hodgkin's disease and childhood leukemia. The company that manufactures these drugs receives a handsome return, but little goes back to the country of origin, Madagascar. That is the way such business has traditionally been done.

There is a need for arrangements that redress this imbalance, including joint ventures. A country like ours would supply some financial capital, and also some intellectual capital in the form of biotechnology. The other country would supply some financing and maybe some intellectual capital, too, but its major contribution would be genetic capital. Merck, the pharmaceutical company, and Costa Rica's National Institute for Biological Inventory (INBio) set up the first of such ventures. Merck invested some funds and, as useful products are discovered in the course of taking the biological inventory ("biochemical prospecting") and come onto the market, the profits are allocated equitably between Costa Rica and the institute, on the one hand, and Merck, on the other. This is a vital project that could be replicated in many different ways elsewhere.

One of the major problems regarding biological diversity is our tendency over the last few centuries, in the West, to become perceptually isolated from it. An Amazonian Indian still knows precisely where everything in his or her daily life comes from — where tonight's fish had been in the river and which edible products came from which tree or plant. But we ourselves lack that knowledge. When the doctor diagnoses your sore throat, you have no idea that a bit of slime from Yellowstone is responsible for the quick identification. Something about our educational system needs to be corrected, to make people appreciate their own biological nature more fully and learn how it connects with the rest of the biology of this planet.

Awhile ago, I was supposed to spend the weekend on Bainbridge Island in Puget Sound. On a Saturday, I flew from London to Seattle and took the ferry to Bainbridge Island. I got there in time for a shower; then all the dinner guests arrived. You can imagine what sort of jet-lag condition I was in. When we sat down for dinner, the topic that came up in the first three minutes was, of course, the *owl!* Oh no, I thought, I don't feel like arguing about anything right now, let alone the spotted owl. But the dinner guest who had asked the question was the president of a major university. So I asked him, "How do you feel about libraries and books?" He seemed completely baffled, and my hostess told me later that she thought I had really gone off the deep end. Until I explained:

We all have a deep vested interest in the life sciences. Each species, as a unique set of solutions to the sorts of biological and ecological problems I mentioned before, has aspects upon which one can build a deeper knowledge about the life sciences. Some of these might possibly do for us what *Thermus aquaticus* from the Yellowstone slime has already done. One of my particularly favorite examples is a New World tropical forest snake that grows to about eight or nine feet in length, the bushmaster. It is not the kind of creature that people cozy up to, particularly when they learn that its venom kills by causing the victim's blood pressure to drop to zero, permanently. But scientists studying how that venom worked uncovered, in humans, a previously unknown system of blood pressure regulation called the angiotensin system. It is not possible to take venom as a pill and have it work, because digestive juices denature the protein, but knowing that this system existed, pharmaceutical chemists at the Squibb company were able to build a molecule that works on the angiotensin system. Squibb markets it as Capoten, and today it is widely used in this country and in Europe for high blood pressure. Millions of people are living longer and healthier lives because of new knowledge about how the poison of a nasty snake, in a faraway jungle, actually works. That is what is possible from learning about just one species, and why biological diversity, as an intellectual resource, is extremely important to us.

There are many causes of biodiversity loss. A major one is adding ninety million people a year to this planet — an additional billion mouths to feed, bodies to clothe, sets of needs to satisfy, every twelve years. But that is not the only problem. If we all stopped reproducing right now and added not one more individual to the human population, we would still have some very serious environmental problems to deal with. It is a complex issue because you have to work on so many different aspects of the environment at the same time. But if you do not include population growth as a prime target, I think the game is lost.

How can we motivate society to take action on some of these vast environmental issues, especially when people do not understand them well? Part of the answer has to involve a major change in our values. The only way we are going to change the value system is if people who think like us talk to people who are different from us. Further, we must talk to those elements in society that play major roles in influencing values. The arts are an important segment in this discussion. The media play a different, but also significant, role. The educational system is perhaps, in the long run, the most crucial element of all. We must learn to value living things, with all of their marvelous complexity and fascinating attributes as well as their practical value, the way we value books. After all, what people would ever suggest discarding books from the Library of Congress just because they themselves will probably never read them? But unless we transfer to plants and animals some of the value that we presently give to books, to data banks, and to our own works of art, and unless we do it soon, I think we will be doing ourselves, and our descendants, a great and irreparable disservice.

Chapter 11   HOW NOT TO PARACHUTE

MORE CATS

Saving the Earth for Fun and Profit

AMORY B.   Rocky Mountain Institute's guiding parable is a true
LOVINS   story from Borneo. In the mid-1950s, many of the
Dayak people had malaria. The World Health Organization had a solution—spray DDT—which they did with generous
enthusiasm. That killed the mosquitoes, and the prevalence of malaria
declined; so far, so good. But there were side effects. One of the first was
that the roofs of houses began to fall down on people's heads. The DDT,
it seemed, had also killed a species of tiny parasitic wasp, which had
previously controlled thatch-eating caterpillars. The colonial government had an easy answer: give everybody tin roofs. But then the people
were driven nuts by the racket of tropical rain on the sheet metal at night.

Meanwhile, the DDT-poisoned bugs were eaten by geckos, which
were eaten by cats. In due course, as the DDT built up in the food chain,
it killed the cats. But without the cats, the rats flourished and multiplied.
Soon the World Health Organization found itself faced with potential
outbreaks of typhus and plague, which the agency had itself created and
was thereby obliged to remedy. So it did—by parachuting fourteen thousand live cats into Borneo. "Operation Cat Drop," courtesy of the British
Royal Air Force (1959), elegantly showed that when you don't understand connections, often the cause of problems is solutions.

At Rocky Mountain Institute, we seek a better understanding of the
connections between things—in particular, sustainable corporate practices, farming, and forestry; community economic development; green
real-estate development; global security; profitable climate protection;

Many of the themes described here are considered in greater depth at RMI's Web
site, www.rmi.org, and the linked www.hypercarcenter.org and www.hypercar.
com. A state-of-the-art compilation by Paul Hawken and Hunter and Amory Lovins, *Natural Capitalism: Creating the Next Industrial Revolution,* was published
in 1999 by Little, Brown (New York) and Earthscan (London) and is posted at
www.natcap.org.

and efficiency in transportation, water, and energy — so that we can try to make the causes of solutions be solutions. That is, we focus on finding ways of solving (or, better still, avoiding) one problem in ways that solve or avoid many others at the same time, without creating new ones, before someone has to go parachuting more cats. In that spirit, my purpose here is to explore some strategies that may make most of the problems the world now faces go away — and not at a cost but at a profit.

I want to begin by providing a conceptual framework for thinking about the energy-related environmental problems we face today. I'll start with the familiar Holdren-Ehrlich equation that states that the harm done by people equals the number of people, times how much they do, times the impact of each thing they do.

harm = population $\times$ quantity of actions per person $\times$ impact per action

It's useful to expand this into five terms: population, times the amount of stuff (defined as the stock of material artifacts) per person, times the throughput of resources needed to create or maintain a unit of stock, times (say, for specificity) the energy needed per unit of throughput, times the impact per unit of energy used. Thus:

harm = population $\times$ stuff per person $\times$ material throughput per unit of stuff $\times$ energy use per unit of throughput $\times$ impact of energy use

When the problem is disaggregated in this way, it becomes more interesting, because there is so much you can do to affect each term, and the results multiply.

The population term pertains to the realm of family planning — basically, making contraceptives available to the enormous numbers of people who want them but can't get — or afford — them. It could also include such social factors as female literacy, social welfare, the roles of women and of men, land tenure, and so on. Complicated social issues, yes, but in fact, just meeting the world's unmet contraceptive demand would get us much of the way there.

I am not an expert on population, but I am very concerned about it. I think the dozen years that we lost on this issue in the "Period of Stagnation" (the Reagan-Bush years) we will be paying for very dearly for a very long time. But I have become convinced that in virtually all countries, regardless of social or religious conditions, there is a large unmet demand for contraception. Simply providing the services — and subsidizing them where necessary — is a necessary and very sound investment. The amount our government is spending now on international family planning is approximately what American families spend each year on costumes and candy at Halloween. That is not the right priority; roughly two or three times that would be about right. It would not take a great deal of money. There are many other very complex layers of the problem. Indeed, in the first Bush administration, I unsuccessfully floated the idea of an organization that Barbara Bush would head, along with all the former First Ladies, whose purpose would be to promote female literacy worldwide. Only those who want to keep women barefoot and pregnant could object. There are a number of other initiatives of that sort that are nonthreatening, and I think we could get a very broad political base behind them.

The second term in the equation is how much stuff we have per person. This depends on values, prices, and full costing; on what we want and how much is enough. We know very little about the degree of flexibility in social values, except that political events since the 1990s suggest that it may be greater than we thought, and that when an idea's time has come, things can happen quickly.

Then there is the term related to what might be called "materials policy." Collectively, this is extremely powerful. How much resource flow we need to maintain the current stock of tables and overhead projectors, cars and houses, and so on, depends on how long products last, what they are made of, and whether such techniques as minimum-materials design, manufacturing with resource-sparing techniques, and scrap recovery are used. Resource flow also depends on whether organizations recycle, reuse, repair, and remanufacture. The dematerialization of the Japanese economy is a prime example of the possibilities: there has been roughly a 40 percent drop in materials intensity in less than a decade in Japan, without much effort, and with far more still to do.

What I have mainly focused on in recent years is the fourth term — the energy per unit of throughput — mostly in the sphere of end-use efficiency. We know how to save roughly four-fifths of the electricity and oil we use now, at less than short-run marginal supply costs. There are also important developments in conversion efficiency and distribution efficiency. For example, system integration could save about one-third of the energy in many industrial countries just by cascading process-heat to lower-quality uses within economically feasible distances, and nearly another one-third by combining the production of electricity, heating, and cooling. Just the waste heat currently thrown away by U.S. power stations equals the total energy use of Japan!

Process redesign is another major area for innovation. Ernie Robertson of Winnipeg's Biomass Institute explains that there are three ways to make limestone into a structural material. One is to cut it into blocks; that is beautiful but not very interesting. Another is to grind it up and calcine it at over 1,200°C to make Portland cement. That is inelegant. A third option is to grind it up, feed it to chickens, and a few hours later, at chicken temperature, eggshell emerges—a material several times as strong as the best Portland cement. Or, if we were as smart as abalone, we could do essentially the same thing, albeit slowly, in sea water, at about 4°C; indeed, abalone's self-assembling inner shell is twice as tough as our best ceramics.

As we start to treat nature as model and mentor, rather than as a nuisance to be evaded, we will find many elegant enzymatic and other means of making things, eliminating brute-force, heat-beat-and-treat techniques like super-high temperatures and pressures. That would be good because we are going to have to undiscover fire. Historically, most of our production processes have changed from being fed by wood, to coal, to oil, to gas, to electricity. The next logical stage involves low-temperature, low-pressure processes in convenient, low-tech solar ranges. After all, while we need boiling sulfuric acid and high-pressure extruders to make polyaramid (the Kevlar in bulletproof vests), spiders make a tougher fiber out of digested crickets and flies in their bellies under life-friendly conditions. Janine Benyus's *Biomimicry* (New York: Morrow, 1997) offers many such examples.

Careful study of the five terms in our equation tells us the good news—that energy can be the least important factor to be worried about in the growth of population and affluence. The bad news is that all of the other factors—population, the stuff we buy, the materials-throughput required for it, and the impact of the energy we use—catch up with us first. What we ought to be most concerned about is not the depletion of nonrenewable resources, like oil and copper, but rather the destruction of what ought to be renewable resources, like biodiversity and soil fertility—the "natural capital" that provides ecosystem services we can't live without. Those are much tougher issues to deal with; hence our recent synthesis, *Natural Capitalism*, which explains how to make the productive use of—and reinvestment in—natural capital turn into a source of profit and competitive advantage.

Despite its simplifications, I suggest the equation as a useful framework for thinking about a very wide range of issues, not just environmental harm from using energy. This model is applicable to things like soil fertility, transport, health, and urban stability. Often, there are ways to disaggregate problems into bite-size pieces — bearing in mind, of course, the reductionist trap that there are often interactions and feedback among the terms of the equation. But some of those interactions can be very helpful as well. In that context, I would like to suggest that virtually everything we ought to be doing to protect the environment ought to be not costly, but profitable.

As an example, a little quadrupled-efficiency compact fluorescent lamp will, over its life, save enough coal from burning to keep a tonne of CO_2 out of the air, as well as eight kilograms of SO_x (sulfur oxides) and various amounts of NO_x (nitrogen oxides), metals, and other bad stuff. Or, if it were replacing nuclear production, it would obviate the production of half a curie, which is a lot, of high-level radioactive waste. Or, if it were saving oil-fired electricity in Hawaii, it would save enough oil to run a family car a thousand miles or a Hypercar℠ (RMI's design concept for an ultralight, ultra-low-drag, hybrid electric vehicle) from coast to coast and back with oil left over. One lamp does all this — and it actually saves at least $10 more in replacement lamps, installation, labor, and utility fuel than it costs. So, it generates at least $10 (usually several times that) of net wealth and defers hundreds of dollars of utility investment, for which we can probably think of better uses. This is especially important in developing countries, where over a quarter of the capital is going to electrification — capital taken away from investments in female literacy, infant immunization, clean water, and other development areas.

A compact fluorescent lamp is a simple example of a powerful proposition: whenever it is cheaper — or otherwise more advantageous — to save fuel than to burn it, then the pollution you avoid by not burning the fuel is eliminated, not at a cost, but at a profit. It doesn't matter whether global warming will happen or is happening or what it will be like, because we ought to take the same actions anyway, just to make money.

Broadly speaking, a least-cost or profit-maximizing energy strategy would eliminate over half of the threat to the climate by purchasing energy efficiency, which is cheaper than buying fuel in the first place. Another quarter of the threat could be obviated with sustainable farming and forestry practices, and the rest with CFC and related halocarbon displacement. Sustainable farming and forestry are roughly at a breakeven point economically, though practitioners usually do better than that. CFC displacement costs roughly zero, but because we have to do it anyway to protect the ozone layer, it doesn't matter what it costs. So if the cost of abating climate change ranges from strongly negative to roughly zero to irrelevant, what are we waiting for? This is not a matter of decisionmaking under uncertainty. It is a matter of realizing that, in this case, uncertainty doesn't matter, because we ought to act in the same way for economic reasons, no matter how the climate science turns out.

A few more concrete examples of what's happening in energy and some other areas of interest: In a 1976 *Foreign Affairs* article, I was heavily criticized for suggesting that our national energy needs over the next fifty years might not follow the official forecast of rapid and steady increase. What actually happened is that over the first fifteen years, the energy used per dollar of GNP went down by a third — more than I had suggested might occur — cutting $160 billion a year off the national energy bill. Over that time, we actually got four and one-half times as much new energy from savings as from all net increases in supply combined. By now, it is even better. The energy saved since 1973 is now a new national source whose annual output is two-fifths larger than the domestic oil industry's. Total U.S. primary energy demand is now within about 1 percent of the much-derided soft-energy-path curve I published in 1976. So far, so good. Nevertheless, we are still wasting $300 billion a year worth of energy, especially in electricity. That is more than the federal budget deficit was at its peak; it is comparable to the military budget. It is hard to compete when you buy that much of the wrong thing. Remember that the power plants are producing about a third of the fossil fuel carbon dioxide and NO_x and two-thirds of the SO_x — mostly to do things that really do not need that much electricity and, indeed, could be done better with a quarter — or a fifth — as much electricity, at lower cost, with better service quality.

So how is it possible to get severalfold more work out of each kilowatt-hour? Remember that each one kilowatt-hour not used saves *several* kilowatt-hours of fuel — mainly coal at the power plant — because of the conversion and distribution losses in between — so saving electricity at the point of end-use has high economic and environmental leverage.

There are many new technologies for using electricity more efficiently. Now we can save twice as much as five years ago, and at only a third of the cost. At the same time, nine states have reformed utility regulation — and therefore each utility's mission and corporate culture — simply by rewarding utilities for *not* selling more energy. Typically, this is done by decoupling utility profits from how much energy they sell. Then, when they do something smart to cut usage and therefore the consumer's bill, we let them keep part of the savings as extra profit. It is amazing how this can change their behavior. Unfortunately, all states except Oregon got so enamored of utility restructuring that by 2000 they had forgotten this simple principle of rewarding what we want, not the opposite. But here is an example of how well it can work.

Pacific Gas and Electric is the biggest investor-owned utility in the country. A decade ago it had about twenty power plants on the drawing board; today, it has none. PG&E has even dissolved its engineering and construction division, because it never again expects to build a power plant. Instead, by the early 1990s, it expected to get at least three-quarters of its new power in the '90s from more efficient energy use by customers. The rest was to come from privately bid renewables, which are now the second-best buy. The utility adopted this policy, in part, because its profits no longer depended solely on how much energy it sold: it got to keep 15 percent of the savings. In 1992, PG&E invested about $170 million in customer efficiency, which created customer bene-fits with a present value of $300 or $400 million. The customers got 89 percent of the savings in lower electric bills, and the shareholders got 11 percent—over $40 million—in higher profits. If someone runs a seg-ment of a business that adds $40-odd million to the bottom line at no cost and no risk, the CEO is probably going to call you up every week and say, "Is there anything you need?" All the smartest people in the utility will want to work in the efficiency division.

Electricity is being saved—by the end of the '90s, electricity use per dollar of GDP was dropping by about 2 percent a year—not just because of environmental concerns but also because of a basic economic fact: electricity production is expensive, but efficiency in using it is cheap. Customers eventually figure this out, and when they do, they want to buy less electricity and more efficiency. The only question is who is going to sell them the efficiency. Over half of U.S. utilities have discovered that it is smart practice to sell customers what they want before someone else does. The only real choice is between participation in the efficiency revolution and obsolescence. Here are a few examples of what is now possible.

I live at seventy-one hundred feet in a four thousand-square-foot facil-ity in the Colorado Rockies. It can get as cold as −47°F in Snowmass. The growing season between hard frosts is nominally about fifty-two days. (We can get frost any day of the year. We have had frost on the

Fourth of July.) One December and January, we saw the sun for a total of seven days and had thirty-nine days of continuous cloud. A first-time visitor to our place can get a bit of a jolt by coming out of a blizzard into a semitropical atrium, surrounded by jasmine, bougainvillea, mango, avocado, papaya, guava, passionfruit, grapes, and even a banana tree. In fact, we have banana crops in December and January — a total of twenty-seven so far. There may be even more of a jolt when you realize there is no heating system — well, almost none. For years we had Nanuq the Beastoid — a portable 50-watt supplementary space heater of the bull terrier variety, adjustable to 100 watts by throwing her ball — and a couple of small wood stoves, which consume probably a total of about half a cord of wood a year. That is about 1 percent of what you would expect. (We do burn some energy studies occasionally, but they do not have much energy content.)

Ninety-nine percent of the heating energy comes from superwindows and is trapped by superinsulation. Superwindows have high-tech coatings and heavy-gas fillings, so they insulate as well as eight to twelve sheets of glass, depending on the model. The net construction cost for making the house so efficient that it's 99 percent self-heating was negative, because although the superwindows and superinsulation cost more, we saved even more construction cost by not needing a furnace and ductwork.

Excluding office functions, our household electric bill is about $5 a month, before taking credit for our much larger production of solar electricity. The refrigerator, for example, uses 8 percent of the normal amount of electricity for that year's model; the freezer uses 15 percent. (We know how to save two-thirds of what's left, but haven't bothered yet.)

All of the above is accomplished with 1983 technology, when, as a package, the savings of 90 percent in household electricity, 50 percent in water, and about 99 percent in space- and water-heating energy all paid for themselves in ten months. Today it can be done even better.

The same thing has been demonstrated in hot climates because buying less or no cooling equipment cuts construction cost by more than the improvements that displace the equipment increase construction cost. For example, new windows can be nearly perfect at letting in light without heat; they cost more, but they save even more air-conditioning equipment cost. There is an experimental house in Davis, California, where it gets as hot as 113°F. Yet the house itself doesn't get hot. It is very well insulated. It has a dark roof (a bad idea required by the subdivision), and it doesn't even have vegetative shading. Yet the house has no heating or cooling system because it doesn't need them. It does have ceiling fans, which provide 9 Fahrenheit degrees of cooling comfort. For cooling backup, one can take the radiant slab coil already installed for heating and run through it a bit of relatively cool domestic water about to be used for some household task. Basically, passive night cooling — night ventilation flush — is enough to keep the house from getting hot. There are also some other innovative features, such as dumping the refrigerator's waste heat into water heating: this saves water-heating energy, makes the refrigerator more efficient, and from the house's perspective makes the upgrade a space-cooling — rather than a space-heating — device. The house was designed to consume only a fifth of the energy (for all space and water heating, space cooling, refrigeration, and lighting) that is allowed by California's Title 24, the strictest energy code in the country. If its design became general practice, its construction cost would be about $1,800 less than normal because, again, all of the usual heating and cooling equipment and ductwork are not needed. It is a much simpler house, too, and over the years would cost about $1,600 less to maintain because it has no heating or air-conditioning equipment.

My colleagues and I often begin the design of a building by saying, "Can we get rid of some or all of the mechanical systems, and is there a sensible way to do that?" Superwindows make that possible, even in big buildings. We retrofitted an office in California to save about three-quarters of the former electricity consumption. The retrofit was designed to save about 97 percent of the air-conditioning energy, which will rise to 98 percent when we finish replacing the computer equipment, and the place is a lot more comfortable.

To save three-quarters of the energy in existing offices would require combining deep, glare-free daylighting with very efficient artificial lighting (around 0.3 as-used watt per square foot). Workers see better, the space looks better, and the same amount of light is available. Some very efficient office equipment now exists that is severalfold better than what is required by Energy Star ratings, totaling only 0.2 watts per square foot. That change by itself will deduct up to $5 per square foot from the construction cost of a new office by making cooling and air-handling equipment smaller. That is a saving of about 8 percent of the total construction cost. Then put in superwindows that are tuned to have the right optical qualities on each elevation. Although they all look the same, they have different infrared properties, to regulate heat and light flow separately from each direction. Finally, install very efficient comfort equipment, which can easily be passive, eliminating the need for refrigerative air conditioning in over 90 percent of the United States, and even in the other 10 percent, too, if you use heat-driven alternatives (absorption, desiccant, and hybrid systems based on either or both).

In a new office building, one could expect to save not just three-quarters of the energy, but more like 80 or 90 percent. Businesses should always do this in new headquarters because it will *cut* capital cost by several percent and add about 5 or 6 percent in space efficiency. Efficient buildings gain something even more interesting. Our studies have found 6 to 16 percent increases in *labor productivity* resulting from the improved thermal, visual, and acoustic comfort and indoor air quality inherent in green buildings. That is worth an order of magnitude more than eliminating the entire energy bill.

So why do many developers and design professionals fail to seek out greater efficiency automatically? Well, largely because there are roughly twenty-five parties involved in the building process, all of whom are systematically rewarded for inefficient design and penalized for efficient design. We need to change the rules so that architects and engineers, for example, get paid according to what they save, not according to what they spend as in the present system.

Here is another example of the kind of societal leverage available from getting the design right. "Mindware" is the stored knowledge in your head that ripens with age; it does not depreciate. One can calculate, from straightforward assumptions, that a senior mechanical engineer specifies over seventeen hundred refrigerative tons of equipment a year, which adds a megawatt of net peak load per year for a utility, requiring an investment of $2 million a year. Now, suppose that better engineering education in integrated design can make the equipment just 20–50 percent more efficient. (That is conservative: we are empirically finding gains more like 75–90 percent or more.) In terms of present value over an engineering career, the utility avoids investments of $6–15 million per brain, not counting any savings in construction cost, fuel, and pollution. So even if engineers never learned from each other, the benefit-cost ratio of better engineering education must be two or three orders of magnitude. And we are not yet considering the greater comfort that sixty-five thousand office workers, with present-valued salaries of $36 billion, will experience as a result of the better building-services engineering. So the 6–16 percent labor productivity gain that is commonly observed in green buildings in our studies would raise this benefit-cost ratio to roughly four to six orders of magnitude. Where else does our society enjoy that kind of potential leverage from improving the design mentality?

Another example is industrial motor systems. Motors use over half of all the electric energy in the country. They use more primary energy than highway vehicles. A big motor consumes electricity equivalent to its capital cost every few weeks. Most people do two things to improve the performance of motor systems: they use slightly more efficient motors, and they install adjustable-speed electronic drives. That is fine, but doing about thirty-three additional things to most motor systems results in saving not just 15 or 20 percent of the motor system energy but more like 50 percent, and instead of a payback of four or five years, there is a payback time of about a year and a quarter at a 5-cent-per-kilowatt-hour tariff. That saving is sufficient to displace 160 GW nationwide, which is about a quarter of the electricity consumed in this country. (The reason this upgrade is so cheap, incidentally, is that one only has to pay for seven of those thirty-five energy-saving measures, the other twenty-eight are free by-products of the first seven. All thirty-five are part of a complex interactive system in which most of the design interactions are favorable.)

Then, too, there are the downstream savings. Many motors run pumps, and out of the pumps come pipes. If the pipes are made just a little bigger, drag decreases as nearly the fifth power of the diameter. Every unit of friction saved in the pipe will save about ten units of coal — and its cost and pollution — at the power plant. It does not require eliminating very much friction to make the pump, motor, inverter, and electricals far smaller — and therefore cheaper — reducing total construction cost. Indeed, a 1997 redesign of a supposedly optimal industrial pumping loop cut its pumping power by 92 percent while reducing its total capital cost and improving its performance in all respects. This required no new technology, but only using fat, short, straight pipes rather than skinny, long, crooked pipes.

There are, however, some obvious barriers to implementation. Consumers expect to get their money back from efficiency investments ten times as fast as utilities expect to get a return from their power plant investments. That is why utilities have supplemented their usual information programs for marketing "negawatts" — units of saved energy — with a variety of financing options: concessionary loans, gifts, rebates, prizes, leases, and so on, so that people can evaluate ways to save energy at the same low discount rate that utilities use to produce energy. If we compare generated and saved energy — megawatts and negawatts — on an equal basis, efficiency looks much better; but if we don't, there is an approximately tenfold price distortion, so we end up buying too little efficiency and too many power plants.

If all Americans saved electricity as rapidly and extensively as ten million people did in the early 1980s in Southern California, we could expand the economy by several percent a year while reducing total electricity use each year. The cost for doing that would be about 1 percent of the cost of building new power plants — not bad for old methods.

But we are still leaving a lot on the table if we stick with the old methods of marketing negawatts. With good marketing we can maximize participation in energy efficiency programs, and with good technology bundling we can maximize savings per participant, but we still can't maximize *competition* in who saves energy and how they do so, so as to keep driving the cost down and the quality up. To do that, we need to make a market *in* negawatts. We need to make saved electricity into a fungible commodity subject to competitive bidding, arbitrage, secondary markets, and derivative instruments — all the financial arrangements that work for other commodities like copper, wheat, or sowbellies.

Central Maine Power Company offered grants for modernization to whichever factories offered to save the most electricity per dollar of grant. In eight states, that grew into a general auction. If the utility wants more power, it takes bids from whoever wants to make — or save — electricity. The low bids are typically from savings, not increased supply.

There are also ways — already in practice — to trade saved electricity between utilities. Utility A signs a contract with Utility B to save electricity and sell it back to A. This can also be done between customers. These exchanges are already happening with water. When Morro Bay, California, was short of water, the town authorities told homebuilders that they first had to save twice as much water as each new house is going to use. So the builders went door-to-door, installing water-saving fixtures in a third of the housing stock in the first two years. Exactly the same thing can be done with saved electricity.

Saved electricity can even be traded between countries, thereby capturing the arbitrage spread between the cost of making and saving electricity. Pretty soon there will be spot, futures, and options markets in saved electricity, and ways to buy back customers' reduced demand — or reduced uncertainty of demand. Electric companies can also market efficiency in each other's territories: there is no monopoly on negawatts. Puget Power, for example, had a subsidiary that sold efficiency in nine states, even though the parent utility only sold electricity in one state.

Gas utilities can sell electric efficiency, too; they can do so just as well as electric companies, but have none of their potential inhibitions.

Another strategy: utilities can charge a fee for inefficient new buildings and use it to pay rebates to efficient new buildings. We call this a "feebate." It is a much more powerful motivator than building codes because there is an incentive for continuous improvement. For all of these kinds of improvements, the more we make them into commodities, subject to market mechanisms, the greater the savings we are going to have.

We could even use feebates to promote the transition to Hypercars: someone who buys a new car could pay a fee or get a rebate. That is simply a transfer of wealth from those who buy inefficient cars to those who buy efficient cars. The fees pay for the rebates; this is not a new tax but is revenue-neutral. The amount of the rebate for efficient new cars could even depend on the *difference* in efficiency between the new car that is purchased and the old car that gets scrapped. This can quickly get the worst cars off the road, with disproportionate air and oil benefits.

An ultralight car, weighing about a thousand pounds for a family sedan or seventeen hundred pounds for a big SUV, can be made of something akin to a jumbo jet floor, which happens to be a honeycomb or foam faced with carbon-fiber composite. This is enormously strong material. There have been head-on crash tests between ultralight two-meter-long city cars and an Audi that weighs twice as much. The Audi is run at half the speed, but with the same momentum. A little composite beam stuffed with foam is wrapped around the inside of the ultralight car. In the collision the beam deforms 6 inches, then bounces back 5.5 inches. The dummies are constrained by their belts and airbags, and they survive. The Audi, however, crushes into the passenger compartment; its dummies are dead. In another interesting approach, roughly 6-by-6-inch hollow conical shells are injection-molded out of thermoplastic and stuffed with carbon fibers pointing toward the apex. To crush this kind of shell into a plastic cow-patty, it must be folded in on itself one small piece at a time, continuously microfragmenting the carbon fibers, which are stiffer and stronger than steel. Their huge surface area also has to be separated from the matrix around them. It takes so much energy to do these things that less than ten pounds of such cones will smoothly absorb the entire crash energy of a twelve hundred-pound car hitting a wall at 25 miles per hour.

The costs of building a Hypercar are comparable to those for a conventional auto and may well be less. Let me explain. We all know that the materials required are expensive. When GM's "Ultralite" concept car was shown at the end of 1991, the *Wall Street Journal* condemned it as economic folly because carbon fiber costs a hundred times as much per pound as steel. That was true for aerospace-grade carbon fiber at that time, but it is no longer true today, especially not for the kind of carbon fiber you would use to make a car. Regardless, what matters is cost per *car*, not cost per pound. Several times less carbon fiber than steel is used to achieve the same strength, and only a small percentage of the car is carbon (approximately 40–50 kg), together with some other fibers that are cheaper. Also, though this material is costly, making a car out of it is cheap, with simpler tooling and manufacturing roughly offsetting the costlier material—just the opposite of steel, which is a cheap material but costly to fabricate. The reasons for the cheap manufacturing are fundamental. For example, the body parts count for an ultralight is one or two orders of magnitude less: the body has 2 to 20 parts instead of 300 or 400 parts, since large complex pieces can be molded in one shot. Assembly labor and space go down by an order of magnitude, as does tooling cost, because there are fewer parts, one die set per part rather than an average of four for progressive hits, and the tooling can be made out of a cheap material such as coated epoxy, which is cheap to fabricate. Because color can be laid in the mold, painting—the toughest part of making a car—is eliminated. Painting costs account for one-fourth to one-half the finished price of a painted steel car part. Collectively, these economies offset—or more than offset—the higher per-pound cost of the carbon fiber. In addition, current model cars have an average 50 percent markup to cover the costs of selling and unsold inventory. In contrast, a Hypercar would be made to order only when someone bought it. The business model would be somewhat like a Dell mail-order computer with a GE service contract.

I should mention that ultralight cars will be easier to recycle. One can recycle the composite cars, say carbon-epoxy composites, by brute force—by methanolysis or by low-temperature catalytic pyrolysis, recovering the original fiber at or very close to its original strength. The salvage value of the fiber, plus the avoided solid-waste disposal cost, justifies doing that; however, it is a less elegant approach than some that could be developed. For example, we could design resins to unlock with a chemical key, at a slightly elevated temperature or pressure. As an institutional matter, we would probably want to adopt the German system: the car maker owns the car forever, and has to take it back. In fact, the manufacturers probably should not sell your car to you in the first place. Rather, they should lease it to you, like airframes. From time to time the customer would just renew the color skin and the seats, plug in new electronics, and upgrade the software. Think of a car as a computer with wheels rather than a car with chips. By implementing in software most features now implemented in hardware, it becomes completely customizable, upgradable, and very long-lived, matching the properties of the composite body, which does not rust, dent, or scratch.

General Motors built a small, four-passenger ultralight concept car in 1991. It took them a hundred days. It seats four passengers and has four airbags. On the inside it is as big as a Corsica; on the outside, as small as a Miata. It can travel as fast as 135 miles an hour, going from zero to 60 miles per hour in 7.8 seconds. It out-accelerates a 12-cylinder BMW with an engine smaller than a Honda Civic's, and gets very high marks in emissions standards. It is safer than what we drive now, yet weighs less than half as much, and has less than half the normal aerodynamic drag. It also averages 62 miles a gallon and cruises at 100 miles a gallon with only four horsepower delivered to the wheels.

And more is possible: if one were to make an ultralight like this even lighter and more aerodynamic and to put a hybrid-electric drive in it (that is, making the electricity onboard from fuel as needed, instead of withdrawing it from half a ton of batteries), the result would be a Hypercar that could get even better mileage — around 100–200 miles per gallon depending on size, body style, and whether the electricity is made by an engine or a fuel cell. Even with present technology, this approach will ultimately save as much oil as OPEC now sells, yet provide superior light vehicles at competitive prices. By the way, Hypercars will also greatly accelerate the shift to climatically benign hydrogen production and use, particularly in high-efficiency, low-cost fuel cells. This is part of a general shift toward decentralized ways of producing electricity, driven largely by the compelling economics of appropriate scale. A side effect of this shift will be to put today's coal and nuclear plants rapidly out of business, reducing pollution and risk. Part of that happy result will come from using fuel-cell Hypercars, when parked (about 96 percent of the time), as plug-in mobile power plants that repay up to half their purchase price by their sale of electricity back to the grid.

There are some interesting extensions of this end-use efficiency approach to pollution prevention. Consider the sulfur dioxides emitted by Midwest power plants. Suppose that instead of putting scrubbers on the dirty plants and raising everybody's bill to pay for them, the utilities were instead to help people get superefficient lights, motors, appliances and so on, thus reducing the need for electricity and consequently burning a bit less coal. The biggest effect would be that the utilities would save a lot of money, because efficiency is cheaper than coal. Then suppose the utilities used the saved money to clean up the remaining plants by whatever their operators think is the cheapest method found through emissions trading — probably fuel switching, co-firing, some scrubbers, and numerous other substitutions and add-ons. Even if the plants are cleared up in a fairly expensive way, the Midwest power pool could end up reducing the amount of sulfur it produces by half — not at a $7 billion cost, but at a $7 billion profit.

The South Coast Air Quality Management District drew a supply curve that showed that roughly a fifth of the NO_x in the basin could be eliminated, at a cost of almost $4 billion a year, by standard end-of-pipe technology. Then Art Rosenfeld, then at the Department of Energy, said, "Wait a minute. Suppose we start by making the pavement and the buildings a lighter color, so the city becomes several degrees cooler — then we don't need to run so much of those NO_x-emitting combustion turbines on hot afternoons in Glendale and Pasadena." Well, white paint and white sand are a lot cheaper than middle distillate, so this tactic has a strongly negative cost, even though it does not save a whole lot of NO_x. But then we can use the money saved to put double — or triple — the current amount of rhodium in catalytic converters or to improve exhaust gas recirculation. We could thereby achieve roughly a two-fifths reduction in NO_x, at zero net cost — instead of one-fifth at $3 billion a year.

But we have left out something — Hypercars. They will be much cleaner, so they will have extremely low or zero NO_x emissions, and they save a lot of fuel cost. We can then end up with an 80 percent — perhaps 90 percent — NO_x reduction at negative net cost.

Next, try the same approach for CO_2. The cost of reducing the carbon emissions by, say, half would be slightly less than zero. If we used modern high-efficiency technologies, the cost of eliminating something like 80 or 90 percent of the CO_2 and equivalent emissions is still less than zero.

We have done this same exercise for cobalt, chromium, the platinum group, manganese, and even for water. A good example is the EPA's Two Forks Decision. It was proposed at the time to build a dam near Denver that would provide a little over 100,000 acre-feet of water a year and, including the associated pre- and post-treatment plants, would cost a little over $800 per acre-foot. RMI showed that it was possible to get at least that much water from efficiency — improved showerheads and toilets plus efficient lawn-watering equipment — at about a fifth the cost per acre-foot, or an eighth as much if one counted the energy saved from not having to heat so much water for showerheads and other fixtures. The Denver Water Board ended up taking this approach by creating saved water markets in exactly the way that I described. The proposed dam died of an acute attack of market forces.

We are beginning to realize that we ought to do what is profitable first, and help it happen in markets, just as entrepreneurial programs—like the EPA's Green Lights, Energy Star, and Green Buildings—are doing now. If we did that really effectively, the economy would improve markedly, and national security would increase. Best of all, we would not need mandatory regulation because that would be necessary only for residual inefficiencies and pollution—for toxic chemicals, in particular—and many of those would disappear as competition to make industrial production more efficient and agriculture more sustainable designed out the toxics, at a profit.

I end with one subversive remark, since I have not said anything controversial so far. As you may have gathered, I am very fond of markets— I use them a lot. I think creatively used market forces are the most powerful tool we have for environmental protection. Their dynamism and diversity are responsible for our current unsustainable system: markets, said Lewis Mumford, tend to harness all of the Seven Deadly Sins except sloth (though that might be the entertainment industry), and the same characteristics can be turned to doing good. Yet there are some things markets cannot do.

Market economics treats the economic process as an endless closed loop of production and consumption, ignoring the fact that much of what goes on is the linear flow outside that loop that steadily converts natural resources into pollution. As economist Herman Daly said, it is as if we tried "to understand animals only in terms of their circulatory systems, without recognizing that they also have digestive tracts which tie them firmly to their environment at both ends." Markets ignore most thefts from the future by counting depletion of natural resources at extraction cost, and pollution at zero. This approach tends to treat capital consumption as income. I wish I knew how to increase my bank account by withdrawing money from it, but I have yet to figure that one out. Yet that is exactly what we are doing with resources. We are treating bads and nuisances as if they were goods and services and are counting only what's countable, not what counts. We are assuming infinite substitutability of artificial—for natural—capital, even though we do not know how to make the natural systems we are destroying. We are applying market-based concepts like discount rates to things one cannot bank at interest, like safety and genes.

Those are severe defects in the market approach. Even if we fix those flaws, market economics still could not answer the questions, What is the right size? and How much is enough? Daly reminds us that a boat that tries to carry too much weight will sink, even if the weight is optimally allocated.

Markets do not address issues that pertain to community, beauty, integrity, justice, or aesthetics. Markets are meant to be efficient, not sufficient; greedy, not fair. Markets cannot ever substitute for ethics or politics; we are in deep trouble if we suppose that they can. If markets do something good for whales or wilderness, God or Gaia or grandchildren, that is purely coincidental. Markets are very good at what they do, but taking care of the planet has not been one of them. Markets make a splendid servant, but a bad master, and a worse religion. While there are good reasons to keep on doing many of the market-based things we are doing, there is an essential point that, I feel, we must always keep in mind: markets are extremely efficient and effective as short-term allocators of scarce resources, but their purpose is far from the whole purpose of a human being.

Chapter 12   FREE-MARKET
ENVIRONMENTALISM

*Protecting the Environment via
Private Property*

FRED L.
SMITH, JR.

There is an alternative to the traditional approach
to environmentalism that must initially strike many
readers as foreign, paradoxical, or counterintuitive — the idea that the environment is protected best if it is protected
privately. And yet that approach continues to draw serious attention,
and it has demonstrated some significant successes.

I worked at the EPA in the 1970s, and many of the issues being
debated then — pollution prevention, recycling, emission permits, hazardous waste management, pollution taxes — are still of great concern to
the agency. But while many of the questions have remained the same, the
answers to which I now subscribe are very different. When I was at the
EPA, I was a strong environmentalist. I still am today. At that time,
however, I had a deeper faith in the efficacy of government than I do now.
That broad philosophical turn has influenced my thinking on environmental issues also.

My personal odyssey from True Believer to Skeptic is not unique. In
Eastern Europe, Southern Africa, Central America, Russia, and even
in the District of Columbia, people are questioning in field after field
whether politics is the most appropriate means of advancing the public
interest. Throughout the world, there is increasing reliance on the private sector and a greater tolerance for individual freedom, action, and
responsibility. Moreover, the mood of the intellectual community has
also changed; policy analysts are far more likely to consider the pros and
cons of private versus political approaches. Whether such trends will
continue is unclear, but at least for the moment, politics is in decline; individual voluntary arrangements are in ascendency. This essay describes
how these reforms might be extended into the environmental arena.

Garrett Hardin's 1968 article in *Science*, "The Tragedy of the Commons," serves as a useful template for examining many environmental
problems. Hardin demonstrated that where there is open access to a
commonly held resource, incentives for responsible stewardship will be

weak and the quality of the environmental resource will deteriorate. Hardin illustrated this principle with an example of a common grazing pasture. As long as grazing on the common pasture remains below carrying capacity, each herdsman may add another cow without negatively affecting the grazing of the other cows. Once carrying capacity is exceeded, however, every herdsman who adds another cow will realize a private gain but impose a social cost — the reduced grazing quality of the pasture — on the other herdsmen. It is in the common interest of all herdsmen to limit the number of cattle, but it is in the individual interest of each to graze as many cows as possible; whatever forage a herdsman leaves behind will not be conserved but will be exploited by neighbors less mindful of the need for conservation. Such incentives encourage a "use it or lose it" attitude toward pasture management, under which each herdsman rushes to stock the pasture with his cattle before others do. The result is the tragedy of the commons, a rapid deterioration of the pasture. The tragedy is the inevitable outcome of uncoordinated, self-interested parties operating in an open access regime.

To Hardin, the tragedy of the commons could be resolved either politically or privately. The first approach requires that one establish a political agency with the authority to devise and enforce the rules necessary for wise range management. The private alternative requires that the rangelands be privatized, that the pasture be divided into plots, with a plot deeded to each herdsman, and the rights then enforced through various mechanisms — fences, branding, legal recourse for trespass.

Despite Hardin's balanced treatment, few environmentalists are aware of how large a role private property constraints already play in environmental protection. Fewer still are aware of how this private environmental stewardship role might be expanded. In fact, many speakers in this series might view things quite differently. John Kenneth Galbraith, for example, noted that in America, our private homes are often beautiful but our public parks are frequently filthy. But, from that astute observation, Galbraith drew the conclusion not that we should privatize the public parks but that we should expand the power and scope of the public sector.

Barry Commoner argued that collective ownership of the means of production was vital. To Commoner, who still seems to believe that socialism is the wave of the future, this meant that environmentalists had best start using what he called the "s-word." Only socialism, he argued, could adequately protect the environment. Commoner went on to emphasize pollution prevention. Cleanup, he argued, was a waste of time. I can only wonder how Commoner deals with dirty dishes and underwear.

Jacques Cousteau presented the case for the Holy Trinity of modern environmental policy: stronger environmental regulations, an expanded environmental education program, and green consumerism. Paul Ehrlich tackled the problem of population, arguing that there were too many people in the world, and he spoke approvingly of China's stringent approach to family planning. Lester Brown thought that the environment was going down the tubes and that something should be done about it. He also was the first, I believe, in this series to bring up the now widespread concern over global warming.

While these individuals addressed a range of environmental issues, they shared a common vision. That vision is very powerful and dominates environmental policy today. Essentially, the view is that America's traditional institutional arrangements — limited government, individual liberty, free markets, reliance on private property — are inadequate for today's complex and vulnerable world. Pollution, they believe, is a natural result of individual self-interest operating in an insufficiently regulated marketplace. To them, and I would imagine to many others, free-market environmentalism seems an oxymoron.

One can argue, however, that the kinds of reform that are in ascendancy in much of Eastern Europe will eventually reach even the EPA. My confidence is based on the fact that the correlation between economic freedom and ecological quality is just too strong to be ignored. For as almost everybody now realizes, Barry Commoner was wrong about the ecological superiority of socialism. Socialism not only fails economically; it also fails environmentally. Indeed, ever since the iron curtain came down, we have discovered that the former Soviet Empire's environmental problems in many ways are even more disastrous than its economic problems. Eastern European nations use far more energy and raw materials to produce steel, use more fuel in transporting goods around the country, use more pesticides and fertilizers to produce wheat. Why is that? Socialist countries were supposed to be operating for the good of all. The reason, I think, is clear. Waste, in a socialist economy, is a collective cost, and the incentives to reduce it are therefore minimal. Waste, in a capitalist economy, affects managers and owners directly; thus, the incentives to control wastes are more concentrated. Indeed, if Eastern Europe were to do nothing more than to reach our level of efficiency in use of raw materials and energy, their pollution problems would decline sharply.

Eastern Europe does not have a monopoly on environmental problems arising from political overreach. Within the United States, more politicized sectors are characteristically less mindful of environmental values. When the private sector harvests timber, it seeks to minimize the number of felled trees; failure to do so leads to unsustainable production and to long-term losses. In contrast, the U.S. Forest Service routinely diverts large sums of taxpayer dollars to subsidize harvesting throughout the Rockies, Alaska, the southern Appalachians, and the upper Midwest that is not viable economically. Clearly, a free-market economy will build some dams and canals, but nothing the Corps of Engineers has constructed in the last forty years would survive any market tests that I know of. Capitalists do invest in third world projects, but only when they think they can turn a profit. Only the World Bank could think that the highways slicing through remote areas of Amazonian forests were an attractive investment.

Capitalism demands efficiency, and efficiency is an important environmental strategy. Wherever in the world we have had freer markets, we have also had a better managed ecology. Wherever we have had more political control, we have experienced greater ecological problems. To free-market environmentalists, the conclusion is clear: those who favor ecological protection (and I assume we all do) should seek to expand the role of private stewardship arrangements to those resources that have historically been denied its protection. We believe that those who take environmental values seriously should seek to transfer the world's wildlife, forest and grazing lands, streams and lakes, beaches and shore areas, even air sheds, to private groups who would be better able to assume stewardship responsibility for them.

Such a free-market environmental agenda represents a radical departure from current policy. And the idea is novel, or more accurately, it represents a novel application of a very old idea: individual responsibility. Minimally, the idea deserves far more consideration here at the EPA than it has received to date.

In developing the logic of that claim, I organize my remarks into four sections. First, I move from the abstract to the concrete in an examination of the plight of the African elephant, an issue that provides a good way of characterizing the two poles of environmental policy — the private and the political. The second section elaborates on these competing visions, contrasting the "market failure" rationale on which the case for political regulation is based with the "failure to allow markets" rationale underlying free-market environmentalism. The third argues the case for reform, noting the inherent problems of the traditional political approach to environmental protection. The final section outlines areas where a property-rights approach seems immediately applicable and suggests necessary work to explore the concept more adequately. Let me begin by presenting the pachyderm as paradigm and suggest why elephants need private property protection.

Most of us have heard much about the plight of the African elephant. Newspapers and television screens have been filled with disturbing pictures of the piled-up carcasses of these noble beasts. The typical explanation accompanying these images is that human greed, market forces, and unchecked selfishness are to blame. Americans, Japanese, Europeans, use ivory for trivial purposes: cufflinks, earrings, billiard balls, piano keys. As the West grows wealthier, such demands increase. Since affluence-driven demand increases ivory prices, there is increasing pressure to harvest these animals. The higher prices encourage poaching, in particular, which is very difficult to police, especially in the poor nations of Africa. Mindless consumerism thereby threatens the future existence of this species, at least in the wild.

The solution, it would seem, is obvious. Markets created the problem, so eliminate the markets and the threat to the elephants will disappear. And indeed, the United States and other nations have backed such a ban on the ivory trade through the Convention on International Trade in Endangered Species of Wild Fauna and Flora (CITES).

But might not there be something wrong with the notion that high prices are a threat to anything? Economists, at least, view the world somewhat differently. When the price of a commodity goes up, more people will seek to profit from supplying it. This is true when one is dealing with haircuts, cars, or education. There is, however, one crucial difference with elephants — namely, poaching.

In the Wild West days of America, we also had a problem with poaching — we called it cattle rustling. In the mid-nineteenth century, Americans, flush with new wealth, developed an appetite for meat. That demand, coupled with improved transportation, made the meat trade very profitable. It also made poaching more lucrative. Poaching was largely restricted to the Great Plains, a region containing large cattle herds and relatively few policemen. That situation is similar to what Africa faces today. To combat rustling we could have banned the beef trade west of the Mississippi, as we have in the case of elephants. We could have taken this path, but of course we did not. Why not?

In America, we understood that what made rustling attractive also made ranching more attractive. Increased demand was more than offset by increased supply — which, in turn, stimulated more creative and effective antirustling efforts. As cattle ranchers gained revenue, they responded to the poaching threat by taking care to protect their cattle herds. They built more fences; they hired more cowboys and equipped them with superior weaponry and horses. More important, this dynamic not only encouraged ranchers to think more carefully about conserving their resource; it also encouraged the participation of people who had no direct concern for the welfare of cows. The demand for superior methods of protecting cattle was increasing, and the profits to be made by meeting that demand grew commensurably. Elaborate branding techniques and eventually barbed wire emerged in response to the increased demand for cattle protection. The end result was that while rustling was certainly widespread in the American West, it never became a serious problem. In America, private cattle herds flourished. There was nothing magic about this development — cattle were protected because there were incentives to do so. Had the cattle trade been outside the legal economy, had there been no private ownership, this outcome would have been far more problematic.

Consider, by contrast, the case of the American buffalo. Unlike cattle, the buffalo was not owned; it was the common heritage of humankind. As a result, the American buffalo was hunted into near extinction. The moral is clear: high prices, when the resource is owned, pose little threat to the survival of the resource. Increased values may encourage poaching, but they also encourage antipoaching efforts, and the restoration of the balance typically moves in one direction. Private ownership links resources into a rich system of interactions that not only benefits us economically but also helps to protect our resources. Not surprisingly, the Competitive Enterprise Institute (CEI) and other free-market groups have concluded that elephants are far more likely to survive in Africa if they are treated more like cattle and less like buffalo.

Unfortunately, in most of Africa, this is not happening. Elephants remain essentially wards of the state. Richard Leakey of Kenya, the great hope of American environmentalists, has long been a champion of this policy and has been showered with praise throughout the world. But some of you may have seen the article that appeared in the *Washington Post* on October 1, 1989, "Save an Elephant — Buy Ivory." Randy Simmons and Zimbabwean wildlife game specialist Urs P. Kreuter undertook a comparative analysis of private and political approaches to protecting elephants. In eastern central Africa and in Kenya, in particular, government protects elephants. In those countries, elephant populations are plummeting, having dropped from about 800,000 a decade ago to

400,000 today. In contrast, Zimbabwean elephant populations have increased at about 5 percent a year over the last decade. Zimbabwe changed its wildlife law in a conscious decision to ensure that the elephant is worth more to the African farmer alive than dead. This has been very successful; unprecedented numbers of Africans have contributed to the preservation of elephants as a result.

Elephants are dying in Africa because they are being poached. They are being poached because the local people do not object to poaching. Consider that if the elephant has no value to the local people, it becomes a kind of giant rat. People get upset when the neighbor's dog runs in their backyard. Can you image how upset you would be if your neighbor's elephant broke into your yard? When elephants have only negative value, the poacher is a hero. In contrast, when the elephants can be harvested and create local wealth, poachers are not as tolerated as they once were in these areas. Robin Hood, who was, after all, a poacher, loses his popularity when he shoots the livestock of the poor rather than taking from the rich on crown reserves. Marshall Murphree, an official in the Zimbabwean Conservation and Parks Department, recently noted how even the language of the people has changed under this decentralized institutional arrangement. Locals used to talk about how your elephants are causing us a problem; now they talk about how our elephants have to be protected. Officials like Murphree now advise owners on the numbers of elephants they might cull, and the local tribesmen sometimes reject them for being too high. Locals act in a more conservative strategy than even the national government considers necessary.

Despite all of this, the United States Department of the Interior, yielding to the lobbying pressures of traditional environmental groups, continues to support the ban. Environmental groups have profited handsomely from the deaths of poached elephants, as they have used the emotional response to the images of poached elephants to garner funds and advance antimarket policies. If this ban is sustained, Zimbabwe and the other countries that were exploring novel conservation-through-use approaches to wildlife protection will find their tasks far more difficult. The result of continued bans will be a lose-lose situation. Africans will be unable to capture the economic value of the elephant deaths, and elephant populations will drop precipitously. Yet, it appears impossible to challenge the policy. Apparently, some environmentalists would prefer that elephants disappear under political management than flourish under private ownership.

An even broader objection to the idea of ownership exists — one based on the grounds that it would seem to require that we domesticate nature, subjecting the flora and fauna of our planet to human control. We need to look at that from a slightly different perspective. The late Kenneth Boulding, perhaps the first ecological economist, once noted the fact that man is by far the most successful species this planet has yet produced. From that observation, he concluded that any species — any plant or animal — that does not *in some sense* become domesticated is doomed. Boulding was not, of course, limiting domestication to a plant placed in the backyard garden or an animal kept in a cage, but rather to the broader idea that humankind would have to relate to that species, to become a conscious steward. For Boulding, Noah's Ark is being played out in the modern world — only those species that Noah consciously elects to save are saved.

In a world of extensive environmental property rights, many resources would be protected by their owners. In such a world, elephants would be privately owned and the owners would decide how they were to be used, if at all. In the poorer areas of the world, such as Africa, economics is likely to be the dominant motive. There, elephants will be preserved if — and only if — they are worth more alive than dead. In wealthier nations, however, species may well be preserved because people like ourselves will care about their preservation, rather than because we expect to profit from that conservation. As the world becomes wealthier, such intrinsic valuations of nature are likely to become more important. The motivation will be less economic in nature than an aspect of humankind's collector instinct.

In any event, the role of private ownership is essential. Private property links humankind and nature and creates many reasons for us to care about the things we own. Consider that when the United States was discovered, there were on this continent two billion passenger pigeons and no chickens. Now there are two billion chickens and no passenger pigeons. The owned species survived; the species that was common property became extinct. Property rights worked for chickens. But property rights have also worked for goldfish and parakeets and collies and the thousands of pets and domesticated species that we own because we care about nature, not for economic purposes.

As we become wealthier, it becomes ever more possible for this intrinsic valuation process to protect an ever-expanding fraction of the world's resources. In the free-market environmental world, ownership of all wildlife would become feasible. Some people will own elephants just as people now own cats and dogs. In fact, this is not as strange as it sounds.

Former senator Lloyd Bentsen's brother is raising black rhinos in Texas right now. Black rhinos are an endangered species. Because this individual has both wealth and influence, he was able to obtain a breeding stock of this endangered species. He now possesses a captive breeding stock of rhinos that provide an insurance policy against their becoming extinct in Africa.

The image of dying elephants leads into a critical question: Do markets "fail," or have we "failed" to allow markets to operate? The elephant situation suggests that the idea of private property may serve an important ecological purpose. Moreover, it crystallizes competing visions of environmental protection. The dominant vision sees environmental problems as resulting from greed and capitalism run amok. The arguments are familiar — corporations cause pollution; capitalism causes cancer; only political action can possibly preserve environmental quality. The other approach — today a neglected alternative — argues that it is the very lack of private stewardship institutions (specifically, private property and the legal defenses necessary to give it meaning) that threatens the environment. Free-market environmentalists suggest we integrate (via an expansive policy of ecological privatization) into the market a broad array of environmental resources now largely defenseless.

Perhaps the greatest obstacle for the wide acceptance of private property approaches to environmental protection is the perception that "markets fail." Market opponents have long advanced such criticisms whenever a specific market failed to respond exactly (or as quickly) as we had hoped. In such cases, the critics have seen the case for political action as obvious — after all, the market had "failed." To the late Nobel Laureate George Stigler, this approach was akin to a singing contest in which the first singer delivers her performance — after which the judges carefully note her timbre, her difficulty with high notes and breathing control, and without any further ado, award the prize to the second singer. Before accepting market "failures" as prima facie justification of political intervention, we must compare the performance of political approaches. Certainly, it is unrealistic to compare real markets with theoretical ideals. Political institutions have their own "failures." A comparative institutional analysis — case by case, environmental problem by environmental problem — would find far fewer cases where political intervention was the "obvious" choice.

There are good reasons why free-market environmentalists are skeptical of the dominant political intervention approach to environmental protection. Everyone wants a world that is both free and clean. Most people are concerned with both the house of humankind (the "economy") and the house of nature (the "ecology"). Our challenge is to find ways to integrate our growing emphasis on ecological values with our more established economic values. That integration must take account of the fact that many people in the world remain far poorer than we in the West. Free-market environmentalists suggest that ecological central planning is no more likely to advance ecological values than economic central planning was to advance economic values. Yet we fear that the dominance of the market failure model is taking us very far down that dead-end path.

Take the implication of the approach. The market failure model says that markets, while beneficial, nevertheless fail, and therefore political solutions for "externality" failures like pollution are essential. Of course, the logic requires that only those economic activities that have environmental consequences must be regulated. Unfortunately, it turns out that all economic activities have some environmental consequences; thus, we quickly find ourselves committed to regulating the entire world. That, of course is impossible, so we compromise by regulating certain sectors and pollutants. The resulting priorities inevitably exclude important concerns, which creates tensions and suspicions which can only be addressed by expanding the scope and severity of regulation.

Consider this example from Irish history. For a period of time, land tenure in Ireland was restricted to nine-year leases. The nine-year lease had a very predictable pattern. For the first three years, the leaseholder would busily repair the damages done by the prior possessor. For the next three years, the holder would manage the property thoughtfully. For the last three years, he would exploit the property because any further investments would only benefit the next leaseholder.

Institutional arrangements create incentives that affect the time horizon. Permanent, transferable property rights create powerful incentives to consider the future impact of current actions. Under a stable private property rights regime, even if one is eighty or ninety years old, one can still sell that property or leave it to one's children. Thus, one still considers the question of how present actions affect future values. The ability to transfer ownership encourages even the shortsighted and the elderly to consider such trade-offs.

The literature on the problems of economic central planning and its difficulties is extensive and persuasive. Central planning fails because a central authority cannot amass the knowledge needed to set priorities — do we want more wheat or more pumpernickel bread? Do we want less nitrogen oxide or less sulfur dioxide? We have sought to address this problem by creating an array of specialized environmental laws that champion the reduction of specific pollutants or the protection of specific environmental amenities. Yet, such agencies have no way of engaging in meaningful trade-offs when their actions cause (to some degree) environmental harms elsewhere, as they inevitably do. The result is an inconsistent and highly variable control program with no ready logical defense.

In brief, the case against central planning is the impossibility of mobilizing, in any timely sense, the dispersed information that is essential to the smooth functioning of a modern society. Absent such information, there is no way to design the incentives essential to coordinate individual actions. The empirical case against central planning is readily available from the experiences of Russia, Eastern Europe, and the third world.

That knowledge was hard-won. When I began my training as an economist, there was a prevailing view that America faced a difficult choice. We could retain our decentralized free enterprise system and suffer an inevitable loss of economic growth. Or, we could follow the lead of the planned economies, trade in our outmoded freedoms, and reap massive gains in efficiency and wealth. Efficiency and freedom were, it appeared, mutually exclusive. The Soviet Union, Eastern Europe, and even the planned economies in the third world were slated to be the wave of the future. For many years, World Bank statistics and leading economic texts (including that of Paul Samuelson) reported that this was actually occurring. It did not, of course. The central planning of socialism proved incapable of mobilizing the energies and the genius of a dispersed and diverse population. Similarly, the most heavily planned central economies — those of Eastern Europe and the Soviet Union — fell far short of the United States in advancing ecological goals.

The point, of course, is that in the last century — the century in which environmental values became salient — America came to view resource management as a political, not a private, issue. Private ownership of resources — as a way of advancing the public interest in environmental and other resource management areas — was and has continued to be neglected. Rather than allowing newly valued or discovered resources to pass quickly into private hands via homesteading and privatization, the tendency has been to manage such resources collectively via political rules and regulations. Resources that came into public prominence prior to the Progressive Era (around the onset of the twentieth century) remained largely in private hands; newer resources came under state control. Thus, underground oil reserves are largely in private hands, while underground water supplies (aquifers) are typically managed politically. Ronald Coase, the Nobel Prize economist, discussed this tendency in his work on the use of the electromagnetic spectrum for radio broadcasting, a resource that first became economically valuable in the early part of the twentieth century. Initially, the resource was privately homesteaded by early broadcasters, but Progressive Era politicians viewed this as a mistake and moved to nationalize the spectrum and place it under the newly formed Federal Communications Commission. Today, steps are under way to reexplore the privatization option. I would argue that a similar reappraisal of the role of private stewardship is overdue in an array of environmental areas.

The fatal flaw of the centrally planned economy is lack of knowledge, a problem that is becoming more pronounced in environmental policy. In today's sophisticated economy, EPA policies are too crude to address effectively the full array of environmental problems. The first wave of EPA programs consisted of hasty responses to massive discharges of a small number of air, water, and ground pollutants from a limited number of point sources. Even such crude interventions could achieve some results, although some data indicate that America was enjoying environmental improvements through local ordinances and fuel switching far before the EPA was created (as suggested by the work of Indur Goklany, an economist at the Department of the Interior, included in CEI's publication *True State of the Planet* and again in our just published *Earth Report 2000*). In any event, the EPA now seeks to control minimal discharges of a vast array of residuals from hundreds and thousands of minor sources in dispersed locations. The knowledge, enforcement, monitoring, and coordination problems arising from this complexity make it clear that we need to find more creative ways of addressing environmental problems.

Another problem with technocratic governance is the lack of stability. Today, the environmental movement is a dominant political force, and few dare to challenge the EPA's decisions. But politics is fickle; today's hero may be tomorrow's villain. Consider the "energy crisis" of the Carter administration. Jimmy Carter, by all accounts, was a green president. But when the energy crisis arose, Carter shifted emphasis, seeing energy self-sufficiency as paramount. His administration moved to accelerate the approval of energy production facilities, to reduce environmental restrictions, to increase funding for a wide array of alternative energy technologies (the Synfuels Corporation), and to increase access to public lands for energy exploration purposes. All this from an environmentally sensitive leader!

Environmentalists should be cautious. A political consensus is always fragile and often ephemeral. Today's polls indicate that people will pay any price for any trivial amount of cleanup, but recent political history is replete with the wrecked careers of politicians who were assured by polls that they were shoo-ins. To pin one's hopes on something as fickle as polls is dangerous, especially when those same surveys show that few people rank environmental issues as among the most significant.

Moreover, most environmentalists seem to believe that environmental priorities can be determined objectively and carried out effectively by the EPA. That is naive. The EPA is a political agency, and its priorities are determined politically: professional input has little weight in this process. Indeed, that was the conclusion of a 1987 EPA internal study entitled "Unfinished Business," which compared environmental priorities as assessed by EPA professionals with what was actually realized in the budget and staff allocations that programs received. The study asked a simple question: If environmental policy professionals were given total discretion, where would resources likely be allocated? They then examined where resources were actually committed. As a first approximation, the two priority rankings were almost inversely correlated. Those programs that were politically salient and had received considerable media attention received the most resources, despite the fact that EPA professionals considered them less urgent. In politics, perceived reality dominates; the sensational trumps the serious. This problem means that shifting political emphasis, as was the case with the Carter administration, and sensationalized media coverage have a profound influence on EPA policy. The agency is, to some extent, at the mercy of its interest groups.

A system that plays political favorites will not view all pollution equally. Pollution by politically powerful groups will be discounted because of those groups' political clout. Enforcers will target those polluters already viewed as villains and will be more lenient toward groups perceived as virtuous. When a supertanker releases millions of gallons of crude, going after the oil company is fun; it makes us feel good. It is easy and it attracts favorable headlines, but it fails to recognize that most river pollution comes from municipalities and farms, not from industries. Municipal sewage treatment plants lag considerably behind industrial cleanup facilities. Why? The obvious answer is that it is much easier to haul an industrialist into court than it is to haul in a city mayor. Going after mayors who face many problems and who enjoy much public sympathy may make the EPA look like a bully and does nothing for the hero image sought by crusading attorneys. Common-law remedies that allowed downstream interests to enjoin pollution by any party may well prove a far more effective strategy for protecting water quality than this errant political process.

Current law, moreover, makes the EPA the fall guy no matter what happens. The agency is always set up to look feckless and stupid. Congress passes regulatory laws filled with wonderful statements: zero pollution, 100 percent cleanup, eliminate all waste in America. These are often written in the spirit of utopian idealism and typically are unsuitable for practical implementation. Yet they become laws, and sooner or later they are not met. When they are not met, what happens? According to Michael Greve: "The EPA's inevitable failure to meet statutory goals and deadlines strengthens the environmental movement's ability to sustain its momentum. It is very easy for the public to understand the environmentalist point. Once again, the government has failed to keep its promise. It is much harder for the other side to explain that the government cannot possibly have kept those particular promises even under the most favorable of circumstances; and the assertion that failure was built in just doesn't even register as credible." The consequence of such failures is not policy reform but the assignment of even more stringent standards to the EPA: more draconian timetables and penalties, the extension of old unattainable standards, and further reduction of its operating flexibility, lest it repeat the same mistakes.

One last point — while our EPA is not responsible for the global environment, the global environment does concern us greatly. And here the tragedy of America's sole reliance on political means of environmental protection is perhaps most explicit. We have adopted an environmental policy that does not export very well. Our approach, for better or worse, has required that we spend hundreds of billions of dollars over the last three decades and that we mobilize large numbers of highly skilled technocrats, engineers and scientists in industry and government agencies, federal and state EPAs. We are fortunate in that the bureaucracies charged with administering the rules are relatively honest — not a characteristic often attributed to third world bureaucracies. Since the rules that the EPA produces are largely the result of interest group politics, and since industry can be expected to play an aggressive role in seeking to hold down costs, the current strategy also requires that a countervailing force (an independent public interest environmental movement) be in position to aggressively police EPA conduct and policy.

The wisdom of applying this policy domestically is questionable, and it clearly could not work in most of the third world. Third world countries do not have hundreds of billions of dollars to spend on anything, much less the environment. They do not have a surplus of highly trained technical people. And the dangers of requiring civil servants in the third world to resist the financial temptations involved in pollution control should be considered very carefully. Given the scarcity of resources and the lack of civil liberties in many of these countries, the likelihood that an aggressive independent force will prove effective at disciplining governmental actions in these nations is even more fanciful. Thus, those concerned about protecting all of "Spaceship Earth," rather than just its first-class cabins, must find more creative ways of addressing environmental issues. Fortunately, there is an effective alternative — free-market environmentalism based on private property rights.

The EPA has two distinct missions: environmental risk management and environmental property management. First, it is responsible for addressing a wide array of environmental risk issues — the regulation of technologies, processes, plants, waste disposal, biotechnology, all of those kinds of questions. The broad market approach in these areas involves thoughtful principles of legal defense against prospective harm and an institutional setting in which the risks of regulation are compared with the risks that the regulation supposedly reduces. That issue is important, but I will focus here on the EPA's second role, that of environmental property manager, and how that role might better be handled by private property arrangements.

Consider, for example, what should be done about resources in sensitive environmental areas, such as oil in the Arctic National Wildlife Refuge (ANWR). The debate over the ANWR is representative of a typical development issue in environmental politics. It also illustrates well the tendency in such political areas to exaggerate one's case. Here, energy developers have argued that failure to develop the ANWR endangers national security and will impose massive costs on the American economy. But environmentalists are equally guilty of hyperbole, arguing that caribou herds will perish if even one additional well intrudes into this massive area. In such political "debates," both parties argue the most extreme position that appears plausible. That reflects the zero-sum nature of politics. Neither side gains anything by recognizing any legitimacy in its opponent's claims. The resulting stalemate often goes on forever, while the ecological and economic values involved remain at risk.

The free-market environmentalist views such a stalemate as stemming from the lack of property rights. Were the resource owned by some party — be it Exxon or the Wilderness Society — there would be far stronger incentives for compromise. Indeed, free-market environmentalists have long argued that we would get more oil from Alaska if the lands in question were owned by the Wilderness Society — and that they would do a better job of protecting the ecological values there than would the Interior Department.

An excellent example of how private property better reconciles environmental and economic values is that of the Rainey Wildlife Refuge. This 28,600-acre bird sanctuary, owned by the National Audubon Society, is in the extensive wetlands of coastal Louisiana, located above a natural gas and oil field. Interestingly, oil companies approached the Audubon Society, declaring their interest in drilling on their refuge. The society rejected the proposal at first but then elected to permit drilling under careful guidelines so as to minimize environmental impact. Both parties were able to reconcile an economic and an environmental goal, because as private property owners they had every incentive to do so. If the Audubon Society had taken the purist path, they would have forgone the royalty payments of a producing hydrocarbon field, and thus been less able to address their many other concerns. Had the oil company ignored environmental values, they would not have gained the right to drill.

There are numerous stories demonstrating ecological sensitivity where companies, power companies in particular, cultivate buffer zones around their plants. Often these buffer zones are used for environmental purposes. Utilities need the buffer zones for safety reasons or as wetlands for thermal cooling operations, but they gain goodwill by managing them for ecological purposes. Again, this illustrates the linkage between economic activities and the environmental concerns of others — something that a decentralized institutional structure facilitates. Environmentalists do not have to care anything about economics to become better economists; market-oriented groups need not worry about the environment in becoming better environmentalists. The need to reach voluntary agreements encourages each side to understand better the values of the other; to consider seriously values that are not their own.

Private ownership, moreover, decentralizes decisionmaking. Many different choices will be made in similar circumstances. This fosters experimentation. Some people will arrive at solutions that would not occur to most of us; some will take decisions that would be rejected by the

majority. In a world of private property, unpopular values can be protected. In the political world, a resource will only be protected if it
garners sufficient support, generally a majority of the population.

A good example of the ability of private property to protect minority
values is Hawk Mountain, in Pennsylvania. Raptors (birds of prey, including hawks, falcons, eagles, and owls) were not well regarded in
America early in the twentieth century; they were viewed as vermin. The
Audubon Society, the premier conservation group of the time, had little
interest in protecting hawks. Their plate was already filled with the de-
manding task of protecting songbirds, birds of plumage, and game birds.
Nobody, it appeared, was willing to stand up for hawks — except for one
individual, Rosalie Edge, in New York City, who championed the birds
of prey and deplored their slaughter. She lobbied the government, but at
the time, the government, serving agricultural interests, was paying
bounties to reduce hawk populations to "protect" game bird populations. Nor could she persuade the Audubon Society to broaden its hori-
zons. She was, however, able to buy land. She and her friends bought
a mountain ridge in Pennsylvania where hawks congregated on their
southern migration. By buying that land, posting it, and fencing it, she
and her few friends were able to reject the tastes of the majority and
protect the birds. Now, of course, we all agree with her, but that is almost
seventy years later.

Speaking of birds, a critic once asked me to consider this horrific
scenario in my perfect property rights universe: Suppose that a wealthy
individual elected to purchase a rare bird and then barbecue it. What
would I say to that?

My reply was that the possibility does exist; anything is possible. But,
we do not spend much time worrying about people buying van Goghs
(or even the work of the local neighborhood artist) and then using them
for dartboards. There may be people in the world who might buy resources to destroy them, but such people are rare and are unlikely to
command any large fraction of the world's resources.

Under a private property regime mistakes will be made, but mistakes
will also be made in a political world. The Glen Canyon Dam was not a
private sector decision; the roads cutting through the Amazon rain forest
were not privately financed. Again, mistakes are going to be made in the
private sector; they are going to be made in the political sector. The
question is, which institutional arrangements reduce the likelihood and
seriousness of such mistakes? In which institutional setting are errors
most likely to be discovered and corrected? Arguably, the wide variety of

choices made in the private sector result in much more learning, much greater ability to do better over time.

A British fishing club, The Pride of Derby, demonstrates how property rights can prevent stream pollution. In England, clubs own the right to fish along some rivers and are thus sensitive to pollution threats. When the Pride of Derby's salmon populations began to decline because of upstream pollution, the angling club brought a suit against the primary polluter, who happened to be a municipality. The municipal government argued that its interests outweighed those of the club; the club prevailed, and the court ordered an injunction.

If we could transfer such fishing rights to more groups around the world, especially in the third world, the fishermen in these regions would be equipped with a relatively inexpensive self-regulating mechanism to protect their rivers and lakes. Our view is that the ocean reefs in the South Pacific, the Indian mountaintops, river valleys in the Amazon, whales, elephants — all will benefit if we can find ways of engaging private individuals to protect resources today rather than trying to persuade the government to take action in some distant tomorrow.

Or consider the EPA's efforts to protect groundwater. Many groundwater studies find that it is being rapidly and seriously depleted and contaminated. What to do about it? Typically, the answer is a form of national land-use planning. Well, do we really want Washington, D.C., or even the fifty state capitals, to plan the use of every plot of land in the United States? Both state and national land-use planning would encounter the central economic planning problems discussed earlier. Before we rush to endorse that approach, we should explore ways in which the resource might be owned and managed privately.

To see how this might be done, consider how the oil industry manages its underground liquid resource pools of oil. Oil is managed through a process called unitization. Oil pools are typically located under the surface of multiple plots of land; as a consequence, many different individuals can hold a property stake in a single deposit. This is the case with many natural resources; the difference with oil is that individual extraction from the pool imposes externalities on all other oil field owners. The externalities are threefold. First, individual extraction siphons from the entire pool, not just that which lies directly beneath the surface of the individual's property. Second, each oil field owner has every incentive to pump as fast as possible because if you do not, your neighbor surely will. This encourages premature and ultimately wasteful extraction. Third, because pumping costs are directly proportional to pool pressure, any decrease in pressure (the natural result of pumping) increases the cost of extraction.

The oil industry addressed this problem through unitization. Unitization consists in the multiple owners of the fill forming a "unit," a form of cooperative management agreement to which the individual property rights are transferred. The individual owners are then reimbursed according to the contractual terms bringing them into the unit. The unit manager then decides which wells will be operational, which will be closed down, and which will be used to flood the field with water to increase extraction levels. By overcoming the coordination problems, the unit manager acts as a conservator of the resource. Unitization reduces the incentives for waste and premature extraction and fosters a more conservative method of resource use. Is it possible that this kind of idea could be applied to aquifers? No one knows, because no one has yet looked at this issue very deeply.

How do you handle large lakes, rivers, and oceans? Property rights solutions in these areas are not apparent; there are no well-developed models to address these problem areas. One avenue, however, is to note that one does not need to own a whole resource to protect it. After all, pollution occurs somewhere before it occurs everywhere. What type of resource protection might be provided the Chesapeake Bay, for example? There are limited applications of property rights in the Chesapeake. Virginia has ownership rights in oyster beds, as does Washington State. Oyster bed owners might act like the fishing clubs in England, becoming sensitive to early indications of pollution. We are a long way from the English paradigm, because only parts of those resources are currently owned, and only certain parts are available for appropriation. However, some promising case studies of how such limited property rights schemes might be extended even here have been highlighted by the Center for Private Conservation.

A number of new technologies that reduce the costs of monitoring and policing such areas have emerged in recent years. The use of branding technologies like sonar and satellite tracking invite the possibility of whale ownership; autonomous underwater vehicles enable the herding of fish schools; and the development of artificial reefs and aquaculture permits fishermen to "fence" in their resources.

My conclusion from all of this is that the environmental values that motivated the creation of the EPA are important, but the agency and its supporters have, to date, been uncreative about addressing them. The predominant view in environmental policy today is, if it isn't political, it isn't real. Regulations and other coercive measures are viewed as the only way to protect our environment.

But free-market strategies should become a part of the toolchest of any serious environmentalist. How else can we escape the current dilemma in which the environment is everyone's problem, in which we continue to chatter fecklessly about the need to preserve humankind's common heritage? Protecting our common heritage does not result in effective action and does not tap very much into our available daily energies.

One story that epitomizes the problems of the socialist solution emerged from the Soviet Union. If a cow owned by a collective farm gets sick, who stays up every night taking care of it? The answer, all too often, is no one. (This is to be contrasted, of course, with how people acted on the very small private plots that persisted under communism.) No one is going to take care of Spaceship Earth if we do not create incentives and institutions that will encourage people to do so. They could, and should, be employed far more widely than is currently the case.

Free-market ideas have done much to advance economic welfare around the world. Free-market environmentalism might similarly free the entrepreneurial energies and creativity of the people of the world to advance ecological goals. It is time to explore that option further.

Part VI   TOOLS FOR
MANAGING CHANGE

Mathematical Models, Risk Analysis, and Communication

Chapter 13   HUMAN-CAUSED

CLIMATE WARMING

Implications for Practically Everything

JERRY D.
MAHLMAN

At the beginning of the twenty-first century, what do we know and not know about human-caused climate warming, and what implications does it have for the future of life on Earth?

Human-caused climate warming has very significant implications for policy decisions on a global scale but, as a climate scientist, I will avoid advocating any specific policy positions on this issue but instead will discuss primarily the science itself, and what it means. It is only by starting with the science that we can glean any real sense of what is in store for the climate — just how hot it actually might get, and when and where, and what the consequences of that might be. Science should be the foundation upon which to build responsible policy decisions concerning future climate changes.

For more than thirty years, NOAA's Geophysical Fluid Dynamics Laboratory (GFDL) has performed model calculations of climate warming caused by added greenhouse gases. The examples I offer are mainly from our own calculations. Other model results, however, are readily available to anyone who wishes to evaluate our results in the light of other findings. The extensive 1995 report of the International Panel on Climate Change (IPCC), in particular, is an invaluable compilation of data analyses and model-based climate change projections.[1]

The basics of the greenhouse effect are fairly simple. Everyone knows about the visible radiation coming from the Sun, which lets us see one another, but most people are less familiar with infrared radiation, the other half of the dominant radiation on the planet. We and everything

I am grateful to Anthony Broccoli, Mack McFarland, Ronald Stouffer, and Anthony Wolbarst for their helpful suggestions for the manuscript.

1. J. T. Houghton et al., *Climate Change 1995: The Science of Climate Change* (Cambridge: Cambridge University Press, 1996, for the Intergovernmental Panel on Climate Change).

else in our surroundings are emitting it and absorbing it. Our eyes cannot see it, but our bodies can feel it, as heat. It is crucial to the radiation balance of the planet, because incoming visible radiation from the Sun is balanced by infrared radiation escaping back to space.

Perhaps the simplest way for laypersons to think about the greenhouse effect is from everyday observations of the world around us. Everyone is aware, for example, that if it is a clear evening with stars sharply visible, it is likely to cool off substantially by morning. On the following night, if the temperature is the same but it is cloudy, we would know that it probably will not be as cold the next morning; the clouds trap much of the infrared radiation that is trying to escape to space, and so the air remains warmer near the ground. Clouds are tricky, though, because they also reflect solar radiation, as is easily sensed on a hot day when a cloud obscures the Sun. So clouds are a double player in the climate system, exerting both cooling and warming effects.

Now, suppose the third night is cloud-free but very humid. Will it get as cold the next morning as in the clear-dry situation? The answer, which may be less evident, is that the overnight cooling is usually considerably less during a clear-humid night than on a clear-dry night. That is because atmospheric water vapor, somewhat like a cloud, proves an efficient trap for the escaping infrared radiation.

Carbon dioxide (CO_2) also plays a critical role in determining the temperature at Earth's surface. During the International Geophysical Year in 1958, when atmospheric CO_2 was first measured systematically, the CO_2 concentration in the atmosphere was about 315 parts per million by volume (ppmv). It has been going up ever since. Now we also have ice core data that connect the recent record with periods much farther back in time. The ice cores indicate that, in preindustrial times, CO_2 was roughly 275 ppmv, while during the last Ice Age, it was about 190 ppmv. Today we have over 360 ppmv, the highest atmospheric CO_2 level in at least the past 140,000 years and likely much longer than that. It is primarily the substantial climate implications of this upward trend in carbon dioxide that I address here.

I am convinced that the best way to distill the facts related to greenhouse warming as a basis for international policy deliberations is that provided by the IPCC. Through its Working Group 1, the IPCC provides periodic climate assessment reports that represent the consensus of a large, international group of climate scientists. When the IPCC concluded in its 1995 assessment that "the balance of evidence suggests a discernible human influence on global climate," it was a watershed event. This carefully worded statement says, in effect, that we think we see, from observations and from supporting modeling calculations, that human-caused climate change is under way. This very cautious statement contains three caveats: "balance," "suggests," and "discernible." The 2001 IPCC Report statement contains a much stronger key statement: "There is new and stronger evidence that most of the warming of the last 50 years is due to human activities." The IPCC does not attempt to represent what cutting-edge scientists think they see in their most recent work. The IPCC's main function, rather, is to provide broad-based climate information that the world scientific community can accept. So it reflects the consensus within a much wider group than just the hard-core experts on the detection and modeling of climate change.

The IPCC also evaluates predictions, primarily from mathematical models, of how the climate might change over the next century. A climate model is a powerful tool that solves, by numerical methods, the mathematical equations that describe land surface processes, the motions of the ocean and the atmosphere, the heating and cooling effects of solar and infrared radiation, the radiative effects of added greenhouse gases, clouds, and airborne particles (aerosols), plus all the other known factors that act together to drive the climate system. A climate model tries to get all of this correct from a first-principles point of view — in essence, all of the fundamental equations that describe the physics involved. These equations are familiar to those who have studied (and remembered) first-year physics: Newton's second law of motion, the first law of thermodynamics, and conservation of matter. The hard part is that, for the climate problem, these equations are strongly coupled and nonlinear. Such equations can only be solved through the use of powerful supercomputers.

I prefer to make a terminology shift here. The IPCC uses the word "predictions," but many climate scientists prefer "projections": How can physical scientists predict a phenomenon when its very nature depends upon future painful social decisions — or lack thereof? As I stated, we are on a daunting trajectory of increasing CO_2. Most likely, we will more than double atmospheric carbon dioxide over the next century; with even less than our current level of CO_2 emissions, we could well eventually exceed a quadrupling of preindustrial levels. The atmospheric carbon dioxide level we eventually reach is clearly a social choice, not a prediction as normally defined by physical scientists.

Climate change modeling projections for various CO_2 emissions scenarios can provide an invaluable instrument for sorting out society's options to deal, or not deal, with the problem. Such projections carry their own scientific uncertainties, which can vary widely in their levels of scientific confidence.[2] For one thing, today's climate models cannot credibly resolve features smaller than 300 miles (500 km) or so; thus the proper inclusion of smaller-scale processes in the model's physical mechanisms remains problematic. Also, there are continued difficulties in modeling aspects of the responses of clouds and aerosols, and their associated radiative processes, to changed concentrations of greenhouse gases.

The 1995 IPCC reports properly claim some degree of confidence in the climate models because they do account for the most important physical processes, to the best of our ability to define them. The models simulate large-scale aspects of climate reasonably well — the annual cycle of seasons, the interannual-to-decadal natural variability of the system, and the broad, national-scale features. Current models are accurate enough to see differences in climate between Washington, D.C., and Miami, Florida, say, and between either of them and Lincoln, Nebraska. Likewise, they correctly predicted what would happen after the 1991 Mount Pinatubo volcanic eruption, which injected tremendous amounts of sulfur into the atmosphere — that Earth would cool down a couple of tenths of degrees Celsius and then recover in a few years. In other words, on a regional scale, the models are basically sound, we believe, and they certainly provide the best way we have — indeed, the *only* credible way, really — to peer intelligently into the future.

Although these words may come back to haunt me, I have suggested that the scientific uncertainties are relatively small, and I do not anticipate any *major* surprises to be forthcoming. To me, one major surprise would be if clouds either amplified or damped climate change in a very large way. I do not know how that would happen, but that is why it would be a major surprise.

When I set up my evaluations of what we know and do not know, I am not trying to be particularly sophisticated. Rather, I believe that I know the theories and the models at a comprehensive level, and I have fundamental respect for what climate data can tell us. Most importantly, I am in contact with and informed by a number of the world's leading climate specialists. We all want to determine if the climate model projections are robust. Partly because of the intensity of the social issues and the potential for misinterpretation, my colleagues and I probably tend to err in the

2. J. D. Mahlman, "Uncertainties in Projections of Human-Caused Climate Warming," *Science* 278 (1997): 1416–17.

direction of scientific conservatism in the publication of our research results. I also believe in the traditional approach to good science, in which we say that this is our best information, and these are our uncertainties, but if we find that we are wrong, we will correct our conclusions and acknowledge our deficiencies.

But surprises will happen. For that reason, I am a very strong advocate of careful long-term monitoring of the climate with real data. Some of the most passionate advocates for better climate monitoring are modelers — we know that our climate change projections need to be checked against the real climate. I never fail to be amazed by how difficult it is to convince national and international agencies how important this is. It is almost as if ignorance about climate change, about surprises that might be in store, is preferable to efforts to evaluate what we are up against.

By the way, while I characterize the so-called scientific uncertainty as being relatively small, there has been a real media-induced amplification of the apparent scientific uncertainties. Controversy sells newspapers. The media's success in heightening the public's sense of scientific controversy has come at a high price: The public is still largely focused on perceived scientific controversy rather than the really hard problem of what the world is going to do about this massive problem.

It is the climate-change projections produced by the models, of course, that people find of greatest interest. One of the most important of these is that climate change, once begun, will continue for hundreds of years. It takes a long time to get this process of human-caused climate warming cranked up — but it will take a *lot* longer to get out of the mess we find ourselves in once the climate has clearly begun warming in a big way and we decide we do not like it. This is hard to communicate to people because we are not very accustomed to thinking of global-scale social or environmental problems that play out on time scales of hundreds of years, perhaps thousands.

For a business-as-usual scenario of burning fossil fuels, with a continuation of current trends in population and industrial growth and in changing patterns of land use, the 1995 IPCC report concluded that global-mean surface air temperature may increase at an average rate of between roughly 0.2 and 0.6°F (~0.1 and 0.35°C) per decade over the next century. Warming is expected to be greater over land than over the ocean; we might expect this because the land heating is confined to a shallow soil layer with small heat capacity, while the oceanic heating is mixed downward over a much deeper layer. The largest surface warming is projected to occur over high northern latitudes in the winter. Considerably smaller changes are expected over the North Atlantic and Circum-Antarctic Oceans, at least in the first half of this century. Precipitation and soil moisture increases over winter are expected for the higher northern latitudes. Places like North Dakota might expect to pile up more snow on the average than they would otherwise, for the simple reason that more water can be evaporated into the air over warmer oceans, so more can precipitate out as the air moves poleward. Yet midcontinental soil moisture is expected to decline in summer because of the higher temperatures, with obvious implications for agriculture. Sea level may rise anywhere between 8 inches and 3 feet (~20 cm and a meter) or so by A.D. 2100. This is a highly uncertain number for several reasons that I discuss later.

It may be helpful here to highlight the distinction between forced and unforced climate change. The Sun shining on Earth provides the heat input that powers the climate system. But even if the Sun's output and the other controlling factors are constant, climate will still fluctuate naturally because of nonlinear interactions between the atmosphere and the ocean-ice-land system. This is called "unforced" change. "Forced" climate change refers to new incremental heating effects on the planet: a changing Sun, volcanic eruptions, added CO_2, added other greenhouse gases, or added aerosols. Separating forced from unforced changes from the observed record can be very difficult because unforced variations masquerading as "trends" can go on for decades.

As I mentioned before, the IPCC made a big impact in 1995 with their statement that "the balance of evidence suggests a discernible human influence on global climate." What does that really mean? The natural fluctuations in global mean temperature are indeed significant, but some people have argued that the entire observed warming over the past century could be due to unforced natural variability — by the system just flopping around on its own without necessarily being nudged by changes in the Sun, or by volcanic eruptions, or by what people do. I assert that the weight of the evidence from climate data and models is generally consistent, with a predominantly human-caused forcing of the observed long-term warming over the past century. Simply put, we have not yet come up with any credible alternative hypotheses involving unforced changes that would have much of a chance of producing an effect large enough to explain the increased temperatures.

The solid line in figure 13.1 shows a time-series of measured global-mean surface air temperature departures from the 1860–1998 long-term

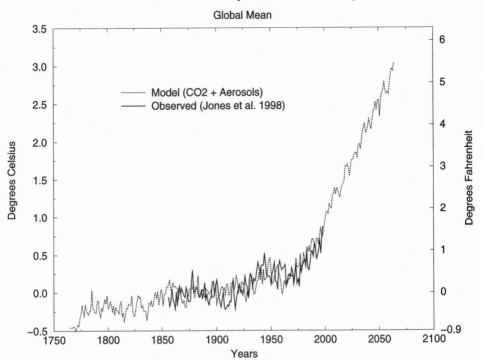

FIGURE 13.1. Time series of observed global-mean surface air temperature from 1850 to 1998 (courtesy Jones et al. 1998, publicly released data analysis) (*solid line*). Time series of GFDL model simulation of global-mean surface air temperature using the most recent IPCC forcing scenario of "equivalent" CO₂ and sulfate aerosol concentrations from 1850 to 2050 (*dotted line*).

mean. That is, it shows yearly variations relative to the 138-year average. Natural variability plays a role here, dominantly so on time scales of less than a decade or so. But the long-term warming since 1860 is readily apparent, even though it is an interestingly bumpy ride on the way up. Note that four of the ten hottest years on record were all in the 1990s, with 1998 clearly a major record breaker, and the other six were in the 1980s. What is the likelihood that this could have happened by accident? How can we unravel a natural change in the climate from one that is forced by greenhouse gases? This is where model calculations can help, by calculating quantitatively what should have been observed versus what the observations actually show.

An interesting complicating factor in all of this is that, when we burn fossil fuels, particularly coal, the emitted sulfur dioxide appears in the atmosphere as aerosols consisting of tiny sulfate particles. These aerosols reflect sunlight before it has a chance to warm the atmosphere, so that they act as an antigreenhouse substance that, in part, provides a cooling offset to the added greenhouse gases. Unfortunately, there are still serious difficulties in calculating the cooling effects of sulfate aerosols. The measurements on them are poor, we do not fully understand their chemistry and how they are transformed in the atmosphere, and we are not sure how to calculate their impacts on clouds. But two important things we do know are that the sulfate aerosols reflect solar radiation and that aerosols appearing in the atmosphere today will be rained out in about a week. Most of the carbon dioxide that comes out of the same combustion processes, in contrast, will be present in the atmosphere for roughly a century. The long atmospheric lifetime of a CO_2 molecule is the major feature that makes the climate-warming problem so insidious. What CO_2 we emit in any one year is relatively inconsequential; the problem is that there is plenty of memory in the atmosphere of the CO_2 we have emitted in all the previous years — and most of the CO_2 molecules that we have personally produced in our lifetimes as users of fossil fuels are still hanging around in the atmosphere, even for those of us over fifty.

A big question is, how much does the climate shift around all by itself without necessarily being pushed or forced by things people do? We now have over a thousand years of unforced climate simulations from three of the leading models. And over that thousand-year segment, there are no hundred-year periods in any of the unforced climate calculations that compare to what has actually happened over the past century. It is easy to argue that the models could have underestimated the magnitude of natural climate variability. But we have recently learned that the amplitude of unforced variability of the climate system on decadal time scales appears to depend strongly upon the same kind of water vapor feedback that so amplifies the response of the modeled climate system to the current CO_2 increases. This leads to a problem for people who argue that the temperature warming over the past century may be explained by natural variability: A high amplitude of *unforced* decade-to-century-scale natural variability appears to require a strong water vapor feedback effect — the same water vapor feedback that acts to amplify the calculated climate-warming responses begun by forcing the system by adding CO_2 and other greenhouse gases to the atmosphere.

What do the models say about the observed record of global-mean surface air temperature for the past century or so, relative to the changes in forcing due to the increases in CO_2 and other greenhouse gases such as methane, nitrous oxide, and chlorofluorocarbons, and in sulfate aerosols? The dashed line in figure 13.1 is from a climate model experiment conducted at GFDL. The measured global-mean surface air temperature (the solid line) shows a runup until 1940 or so, and then a flattening out, and a further runup after 1970. The GFDL results tend to do that, too. A plausible reason for this flattening effect is that, after World War II, there was an explosive increase in the burning of coal and oil, as the IPCC properly incorporated into their forcing scenario. What would happen if tomorrow afternoon, say, we were to double our burning of fossil fuels? By the end of the week, we would roughly double the amount of sulfate aerosol in the atmosphere, but we would have produced only a tiny change in the atmospheric CO_2 amount. Because sulfate aerosols are highly water soluble and rain out efficiently, they reach atmospheric equilibrium within about a week. In contrast, the CO_2 effect is a bit like slowly filling up a large bathtub a drop at a time. So what appears to have happened was that the effect of the burst in sulfate aerosol production dominated the picture for awhile, but the effect of the slowly but inexorably growing CO_2 finally caught up and again took over.

A comparatively small CO_2 source, applied over a long period of time, had a big effect when the offsetting carbon-absorbing sinks are very inefficient. This helps explain why the human-produced emissions of greenhouse gases take so long to cause a substantial effect on the climate. It also tells us that, if we do not like the climate we have produced, it could take us hundreds (and perhaps thousands) of years to get most of the extra added CO_2 removed from the atmosphere.

A major problem that the comprehensive coupled atmosphere-ocean climate models address is the rise in sea level brought about by human-caused global warming. This becomes significant when you look at it over hundreds of years, rather than over tens of years. It occurs, in part, because seawater expands when it is warmed. When the atmosphere, made warmer by added greenhouse gases, heats up the ocean, the whole ocean occupies a larger volume. Because of the huge mass, large depth, and high heat capacity of the ocean, achieving the full ocean warming response requires many centuries. Suppose the CO_2 in the atmosphere doubles over its preindustrial value; after seventy years, the sea level will have risen less than 12 inches (~30 cm) due to this expansion effect, but after five hundred years, it is passing three feet. After a couple of thousand years, the doubled CO_2 equilibrium sea-level rise due to the warmer ocean reaches about five feet. Since nobody currently sees a viable strategy to prevent atmospheric CO_2 from reaching such a doubling, more than three feet of sea-level rise can be considered as a minimum commitment that we have probably already made and tacitly accepted. It is thus our descendants who will have to deal with most of the consequences of a sea-level rise.

But that is just the first part of the sea-level story. Part two involves the effect of melting continental ice. This is still hard to pin down, because there are plenty of reasons for us to think that today's model calculations of melting Greenland ice may be inaccurate. The sea-level rise due to melted Greenland ice in our climate model proceeds at about four times the rate per century that comes from the thermal expansion of seawater effect noted above. If this calculation is to be believed, instead of getting roughly three feet of sea-level rise over five hundred years, we may have to add four times that. Now there is possibly three feet per century of sea-level rise, due to the melting of Greenland ice. This, of course, assumes that the considerably colder Antarctic land ice will not melt appreciably over the next five hundred years or so — and that is not a given.

Since the last Ice Age, the sea level actually has risen roughly 425 feet (~130 meters) — over a meter per century for ten thousand years. The last Ice Age is acknowledged to have been the result of a negative global climate forcing (lowered CO_2 and increased solar reflection off the ice) that was very roughly the cooling counterpart to what warming would occur with a doubling of atmospheric CO_2. Thus, a sustained meter of sea-level rise per century in the future cannot be dismissed as fanciful in the current global-warming context.

Obviously, there are many places where "only" a meter of sea-level rise could make an enormous difference for humans and for natural ecosystems. It would put a good deal of the south Florida and Louisiana seacoasts under water, as well as substantial parts of Bangladesh and all of a number of small island nations. This may prove to be a major societal concern, as well as heightened motivation for climate scientists to perform much better calculations of how Greenland's and Antarctica's ice would actually melt and at what rates.

Human-caused climate warming could bring about very different kinds of events with potentially serious consequences. From the southern U.S. East Coast, for example, the Gulf Stream flows northeastward, bringing the warm surface water that helps keep the climate of much of Western Europe mild. Farther north, part of this great circulation of the North Atlantic Ocean plunges to considerable depths, at a rate of about twenty million cubic meters of water per second, and then heads south again. Our and others' modeling studies project that, under conditions of doubled and quadrupled atmospheric CO_2, the higher temperatures of the upper oceans inexorably produce higher water vapor concentrations in the atmosphere. We calculate that the large-scale cyclonic storms of the atmosphere will precipitate considerably more of this water vapor onto the land and oceans at high latitudes. In the seawater, this would increase the amount of fresh water at the surface beyond what it has been in the past. Fresh water is less dense than salt water, so this lighter water would have a reduced tendency to sink; thus the normal sinking process starts to slow down. The model indicates that at quadrupled atmospheric CO_2, enough fresh water will be available to cause what we at GFDL have dubbed the "drop-dead" result, in which the overturning of the North Atlantic Ocean essentially stops.

What would the cessation of the Gulf Stream mean for life in and around the North Atlantic Ocean? I do not know. But surprisingly little research on the possible impacts of climate change has been focused on this question. (Perhaps this lack of attention is due to a tendency for most countries to focus on the possible climate change impacts expected within their own borders.) But the impacts, should the drop-dead scenario actually occur, could be critically disruptive in parts of Europe.

Another issue of vital importance is the possible effects of climate change on agriculture. As I mentioned before, our modeling indicates that at doubled CO_2, the soil moisture in the interior of the United States tends to decrease considerably more through the summer than in a world without any excess greenhouse gases present. When the summer Sun gets high in the sky, the added greenhouse gas heating further increases the evaporation of soil moisture, leading to 20–25 percent losses; at four times CO_2, we calculate on the order of 50 percent drying. In effect, in a "typical" year in a higher CO_2 world, this evaporative effect overcomes the possibility of higher precipitation arising from the higher atmospheric moisture content, although important uncertainties remain in such calculations. This is another potential effect of greenhouse warming that could seriously harm the affected areas.

What do our climate model projections tell us about, say, the southeastern United States? For people who live in this area, it is clear that uncomfortably warm summertime temperatures already affect the quality of life. The current climate in this region has a daily average temperature in July of roughly 80°F (about 27°C). But at doubled CO_2, the *average* daily temperature climbs to something near 88°F ($\sim$32°C), which

is close to today's average *maximum* daytime temperature. At quadrupled CO_2, the daily average temperature would get up to something
like 96°F ($\sim$35°C).

Unfortunately, that is not all the daunting news. For an 8°F ($\sim$4.5°C)
increase in temperature, the calculated *heat index* increase (which also
accounts for the physical discomfort effect of the additional humidity) is
roughly 12°F ($\sim$7°C). At quadrupled CO_2, all of these numbers roughly
double. Climate models indicate that there are a number of places besides the southeastern United States that would likely experience this
heat index effect. Southeastern Asia appears to be at significant risk, as
well as any subtropical or tropical locations where the local humidity is
controlled by the temperature of the nearby ocean. I expect this will
become a major climate-impact social issue as awareness of its potential
increases.

The items above suggest some areas where society may be especially
vulnerable to climate change. Obviously, agriculture and forestry could
come under great stress. Also, the likelihood of impacted public health
has gotten a lot of attention, and rightly so; we are currently seeing the
migration of some disease carriers into previously unaffected areas, but
so far with limited ability to attribute with certainty such changes to
global climate warming. What about lowland flooding? There is credible
evidence that today's higher rainfall areas will likely get wetter, while
today's arid regions will likely become even dryer.

What does the modeling tell us as to how well the planet could adjust
to this magnitude of change? Let us start in 1990 and assume that we
would operate under what the IPCC calls its IS92a, or "business as
usual," scenario. This assumes a 1 percent per year increase in energy
efficiency, which is roughly what we have been achieving historically,
and middle-of-the-road population growth; it also assumes that all climate convention commitments will be fully honored. The latter is an
interesting assumption, since to date it appears that none of them have
been. For the IS92a scenario, we get to a doubling over preindustrial
CO_2 by A.D. 2050, a tripling around 2100, and a quadrupling around
2150. If you trust that the climate will respond in any way close to what I
have stated about current model projections, these CO_2 levels imply
potentially serious climate changes.

The level of CO_2 we eventually provide to the atmosphere has to be
regarded as a global social choice. We have no hope of keeping it at 360
ppmv, but is it possible to avoid a CO_2 doubling? What are the social and
environmental implications of letting CO_2 quadruple? If we were to

decide collectively to hold to a CO_2 doubling or less, we would soon have to curtail sharply our CO_2 emissions growth, level emissions off in the next decade or two, and then reduce emissions substantially over the next century. Meanwhile, the demand for fossil-fuel energy continues to grow, largely because of the understandable growth in demand per person in the developing world. And, by the way, Earth's population could well double during the twenty-first century, so that we would likely have to fight through roughly a factor of four growth in demand just to keep emissions at today's levels. But holding CO_2 to a doubling or less would eventually require CO_2 emissions that are substantially *below* today's values.

In my opinion, the science of the global-warming problem makes it clear that Earth's decisionmakers will inevitably have to decide to phase down global emissions of CO_2. The big questions are how to do it, when, and at what cost? Will we do it soon, or twenty years from now, or in a hundred years? Climate science cannot contribute directly to the answer to these policy questions, but it will continue to provide climate information to those sectors (e.g., agriculture, public health) that will assess the impacts and costs of human-caused climate change.

To summarize my thinking on the importance of the modeling of climate change: There are significant uncertainties in our projections of what the future holds for the climate; by itself, this means that the potential impacts of climate change will remain poorly quantified for some time. Thus, there are not yet clear indications as to which climate-change stresses on the Earth-atmosphere system will actually have the greatest impacts. That will be determined largely by whether or when and how much we choose to mitigate CO_2 emissions. Unfortunately, there is still much that we do not know about how our social, economic, and biological systems would react to a wide variety of climate changes over the full range of local climate types, natural ecosystems, and sociopolitical circumstances. On a more positive note, virtually all climate scientists agree that modeling science is sufficiently mature that its broad-scale projections for various possible scenarios of future releases of greenhouse gases should be taken seriously by impacts researchers.

It may be appropriate to close with a few comments on the climate-change convention held in Kyoto, Japan, in 1997. Again, it is my long-time principle to not offer any policy solutions, because policy solutions are not really about science. They can and should be guided by science-based information, but they have little to do with physical science directly. I see policy decisions mainly as resolving differences in values, reconciling differing claims for equity, and seeking optimal (least bad?) overall solutions. I believe that climate-change scientists can be of greatest value, in general, if they try to provide the best science possible, such as the projections from the major climate-change modeling efforts, but do not become identified with any particular policy stance. But, Kyoto did have to deal with a number of nonscientific issues that I found fascinating in my self-chosen role as a nonparticipant.

The convention process called for most of the countries of the world to agree on a protocol to begin reducing emissions of CO_2. Almost all six billion of us are visibly engaged in the CO_2 emissions process, including virtually everyone in the United States. Only some of the most desperate of the world's poor are not participating. One might describe the Kyoto Conference as an attempt to get people with intensely regional interests to the same table to begin to negotiate on a problem that is fundamentally global. This global point perhaps needs to be repeated forcefully to our leaders and to others who are mainly focused on national- or regional-scale problems. The fact that a CO_2 molecule added to the atmosphere today has an apparent average lifetime of nearly a century has important implications, mainly because the lower atmosphere mixes itself globally on a time scale of about a year. It does not matter where the CO_2 molecules came from—they all get well mixed together soon enough; so whether one emits CO_2 in the United States, South Africa, or India is irrelevant. What *does* matter is the totality of all the CO_2 and other greenhouse gases emitted, because they all soon get globalized. Similarly, a CO_2 sink in a given region is drawing CO_2 down from the global CO_2 emissions, not local emissions. Thus, the idea of claiming unplanned regional CO_2 sinks as credits applied against willful regional CO_2 emissions strikes me as fundamentally illogical from the perspective of the science of atmospheric CO_2.

Before the Kyoto Conference, the developing countries said that this is a developed-nation problem because almost all of the added atmospheric CO_2 molecules have been put there by the developed countries. They were right. The developed countries said that the developing countries' growth rate of CO_2 emissions is prodigious and within fifty years will totally dominate global emissions. They also were right.

Most fascinating to me was what was *not* directly acknowledged in the Kyoto process, presumably to keep the negotiations from collapsing before they even began. It was widely recognized among the negotiators that no one has identified a viable mitigation path for CO_2 emissions that can prevent a doubling over preindustrial values. Apparently it was tacitly accepted without evaluation that a doubled CO_2 would produce an acceptable level of human-caused climate change. Has anyone actually performed a comprehensive evaluation of the consequences? I do not think so, certainly not the IPCC. Clearly, if the climate change projections described here are close to being correct, then there are many aspects of doubled CO_2 that would very likely be less than acceptable in terms of their impact upon life on Earth, seriously so in vulnerable locations.

The Kyoto negotiation process was intensely focused on the question of who should pay for CO_2 emissions mitigation commitments and how high such costs might be; this is obviously an important concern. But Kyoto chose not to deal with the equally thorny question of who pays the costs of coping and adaptation to the changes that would still occur, even if we all *did* begin aggressive CO_2 emissions mitigation. This hidden coping/adaptation "tax" is virtually guaranteed to be substantial, and it will be levied in ways that will likely have little to do with policymakers' determinations of fairness or ability to pay. This strikes me as a prodigious problem that will likely fuel equity debates over the rest of the century.

So, all we need is the wisdom of Solomon and a universal willingness to make local sacrifices for the global common good, with most of the payoffs to life on Earth coming well after we are gone. And some folks still say that fixing this will be easy!

Chapter 14 FUTURE DIRECTIONS IN ENVIRONMENTAL RISK ANALYSIS

MAX
BAUCUS

The environmental policies that our nation has been developing over the past few decades will have profound implications for all of us in the future, and especially so for our children and grandchildren. These policies will affect not only the quality and safety of the air we breathe and the water we drink but also the livability of our communities and surroundings, the kinds of jobs we hold, and even the shape of our economic and social growth. So it is critically important that we use our best, most fully informed judgment in the formulation of these policies. One powerful tool to assist in this effort is the relatively new science of environmental risk analysis.

By way of background, Congress and the EPA have much to be proud of in what we have already done to improve and protect our environment. Not only have we solved the most readily apparent problems — the Cuyahoga River in Ohio is no longer catching fire, and the smell of the Potomac River in Washington, D.C., has improved greatly — but we have also addressed many of the other highly important, if more subtle, problems such as removing lead from gasoline, cleaning up toxic waste sites, and the like.

These improvements stemmed largely from federal laws, including the Clean Air Act, the Clean Water Act, the Safe Drinking Water Act, Superfund, and the Resource Conservation and Recovery Act. These laws establish the overall policy framework for action but assign much of the responsibility for the details of implementation to federal agencies such as the Environmental Protection Agency, the Nuclear Regulatory Commission, the Department of the Interior, and others — and in many cases, in cooperation with the individual states.

Thirty years ago, the problems were as obvious as the solutions were simple. Factories pouring forth pollution from stacks into the air and from pipes into a river or lake simply demanded laws and regulations to reduce or prevent it. We did not need a variety of sophisticated tools in our environmental toolbox to fix the problems we saw. Command-and-control, the dominant philosophy at the time, worked fairly well. It was responsible for the vast majority of the progress we have achieved in cleaning up our environment, a feat all the more remarkable given that our population increased by about a quarter and our economy grew nearly sixfold over the same period.

To a great extent, then, we have addressed the glaring problems. And although population and economic growth issues will demand our constant attention in order to maintain our progress, other challenging and complex matters must also be confronted. These include national concerns such as nonpoint water pollution and the bioaccumulation of persistent toxic chemicals, global problems like ozone depletion, loss of biodiversity, and climate change, and universal concerns of equity and burden sharing. In these areas, the answers are less obvious, and the needs for economic efficiency are greater. Today, the traditional command-and-control approach often appears ill suited to these new complexities. It seems, simply, too blunt an instrument and no longer up to the demands we place upon it. We need to harness our resources more effectively, including the creativity of scientists and engineers in the private sector, if we are to deal successfully with these issues.

This means that we have to look hard at a range of newer, more innovative ways to address pollution and other environmental problems and determine which approaches will give us the results, and the efficiencies, that we need. At the same time, we must set priorities more appropriately than we have in the past so that our efforts, and the money available, will be directed at our most pressing problems. We require better methods to help us determine which threats are the biggest, which we should tackle first, and how much effort we should expend on each of them. Fortunately, advances in science and years of experience provide us with several possible approaches, one of the most important of which is environmental risk analysis.

Risk analysis is, in essence, a methodology that allows us to formalize and quantify the kind of commonsense thinking we do intuitively every day — namely, determine what potential threats we face, how likely they might be, and how serious they could be. Then, if we have enough financial or human resources to tackle only a few such problems, the threats with the greatest assessed risk of causing harm may well be the ones to try to remedy first. Obviously we do not need to perform complicated mathematical calculations when the situation is very simple. But when things become complex, involving numerous interlinked problems, each with wheels within wheels, risk analysis can provide invaluable guidance in making wise decisions.

In environmental and public health applications, risk analysis typically first asks what the risks might be if a person were exposed to a certain hazardous material or situation — whether it be a pesticide in the soil or the hole in the ozone layer. It then attempts to obtain two independent but complementary kinds of information. The first is the magnitude of risk for any particular degree of exposure to the hazard. (It is commonly found that the greater the exposure, the greater the risks and consequences, although there may be a threshold level of exposure below which no harm occurs.) The other is the numbers of people who might, indeed, be exposed to any particular level of the hazard. By combining these separate estimates, risk analysis can project the harm to the population that the material or situation may cause. In practice, it is important that the risk assessment be coupled with other considerations, such as the distribution and equity of the risk. For example, in some situations, the total number of people at risk may be less important than who is at risk, such as children or the elderly, who may be particularly susceptible to harm, or individuals who may be exposed to many other risks. When risk assessments are used in combination with these other factors, they can greatly assist in prioritizing problems and identifying the best solutions to them.

Risk analysis is one of those notions that sounds so commonsensical and obvious that people are sometimes surprised to learn that there is actually a fair amount of controversy surrounding it. It is a field that has become polarized, with industry often on one side, very much in favor of some of the new approaches, and many of the environmental groups equally opposed to it.

Why the controversy? In large measure, because risk analysis is often oversold. It is touted by some of its proponents as the next silver bullet for our environmental ills. That, in turn, has led others to fear that it will be used to arrive at simplistic answers to problems that, by their very nature, encompass considerations beyond quantifiable risk, such as social fairness or species extinction. Also, there is concern that the inherent limitations in risk analysis — such as gaps in scientific understanding of environmental issues, the lack of analytical methods to estimate important risks, and the sensitivity of the analysis to underlying assumptions — are often overlooked or poorly understood. These limitations mean that we must not rely on risk analysis alone to determine public policy. If we acknowledge those weaknesses, however, and take them fully into account, risk analysis still can be a powerful tool to help inform policymakers.

Risk analysis can be used not just for the assessment of individual situations but also for the comparison of different risks. It is clear that some risks are worse than others. For example, many experts have concluded from comparative risk analysis that global warming and climate change, the kinds of problems we face in the long run, are far more important than some of the problems we are focusing on now, like cleaning up Superfund sites. But the fear often expressed is that such comparisons would be used more to justify reducing efforts at, say, a Superfund site than to increase efforts to combat climate change. I think there would be much greater acceptance of risk analysis and other newer approaches if they would be adopted in a "no backsliding" context; that is, we would basically employ them to go forward but not to reverse the progress that has been achieved.

In the big picture, risk analysis may be thought of as the first of the three faces of the discipline known as risk management. As just described, the job of risk analysis is to help in determining how serious a given problem is and how bad it is compared with others. It also points out which approaches to dealing with the actual physical hazard are likely to work well and which are not.

The second aspect of risk management involves combining what has been learned from a given analysis with relevant information on the economic, sociological, political, and other aspects of the situation to arrive at a strategy for action. How much would the various possible solutions cost, how fair and balanced would they seem, or be, to the various involved parties, and what will the political climate allow?

The third is risk communication, which, in this case, attempts to educate the public and to involve them meaningfully in setting priorities. Its purpose is primarily to include them in the process of making optimal, or at least reasonable, decisions. After all, when it comes to the nonscientific elements of decisionmaking, the public has as much knowhow as the "experts." Effective risk communication is critically important, I believe, and it is largely responsible for the fact that the public supports environmental protection. We have spent more than a trillion dollars to clean up the environment since 1970, when the EPA was established, and people generally think that this is money well spent. The public wants a clean environment, and people believe strong environmental laws are the way to ensure it. I see that throughout my home state of Montana and wherever I travel around the country.

But while clearly very important, effective risk communication is difficult to achieve. People want to feel certain that environmental laws are based on good science and sensible economics, but many of them have a relatively poor grasp of the basics of both. Some become very concerned about isolated risks like Alar on apples and, just as often, are indifferent to widespread threats like indoor air pollution. Furthermore, various special interests can distort scientific and economic data to their own advantage, further confusing the public. All this, of course, complicates the processes of writing fair and protective statutes and regulations.

A few years ago, an article in the *New York Times* demonstrated this difficulty clearly. The authors selected thirty issues and asked experts to rank them according to risk. Then they asked members of the League of Women Voters, a well-informed public interest group, to order the same issues. The two lists had little in common. League members chose nuclear power as the greatest risk of all—above smoking, alcohol, and surgery. Presumably with the strong belief that no Chernobyl would ever occur here, the experts ranked it twentieth. League members ranked x-rays twenty-second; experts ranked it seventh, and so on.

While this example does not demonstrate that either grasp was wrong—they may have been incorporating different considerations into their rankings—it does suggest how hard it is to communicate the idea of relative risk. Part of this is due to the generally low level of science and economic education that most people have been exposed to, certainly most of those who are a decade or more out of school. But it is also due to the changing nature of communication. On the one hand, over the years I have noticed that it is more and more difficult for people just to get access to facts through the traditional means. Nearly all the daily newspapers in the country have shrunk their news content. In Montana there are many dailies, and the amount of national or international news in those papers today is much less than it was, say, fifteen to twenty years ago. There is a dramatic difference, which I think holds true for local papers nationwide.

On the other hand, there is an explosion of new sources of information. Cable and satellite television and the Internet can provide seemingly endless amounts of information—much more, in fact, than the average person is likely to sort through. So it is extremely hard to get the truly important facts out to the public if people are overwhelmed with other information, especially since they tend to choose the particular channels that are most convenient or easy for them to access. Unfortunately, that caters to short-term amusement and distraction, rather than to their long-term interests and needs.

To a great degree, it seems, we have to do a much better job of educating the media, so that they, in turn, will do a better job of educating and informing the public about ideas such as risk and about ways to make and support good decisions on environmental and other important policies. The media will usually tend to sensationalize, because that sells newspapers; bad news always has more potency and travels faster than good news. At the same time, however, nearly everyone has some sense of responsibility; I think that we can encourage the media's responding to that sense by inviting reporters and editors to sit down with us while we show them the facts. We should expose them more to our struggles to find good solutions, so that they can communicate better with their readers and listeners. This is one very important, albeit partial, solution to this problem. Experts, too, need to do a better job of communicating risks and choices to the public; otherwise, so much of our scientific and statistical research and analysis will simply be a waste of time and effort.

We are extraordinarily blessed to be living in a democracy. As a matter of principle, the public must always make the final decision. But this process will reach the right result only if the public has all the facts and understands the context in which they fit. If the people do not get the necessary information and do not have the skills to assess it, they will have a much harder time making good decisions. Our tasks as legislators, environmental workers, educators, or media people, is to try to make sure the public understands the risks and the options before it makes its choices.

So to summarize much of the above, in the difficult task of priority setting, it may be very helpful and constructive to make effective use of the three components of risk management. With risk analysis, one may be able to identify and analyze the most pressing physical dangers. Then it is necessary to combine this understanding with the relevant information on the economic, sociological, political, and other aspects of the situation. And finally, both in general and for the specific case at hand, it is vitally important to try to provide the public with the ideas and tools they require to make good environmental decisions. But it is risk analysis that helps us focus our attention on the real problems in the first place.

There are, I believe, a variety of areas where our understanding of risk can help us overcome some of the more resistant questions in environmental policy. In the past, we sometimes focused so hard on just one topic that we lost sight of the rest. For example, after many years of frustration at the EPA's inaction in addressing threats to drinking water safety, when Congress reauthorized the Safe Drinking Water Act in 1986, we ordered the EPA to identify and regulate twenty-five new drinking water contaminants every three years, regardless of how much risk the new contaminants actually posed to public health. Risk analysis helped us improve this law when we revisited it. The 1996 amendments to the Safe Drinking Water Act direct the EPA to target its resources on the contaminants that pose the greatest threats to human health. After all, if every contaminant is a priority, none is a priority. The Safe Drinking Water Act's use of comparative risk helped us set the right priorities, become more efficient, and do a better job at protecting the public health.

Risk analysis, then, can help us focus on the big picture. It can help local government, industry, environmental groups, and the public to set the right priorities, to make rational choices, by standardizing our estimates of hazards, costs, and benefits. Of course, we cannot assume that the same approach will work for creating or improving all environmental laws and regulations. We are still in the early stages of developing the application of risk-based techniques. A carpenter who picks up a new hammer and gives it a few experimental taps before banging away is using sound, comparative risk analysis. He is careful to use his tool on nails rather than on screws, and on wooden furniture rather than on windows. And when he builds a house, he needs other tools in addition to his hammer. We need to be just as careful and proceed with the understanding that risk analysis is but one part of the decision-making process.

Our understanding of risk analysis is still in its infancy, as is our ability to apply it to specific environmental problems. It would be foolish to ignore it, but we should also resist the temptation to make the opposite mistake by applying risk analysis as broadly as possible or as soon as possible. Indiscriminately applied everywhere, to all problems, risk assessment can create its own problems. At best, it could lead to inefficient use of resources; at worst, it would give the wrong results. Rather, we should begin by looking at our conceptual approach to environmental policy as a whole, to see where risk analysis can best help. Then we should examine our statutes and regulations to see where we can employ risk analysis most effectively.

In the early days of confronting toxic air pollutants, for example, our objective was to develop a health-based approach. It proved very time-consuming and, ultimately, unsuccessful. In this case we found that regulating only by risk assessment proved unworkable. So, in the end, we turned to a technology-based approach. We may well encounter similar problems in other areas. We are still developing ways to know how and when to apply risk assessment to complex problems.

As we refine risk analysis, we must remember that we will use it for a simple purpose: to protect people and the environment. It must never become a substitute for good judgment or, as some hope it will, a way to gut environmental laws and regulations. I am hoping for precisely the opposite — that it will become a tool for setting priorities better and protecting the environment more effectively and more efficiently.

Our ability to improve the performance of this country's environmental laws and to achieve a cleaner environment will depend increasingly on having more tools available to policymakers at the federal, state, and local levels. When used wisely — that is, to inform decisions, not to make them — risk analysis can help us make more effective use of our financial, human, and institutional resources. In so doing, it can contribute to greater public understanding and stronger support of our critically important environmental programs.

Chapter 15   RISK COMMUNICATION

Evolution and Revolution

VINCENT T.
COVELLO AND
PETER M.
SANDMAN

Over the past thirty years, our country has witnessed a tremendous revolution in the way we manage the environment: the public has taken back power over environmental policy. In the 1970s, people were largely content to leave control in the hands of established authorities, such as the Environmental Protection Agency. In the 1980s, however, the public reasserted its claim over environmental policymaking. People became demonstrably upset, distressed, even outraged when they felt excluded.

In this crucible, modern risk communication was forged. It was created, in part, to guide the new partnership and dialogue of government and industry with the public. It addressed a fundamental dilemma made clear by that dialogue: The risks that kill people and the risks that alarm them are often completely different. There is virtually no correlation between the ranking of hazards according to statistics on expected annual mortality and the ranking of the same hazards by how upsetting they are. There are many risks that make people furious, even though they cause little harm — and others that do kill many, but without making anybody mad.

Risk communication is a scientifically based discipline that confronts this dilemma. Where data indicate that a hazard is not serious, yet the public is near panic, it can be used to calm people down; for this kind of situation, its goal is to provide reassurance. But it can also help generate a sense of urgency where data indicate that the hazard is serious, yet the public response is one of apathy. It has been effective, for example, in motivating people to buckle up their seat belts, to quit smoking, to test for radon in their houses, and to evacuate their homes during an emergency. It means shaking people by their collective lapels and saying: "Look, this is dangerous. It could kill you. Do something!"

This is the general context for the interest in risk communication that began in the 1980s and continues to this day. Other factors that have contributed to its rapid growth include significant increases in

— public interest in health, safety, and environmental issues and media coverage of them;
— the demand for information generated by public concern about risks from past, present, and future activities;
— the number and reach of right-to-know laws relating to exposures to risk agents;
— mistrust of risk management authorities, and public demands for the right to participate as a full partner in all phases of risk assessment and risk management;
— awareness by governments and industry that risk controversies often threaten the achievement of their organizational goals; and
— awareness by all sides that the public's response to a risk can be amplified or attenuated by those who wish to manipulate it—that is, that risk communication is a useful tool for advocates of particular outcomes.

The science and art of risk communication was formulated in response to these changes. In the process, several important obstacles had to be overcome: inconsistent, overly complex, confusing, or incomplete risk messages; the lack of trust in information sources; selective reporting by the media; and psychological and social factors that affect how information is processed.

The first of these obstacles derives largely from the uncertainty, complexity, and incompleteness of environmental data. To make effective decisions, risk managers need to know the potential harm posed by threats to health, safety, or the environment. Risk assessments are designed to provide this information, but, unfortunately, large gaps remain in our understanding of many hazards. For example, most environmental risk assessments to date have focused on cancer; there has been much less study of other types of adverse health impacts (e.g., effects on reproduction). In addition, most risk assessments have addressed single chemicals, with much less attention to mixtures of chemicals. This lack of data presents a critical challenge.

Even on those occasions when one can place precise quantitative error bars on a risk estimate, the "lesson" of the assessment may be only that the risk in question is somewhere between serious and nonexistent. So the decision whether to take action to avert a possible catastrophe (e.g., global warming) may need to be made before the magnitude and likelihood of the catastrophe can be estimated with anything approaching confidence.

Largely because of gaps in knowledge, risk assessment seldom provides exact answers. In this sense, it suffers from the same weaknesses as many other fields of scientific inquiry. A variety of confounding factors (e.g., smoking, drinking, exercise, and diet) often make it difficult, if not impossible, to reach definitive conclusions about cause and effect. This is especially the case for health risk assessments, where usually direct testing on humans is ethically prohibited (an important exception being controlled clinical trials). As a result, the outcomes of most risk assessments are best seen as estimates, with varying degrees of uncertainties about the actual nature of the risk. These uncertainties can justify conflicting interpretations of the data, typically grounded as much in value judgments as in scientific judgments.

A second major obstacle to effective risk communication is distrust. Sources of distrust include disagreements among experts; lack of coordination among risk management organizations; inadequate training of experts and spokespersons in risk communication skills; insensitivity to the requirements for effective communication, public participation, dialogue, and community outreach; mismanagement and neglect; and a history of frequent distortion, exaggeration, secrecy, or worse on the part of many risk information providers. A complicating factor is that while industry and government risk communicators often see the lack of trust and credibility as their central problem, activists tend to see the undermining of undeserved trust as a major achievement.

Often the problem of risk communication is not so much how to regain trust as how to function without it. Important lessons can be learned here from the ways companies deal with each other — in contract negotiations, for example — where accountability, not trust, is the dominant value. Organizations that accept the obligation to prove their contentions to the satisfaction of their critics find a wide range of mechanisms to help them do so, such as third party audits. Ironically, it is because they rely more on accountability and less on trust that such organizations come to be viewed as trustworthy.

A third obstacle is selective reporting by the news media. The media are critical to the delivery of risk information to the general public (though they are much less important for communicating with involved stakeholders). A major conclusion from research focused on the news media is that journalists are highly selective in reporting about risk and particularly inclined toward stories that involve people in unusual, dramatic, confrontational, negative, or sensational situations (e.g., natural disasters, technological disasters, emotionally charged town hall meetings). They tend to focus their attention on issues that play to the same "outrage factors" that the public uses in evaluating risks. For example, they look for stories involving dreaded events (e.g., cancer among children), risks to future generations, involuntariness, unclear benefits, inequitable distribution of risks and benefits, potentially irreversible effects, and cases where trust is lacking. They pay much less attention to stories about risks that affect many more people each year but are less dramatic (e.g., heart disease and diabetes).

In addition, many media stories about risk suffer from substantial omissions or present oversimplified, distorted, inaccurate information. Studies have revealed, for example, that media reports on cancer risks often fail to provide adequate statistics on general cancer rates for purposes of comparison, or enough information on detection, treatments, and other protective measures.

Some of these problems stem from characteristics of the media and the constraints on them, such as tight deadlines limiting the pursuit of information and lack of time or space to deal with the complexities and uncertainties surrounding many risk issues. Others arise from the ways in which journalists view their role. They often see their job as simply to present opposing views as equally as possible, without judging their merits; thus, truth in journalism is quite different from truth in science. In addition, people in the media are often forced to rely heavily on sources who are easily accessible and willing to speak out; others tend to be ignored. And reporters often do not have the scientific or technical background and expertise needed to evaluate the complex data and the disagreements that surround many debates about risks. Consequently, their stories may contain inadvertent distortions of reality, or tend to mislead, or even be just plain wrong.

The fourth major obstacle to effective risk communication derives from the psychological and social factors that influence how people process information about risk. At least seven such factors can be identified.

The first consists of the mental shortcuts, or heuristics, that all of us (including experts) employ to calculate the probability that an adverse action or event will happen. As a result of these heuristics, people may make biased judgments or use only a small amount of the available information in making decisions about risk. We tend to assign greater probability to events of which we are frequently reminded (e.g., in the news media, scientific literature, or discussions among friends or colleagues) or to events that are easy to recall or to imagine through concrete examples or dramatic images.

A second psychological factor that affects our processing of risk information is apathy. In many cases, people lack motivation and are simply not interested in learning about a risk. Apathy can indicate true lack of interest, serve as a psychological defense mechanism, or be based on a prior negative experience. For example, people may not be willing to become actively engaged if they perceive a lack of relevance or an absence of opportunities for meaningful participation and dialogue.

A third is overconfidence and unrealistic optimism, which often lead people to ignore or dismiss risk information. A majority of the population, for example, consider themselves less likely than average to get cancer, get fired from their job, or get mugged; only 50 percent, of course, can be "less likely than average" to do anything. Overconfidence and unrealistic optimism are most influential when the risk in question is voluntary, and when high levels of perceived personal control lead to reduced feelings of susceptibility. Many people fail to use seat belts, for example, because of the unfounded belief that they are better or safer than the average driver. In a similar vein, many teenagers engage in high-risk behaviors (e.g., drunk driving, smoking, unprotected sex) because of perceptions, supported by peers, of invulnerability and overconfidence in their ability to avoid harm.

A fourth factor is the difficulty people have in understanding information that is probabilistic in nature, or relates to unfamiliar activities or technologies, or is presented in unfamiliar ways. Studies have demonstrated, moreover, that subtle changes in the way that probabilistic information is framed — such as expressing risks in terms of the probability of survival versus that of dying — can have a major impact on how we view the risk.

Another is the public's desire and demand for scientific certainty. People are averse to uncertainty and find a variety of coping mechanisms to reduce the anxiety it causes. This aversion often translates into a marked preference for statements of fact over statements of probability, the language of risk assessment. Despite protests by scientists that precise information is seldom available, people want absolute answers; they demand to know exactly what will happen, not what might happen.

A sixth factor is the reluctance on the part of people to change strongly held beliefs and their willingness to ignore information that contradicts them. Strong beliefs about risks, once formed within a particular social and cultural context, change very slowly, and they can be extraordinarily persistent in the face of contrary evidence.

A last, but very important, social/psychological determinant of how we *process* risk information involves the factors that affect how we *judge* the actual magnitude of a risk. These components of judgment are often thought of as distortions in public risk perception; they are, perhaps, better seen as aspects of public risk assessment. Beginning in the 1960s, a large research effort focused on the complexity of the considerations involved in nonscientific risk perception/assessment. A major conclusion of this research was that typically there is only a low correlation between the level of physical risk in a situation and the amount of worry that it arouses. Much more important in determining people's responses, it was found, is the presence of what are now called "outrage factors." These include:

— *Voluntariness.* Risks from activities considered to be involuntary or imposed (e.g., exposure to chemicals or radiation from a waste or industrial facility) are judged to be greater, and are therefore less readily accepted, than risks from activities that are seen to be voluntary (e.g., smoking, sunbathing, or mountain climbing).

— *Controllability.* Risks from activities viewed as under the control of others (e.g., releases of toxic chemicals by industrial facilities) are judged to be greater, and are less readily accepted, than those from activities that appear to be under the control of the individual (e.g., driving an automobile or riding a bicycle).

— *Familiarity.* Risks from activities viewed as unfamiliar (such as from leaks of chemicals or radiation from waste disposal sites) are perceived to be greater than risks from activities viewed as familiar (such as household work).

— *Fairness.* Risks from activities believed to be unfair or to involve unfair processes (e.g., inequities related to the siting of industrial facilities or landfills) seem more threatening than risks from fair activities (e.g., vaccinations).

— *Benefits.* Risks from activities that seem to have unclear, questionable, or diffused personal or economic benefits (e.g., waste disposal facilities) are judged to be greater than risks from activities that have clear benefits (jobs; monetary benefits; automobile driving).

— *Catastrophic potential.* Risks from activities viewed as having the potential to cause a significant number of deaths and injuries grouped in time and space (e.g., deaths and injuries resulting from a major industrial explosion) are less acceptable than risks from activities that cause deaths and injuries scattered or random in time and space (e.g., automobile accidents).

— *Understanding.* Poorly understood risks (such as the health effects of long-term exposure to low doses of toxic chemicals or radiation) seem worse than risks that are well understood or self-explanatory (such as pedestrian accidents or slipping on ice).

— *Uncertainty.* Risks from activities that are relatively unknown or that pose highly uncertain risks (e.g., risks from biotechnology and genetic engineering) are felt to be greater than risks from activities that appear to be relatively well known to science (e.g., actuarial risk data related to automobile accidents).

— *Delayed effects.* Risks from activities that may have delayed effects (e.g., long latency periods between exposure and adverse health effects) are judged to be greater than risks from activities viewed as having immediate effects (e.g., poisonings).

— *Effects on children.* Risks from activities that appear to put children specifically at risk (e.g., milk contaminated with radioactive or toxic substances; pregnant women exposed to radiation or toxic chemicals) are perceived to be greater than risks from activities that do not (e.g., workplace accidents).

— *Effects on future generations.* Risks from activities that seem to pose a threat to future generations (e.g., adverse genetic effects due to exposure to toxic chemicals or radiation) are judged to be greater than risks from activities that do not (e.g., skiing accidents).

— *Victim identity.* Risks from activities that produce identifiable victims (e.g., a worker exposed to high levels of toxic chemicals or radiation; a child who falls down a well) are less readily accepted than risks from activities that produce statistical victims (e.g., statistical profiles of automobile accident victims).

— *Dread.* Risks from activities that evoke fear, terror, or anxiety (e.g., exposure to cancer-causing agents; AIDS) are perceived to be greater than risks from activities that do not arouse such feelings or emotions (e.g., common colds and household accidents).

— *Trust.* Risks from activities associated with individuals, institutions, or organizations lacking in trust and credibility (e.g., industries with poor environmental track records) are judged to be greater than risks from the same activities but associated with those who are trustworthy and credible (e.g., regulatory agencies that achieve high levels of compliance among regulated groups).

— *Media attention.* Risks from activities that receive considerable media coverage (e.g., accidents and leaks at nuclear power plants) are viewed as greater than risks from activities that receive little (e.g., on-the-job accidents).

— *Accident history.* Risks from activities with a history of major accidents or frequent minor accidents (e.g., leaks at waste disposal facilities) are perceived to be greater, and are less readily accepted, than risks from those with little or no such history (e.g., recombinant DNA experimentation).

— *Reversibility.* Risks from activities considered to have potentially irreversible adverse effects (e.g., birth defects from exposure to a toxic substance) are judged to be greater than risks from activities considered to have reversible adverse effects (e.g., serious sports injuries).

— *Personal stake.* Risks from activities viewed by people to place them (or their families) personally and directly at risk (e.g., living near a waste disposal site) are perceived to be greater than risks from activities that appear to pose no direct or personal threat (e.g., disposal of waste in remote areas).

— *Ethical/moral nature.* Risks from activities believed to be ethically objectionable or morally wrong (e.g., foisting pollution on an economically distressed community) are less acceptable than risks from ethically neutral activities (e.g., side effects of medication).

— *Human versus natural origin.* Risks generated by human action, failure, or incompetence (e.g., industrial accidents caused by negligence, inadequate safeguards, or operator error) are judged to be greater than risks believed to be caused by nature or "Acts of God" (e.g., exposure to geological radon or cosmic rays).

These findings reveal that people often perceive and assess "risk" more in terms of these "outrage" factors than in terms of potential for "real" harm or hazard. For the public,

Risk = Hazard + Outrage.

This equation reflects the observation that an individual's perception or assessment of risk is based not only on the quantifiable magnitude of the hazard (e.g., as ascertained from mortality and morbidity statistics) but just as importantly on the serious outrage factors.

When it is present, outrage often takes on strong emotional over-tones. It predisposes an individual to react emotionally (e.g., with fear or anger), which can in turn significantly amplify levels of worry. Outrage also tends to distort perceived hazard. But as we have stressed, the outrage factors are not only distorters of hazard perception. They are also, independently, components of the "risk" in question — and may themselves be perceived accurately or inaccurately.

This model implies that a key part of resolving risk controversies lies in recognizing the importance of the various outrage factors that we have just discussed. Thus a fairly distributed risk is viewed as being less risky, and therefore is more acceptable, than an unfairly distributed one; an activity that provides significant benefits to the parties at risk is more acceptable than another with no such benefits; an activity for which there are no alternatives appears to pose less hazard than one for which there appear to be better alternatives; a risk that the parties affected can control — through voluntary choice, the sharing of power, or the acquisition of knowledge needed to make informed choices — seems less threatening than a risk that is beyond their control. An activity that people can assess and decide voluntarily to accept is more acceptable than an imposed risk. These statements are true in the same sense that a risk that is statistically unlikely and/or of small consequence is more acceptable than a large risk.

Thus, risk, in its more general sense, is multidimensional, and its quantitative size (its hazard) is only one of the dimensions. Since people vary in how they assess risk acceptability, they will weigh the outrage factors according to their own values, education, personal experience, and stake in the outcome. Because acceptability is a matter of values and opinions, and because values and opinions differ, discussions of risk may also be debates about values, accountability, and control.

Once the outrage model is accepted as valid, then a broad range of risk communication and management options becomes available for resolving risk controversies. Because outrage factors such as fairness, familiarity, and voluntariness are as relevant in judging the acceptability of a risk as are its assessed magnitude and probability of occurrence, efforts to reduce outrage (to make a risk seem fairer, more familiar, and more voluntary) can be as significant as efforts to reduce the physical hazard. If "Risk = Hazard + Outrage" is taken literally, then making a risk appear fairer, more familiar, and more voluntary *does* indeed make it smaller, just as does reducing the physical hazard. Similarly, because personal control is important, efforts to share power, such as establishing and assisting community advisory committees or supporting third party research, audits, inspections, and monitoring, can be powerful means for making a risk more acceptable.

Not surprisingly, it has taken governments, companies, and others time to absorb these ideas. Indeed, environmental and health "risk communication" has gone through four evolutionary stages in the process, each with its own general philosophy and approach.

The first stage was simply to ignore the public. This is the pre-risk-communication stage, prevalent in the United States until about 1985. The approach is built on the notion that most people are hopelessly stupid, irredeemably irrational. So you ignore them if you can; mislead them if you absolutely have to; lie to them if you think you can get away with it. Protect their health and environment, but by no means let them in on risk policymaking, because they will only mess things up.

And indeed, for a long time the public was content to be ignored. But this approach stopped working in the mid- to late 1980s. There began a broad movement to take back power over environmental policy; and increasingly, when the public was ignored, controversies became larger. That was the experience of the nuclear power and chemical industries; the biotechnology industry is learning the same lesson today.

Since ignoring the public no longer worked, we advanced to the second stage, and the first level of true risk communication: learning how to explain risk data better. This is where many organizations still are today. Although there has been real progress, it remains an uphill battle for spokespersons to explain risk numbers — such as parts per billion — so that people understand what they mean. Techniques are improving for explaining, for example, that a risk that is unlikely and of small possible impact is trivial in importance, that people do not need to worry about it, that they should ask that their tax dollars be spent on averting other, much more serious risks instead. Risk communicators have found that it is also clearly worthwhile to learn how to deal with the media, how to reduce or eliminate jargon, how to make charts and graphs more easily grasped, and so on.

Most important, risk communicators, like many others, have found that *motivation* is the key to learning. While risk communication materials for the general public should be presented at the sixth- to ninth-grade level to be comprehensible, people take in even sixth- to ninth-grade material only when they are motivated. But when they are sufficiently inspired, they manage to learn even very complex material. We all know high school boys who cannot make much sense out of *A Tale of Two Cities* but have no difficulty figuring out from an article in *Popular Mechanics* how to adjust the spark plugs on their car. By any known readability test, *Popular Mechanics* is more difficult than Dickens. In a similar way, concerned citizens without high school diplomas can make their way through a highly technical three hundred-page environmental impact report to zero in on the one paragraph that they believe undermines the entire argument of its authors.

For some risk problems, such as radon, where the hazard is large and the controversy is minimal, doing a better job explaining the data is one of the most important pieces of the puzzle. When people have control over a particular risk and response to it is voluntary, there is need for action at the individual level. Health departments are accustomed to this type of issue, but for many organizations, including environmental regulatory agencies, it is new. Here, the main challenges in bringing about the appropriate action are catching the public's attention and explaining the risk numbers in meaningful, relevant fashion.

When the hazard is not great but people are extremely outraged, however, explaining the data better seldom does much good (and stirring up attention is unnecessary). You can never produce a video that will transform people who are trying to throw rocks at you into a pacified, well-informed audience.

That is why risk communication moved on to the third stage, which is built around dialogue with the community, especially with interested and concerned, even fanatic, stakeholders. The publication of the *Seven Cardinal Rules of Effective Risk Communication* (see the appendix) by the EPA as a policy guidance document in 1988 was an important third-stage event; its central premise is that what people mean by "risk" is much more complicated than what technical experts commonly mean by the same term.

In the third stage, a profound paradigm shift took place. For the first time, risk was properly seen as consisting of two almost independent, basic elements, hazard and outrage. The advantage of the "hazard + outrage" concept was that it served to reframe the problem. It allowed risk policymakers to consider in their decisions all the factors that are included in the public's definition of risk. This new, expanded concept of risk also pointed to the need for real dialogue among all the interested parties. It led to the then revolutionary idea that the essence of risk communication is not just explaining risk numbers — it is also reducing (or increasing) outrage. The problem is not so much that people do not understand the numbers but rather that they are (or are not) angry or upset.

Third-stage success requires that if you have a substantive action to offer in response to a risk situation, and you want people to listen to it, you have to listen to them first. In addition, you cannot just acknowledge people's outrage — you must communicate that they are entitled to be outraged, and why.

An excellent example of this occurred in the late 1980s. Medical waste was floating up on the shorelines of the northeastern United States, and the public's response was powerful. In New Jersey, the Department of Environmental Protection kept telling the people that the stuff was not dangerous, but the public kept on insisting that it was still disgusting, and a battle erupted. In Rhode Island, by comparison, the commissioner of health handled the same issue more deftly. He went public and said (in essence): "This is an outrage; this is unacceptable. The people of Rhode Island will not, and should not, tolerate any hypodermic syringes washing up on our shores. We are going to do absolutely everything in our power to stop it, even though the hazard from it is essentially nonexistent — even though there is a negligible risk to health. We are going to turn our budget upside down if we have to. We will put a stop to it no matter what it takes and no matter how much it costs." The public's reply was: "Thank you for your response . . . but maybe we should wait a minute. If it's really a negligible risk, how much of our money are you planning to spend?" Psychiatrists call this "getting on the other side of the resistance." When you share, and even exaggerate, people's concerns, they pick up that you believe that their anger and their outrage are legitimate. That frees them to feel something else. In Rhode Island, they came to see that the risk was extremely small, and they began wondering whether it was worth spending a lot of money on it.

Stage four in the evolution of environmental and health risk communication comes about when you really believe in stage three and discover that stage three requires fundamental shifts in an organization's values and culture. Stage four involves treating the public as a full partner. It works somewhat like psychotherapy. First, you must commit yourself, at least tentatively, to the goal — in this case, third-stage risk communication. Then you try to carry it out. Then you discover that, for the most part, you cannot. And then either you give up or you recognize that a change in how you deal with others often requires a change in how you deal with yourself.

But the fourth stage of risk communication is difficult to achieve, for a number of reasons, and only limited progress has been made toward achieving those organizational adjustments. First, and perhaps most obvious: It is simply very hard for individuals and organizations to change. Habit, inertia, and the fear of failure in instituting the new all conspire to point us in the direction of old and familiar behavior. Second, the technical fields are dominated by people who, by disposition, prefer clear boundaries, logical approaches, and unemotional situations. They typically do not like negotiation, dialogue, and partnerships with members of the public.

A third cause of limited stage-four progress in the environmental field, in particular, involves the convictions and principles of the people employed in it. Most choose that kind of work because they want to save lives or protect people from hazards. They are convinced that they know precisely what is needed to do that, and so they tend to have strong motivation to resist any competing approaches. They want to deal with risks in a scientific, factual way, and not with people and their emotional problems. Then, too, there is the skepticism of many people in government and industry who doubt that risk communication can actually do much good. They believe that people are irrational and hysterical and that they will stay that way, regardless of how you try to get through to them.

A fifth impediment concerns power. At the core of the third and fourth stages is empowerment of the public. Every profession has at its center an impulse to hoard power and to resist attempts to usurp that power.

Sixth, organizational climate is also important. Researchers have found that people in bureaucracies are often very adept at distinguishing real policies from those that are mere rhetoric. Is the organization's commitment to dialogue sincere? Will I get the time, the staff, the training, and the budget to do the job well? If the dialogue process fails, will it harm my career? Will it affect my performance appraisal?

Finally, the seventh, and perhaps the most important, reason that there has not been more progress toward the fourth stage of risk communication involves one's level of comfort and self-esteem. Managing the risk my way feels good (to me). Sharing control and credit with citizens — especially with angry, hostile, irrational citizens and with the activists who have inflamed them — feels rotten (to me). Even in the face of evidence that reducing stakeholder outrage and settling risk controversies are usually more profitable strategies than continuing a fight, managers frequently put a higher premium on protecting their own comfort and self-esteem than on achieving their organization's substantive goals. The outrage they choose to reduce is their own.

Except for the first stage (ignoring the public), the various stages of risk communication build on one another; they do not, however, replace one another. We still must be concerned about explaining the data better and about making dialogue happen—even as we try to change our organizations.

If this fourth stage is ever fully realized, risk communication will turn out to have been even more revolutionary an idea than its organizers first thought. We knew that it was going to alter the ways in which the public deals with organizations about risk, and in which organizations deal with the public. What we did not realize was that it would transform the way organizations think of themselves as well. We have discovered, at the most fundamental level, that engaging in meaningful, respectful, and frank dialogue with the public involves changes in basic values and organizational culture. But we have also found that much more often than not, the improvements that come of it all prove well worth the effort.

Part VII   HOPE

Chapter 16   SYMBOLS OF HOPE FOR
ENVIRONMENTAL
SUSTAINABILITY

JANE
GOODALL

How is it that a little girl who grew up in London in a family that had very little money — we had enough to eat, some clothes to wear, but we couldn't afford a bicycle, let alone a car — is traveling around the world, addressing groups such as the EPA? How is it that someone who has spent most of her life sitting in the forest gets invited to speak in all corners of the globe?

The answer is that I had a strong and supportive family. My mother, in particular, always impressed upon me that if I worked hard, took advantage of opportunities, and never gave up I would find a way to make my dreams come true. She was the only one who didn't laugh at me when, at eleven years of age, I fell in love with Tarzan and determined that when I grew up I would go to Africa, live with animals, and write books about them. Hardly surprising that my dream seemed absurd: World War II was still ongoing, Africa was still thought of as the Dark Continent — and I was a GIRL!

We couldn't afford the university. My mother suggested secretarial training, so that I could get a job anywhere in the world. A good idea. Then, an invitation from a school friend to spend some time with her family in Kenya. Leaving my job in London to work as a waitress to save up for a return fare by boat. Making an appointment with the late Louis Leakey. And that led to a job as his assistant, a three-month field trip to the now famous Olduvai Gorge, and suddenly I found I was waking, each morning, into my dream. As of 1957, no human fossils had been found in Olduvai. After the hard day's work searching for fossils I was able to walk up onto the Serengeti Plain. There were so many animals in those days — giraffes, zebras, antelopes, ostriches, and many more. One evening there was a close-up meeting with a rhino. Another evening with a curious two-year-old male lion.

It was at Olduvai that Louis Leakey decided he would ask me to undertake a field study of a population of chimpanzees living in the forests that fringed the eastern shore of Lake Tanganyika. He hoped that an understanding of the behavior of our closest relatives, in their natural habitat, might help him better imagine the social behavior of our Stone Age ancestors. He could determine much about their appearance from bone structure, their diet from tooth wear, and their way of life from artifacts associated with living floors. But behavior does not fossilize.

At first I didn't believe he was serious. I had no university degree, surely no proper qualifications. But Louis, with unusual perspicacity, said that this was all to the good. He wanted someone whose mind was uncluttered by the reductionist thinking of the ethologists of the time.

Of course I was thrilled. But there were two major obstacles to overcome. Firstly, who on earth would give money for such a crazy project? A young and untrained female setting off on a venture that was bound to fail! At last a generous American businessman, Leighton Wilkie, agreed to provide funding for six months. Secondly, the British authorities of what was then Tanganyika were shocked at the prospect of a young *girl* going into the bush alone. It was preposterous, ridiculous. But in the end, because of Louis's insistence, they reluctantly agreed — provided I had a companion. Who volunteered? My remarkable mother!

During the four months that she was with me, my mother set up a little bush clinic, supplying local fishermen with simple things like aspirin, saline drips, Epsom salts, and so on. Nevertheless, she effected some spectacular cures. This established an excellent relationship with the local people, which has stood me, my students — and the chimpanzees — in good stead ever since.

When I began my study, the chimpanzees were terrified of the strange white ape who had arrived in their midst. Repeatedly they ran away. But gradually they got used to me. I sat patiently on the peaks and ridges between the thick forests of the valleys, used my binoculars, and did not try to get too close too quickly. One day my cook reported that an adult male had arrived in camp to feed on the ripe fruits of an oil nut palm that grew there. During his visit he found — and took — some bananas lying on my table. He returned again and again. He got used to the camp, to the cook, and, eventually, to me. Then, when I met him in the forest, his calm acceptance of me served to allay the fear of the other chimps. Perhaps, after all, I wasn't so dangerous as they had thought! And so I was introduced to the magic world of the wild chimpanzees — a world unknown to anyone outside the forest.

One amazing day I watched David Greybeard using grasses to fish for termites. Sometimes he stripped leaves off twigs for this purpose — the beginning of toolmaking. This was a breakthrough observation. It had been thought that humans, and only humans, could use and make tools. On the basis of these observations, Leakey was able to secure funding for the continuation of my study. And it was David Greybeard also who first demonstrated meat eating. It had been thought that chimpanzees were vegetarians. Later I saw them hunting and sharing the kill.

As I became more familiar with this world, I began to recognize the chimpanzees as individuals, each with a unique personality. I named them — David Greybeard's close companion, Goliath. The old female Flo and her infant daughter Fifi. Mike, Mr. McGregor, and Melissa. And so on, until all members of a community of some fifty individuals had been named.

As time went on I learned more about the complexities of their social life, how they traveled mostly in groups of up to six, sometimes joining in large, excited gatherings — usually when a favored food was available in one part of the range or a sexually popular female was in estrus. And sometimes they traveled alone. Such a society favored the ability to make rapid behavioral adjustments: a young male might be the most dominant individual at one moment, lording it over the females, but he might need to be very submissive the next when a high-ranking male joined the group.

I gradually understood something of their communication patterns — the many different calls, each of which meant something different, the postures and gestures, many of them so like some of ours, and occurring in the same contexts, too. Like kissing, embracing, holding hands, patting on the back — all in greeting. Tickling with the fingers in play. I realized the importance of friendly physical contact, the crucial role played by social grooming in maintaining friendly relations. Aggressive patterns were similar to ours, too — swaggering, kicking, and hitting — and the contexts in which aggression occurred.

I gradually came to appreciate the nature of the affectionate and supportive bonds that persist through life between a mother and her offspring, and between siblings. A fully grown male will hasten to the defense of his old mother (chimpanzees can live more than sixty years) — and she may even hurl her frail body into some fight on her son's behalf. When a mother dies, an orphaned infant will be adopted by an elder sibling. Young males make excellent caregivers, even though there is no father role as such in chimpanzee society. Infants under three years of age, relying almost entirely on milk, cannot survive the death of their mothers. But one rather sickly youngster of only three and a quarter years survived after he was adopted by an adolescent male of twelve years not thought to be related. Yet Spindle waited for little Mel during travel, carried him on his back, and drew him into his nest at night. Spindle shared food when Mel begged. Without doubt, Spindle saved Mel's life.

The long-term research has pointed to the important role played by early experience in shaping adult behavior. Youngsters lucky enough to have mothers who are affectionate, playful, supportive but not over-protective, and capable of enforcing discipline are likely to become assertive and successful as adults. Those with mothers who are more harsh and punitive, less affectionate and supportive, tend to develop into individuals who are tense and find it difficult to enjoy relaxed relationships with other adults. In other words, maternal techniques play a vital role in determining the future behavior of infants. Of course, a genetic component is involved as well; it has not yet been possible to separate the effects of nature versus nurture.

As an aside, it may be that there is an important lesson for us here. It seems more than likely that maternal behavior and early experience also play an important role in determining the subsequent behavior of humans. Human infants, through millions of years of evolution, have been programmed to expect a predictable environment. When that environment is disrupted — in dysfunctional families, when the mother is working and there is no mother substitute, when there is no paternal role model, and so on — is that likely to affect the future behavior of children? If so, we should be putting far more resources into finding ways to minimize damage of this sort in infancy and childhood. As more women go into the workplace, through necessity or inclination, it becomes increasingly important to provide an alternative environment that tries to address the innate expectations of the child and also provides additional stimulation that will equip the individual for the pace of modern life.

It is now forty years since I arrived at Gombe. We have been able to collect the life histories and family histories of so many unique individuals. We have been able to record the history of a community of extraordinary beings who cannot record it for themselves. It is a history every bit as fascinating as that which we read in our history books: the often dramatic confrontations between adult males vying for the alpha position, the terrible epidemics, and even a series of brutal and aggressive attacks by the males of one community on the individuals of another that resulted in the annihilation of the smaller — except for the adolescent females, who were actively recruited. These events took place during a four-year period and were like primitive warfare.

One chimpanzee, Fifi, was a tiny infant in 1960, and she is still alive today — the only survivor from those early days. She, along with her mother, that great matriarch Flo, has become well known around the world. Two years ago when I went to Korea for the first time, a young woman approached as I walked along the street in Seoul. "You must be Jane Goodall." I was surprised to be recognized. "I never thought I'd see you," she said. And then, "Can you tell me — how is Fifi?"

When I first went to Cambridge University (Louis had arranged for me to get a Ph.D. in ethology, despite my lacking a B.A.), I was told that naming one's animal subjects was considered unscientific. I should have numbered them. Nor should I have described their personalities — only humans had personalities. Nor, it seemed, should I have attributed to them the ability to reason or to experience emotions. All of this was anthropomorphizing. Luckily I had learned about animal mind, emotions, and personality during my childhood from my dog Rusty. It is an interesting thought — if I had been persuaded by that reductionist and homocentric viewpoint, would that young Korean woman have approached? Would she have been touched by the life history of Number 12, described without personality, mind, or emotions? It seems unlikely.

Our study of chimpanzees has taught us not only a lot about the chimpanzee's place in the nature of things but a lot about ourselves as well. There is widespread recognition today, even among scientists, that we are not the only beings with personalities, minds, and emotions. Indeed, scientists are increasingly striving to investigate those once forbidden areas. Where a sharp line was once perceived, dividing human animals from the rest of the animal kingdom, that line has become increasingly blurred. And this is leading to a new respect for the other amazing beings with whom we share this planet.

My own observations in the wild, and those of other field biologists subsequently, paved the way for a greater understanding of the similarities between humans and their closest living relatives. These observations were substantiated by work in a variety of captive situations. It was shown that chimpanzees were capable of many cognitive performances once considered unique to humans — understanding the moods and needs of others, the ability to learn through imitation, and a whole variety of skills demonstrated through the use of specially designed computers. Chimpanzees were taught many signs of American Sign Language, could acquire these from each other, could invent signs for unnamed objects.

Laboratory research has revealed that chimpanzees are closer to humans than was thought: the structure of their DNA differs from ours by only just over 1 percent; their blood is so similar to ours that we could get a blood transfusion from a chimp, or they from us; their immune system is also very similar to our own. That is why chimpanzees are used in medical research to try to find cures or vaccines for diseases like hepatitis and AIDS. Chimps keep those viruses alive in their blood, although they do not get the symptoms.

In 1985 I attended a conference in Chicago that brought home to all the participants the alarming rate at which chimpanzees were disappearing across their range. One hundred years ago there were probably close to two million chimpanzees in twenty-five African nations from the west coast, throughout the equatorial forest belt, and as far east as western Tanzania and Uganda. Forty years ago when I began my study at Gombe there were probably, still, at least one million. Today there are no more than two hundred thousand — probably far fewer — spread over twenty-one nations. Forty years ago one could go by boat along the eastern shore of Lake Tanganyika and see green forests rolled down to the water's edge. If one climbed to the tops of the Rift Escarpment and looked east, again chimp habitat stretched as far as one could see. Today, although the thirty square miles of the Gombe National Park looks the same, outside the park the trees are gone. Cultivated lands press right up to the boundaries. At one time approximately one hundred fifty chimpanzees lived in the park — now there are fewer than one hundred. And these are quite isolated, for beyond the park boundaries the chimps, along with other forest creatures, are gone. Soon the Gombe chimpanzees will show the effects of inbreeding, probably in increased susceptibility to disease.

It is not only the chimpanzees who are suffering. Outside the park the people are suffering also. With the tree cover gone, the soil has lost much of its fertility. During the rainy season more and more of the thin layer of topsoil is washed down the rocky hillsides into the lake, where the fish breeding grounds are becoming silted up. In some places women must dig up the roots of the trees that once were there to get wood to cook food for their families. They have no other way of cooking. These are economically very poor people and they cannot afford to buy food from elsewhere. There are far more human beings living in this area than the land can adequately support — not only as a result of the increase in population that has taken place all around the globe, but also because of the refugees who have poured in from Burundi in the north, and more recently across the lake from the Congo.

How can we justify protecting the precious thirty square miles of forest with its so well known chimpanzees when humans are facing increasing hardship? To try to solve this problem, the Jane Goodall Institute, with initial funding from the European Union, started, in 1995, the Lake Tanganyika Catchment Reforestation and Education project, known as TACARE. Tree nurseries have been established in twenty-eight villages along the lake shore and around the Gombe National Park. These nurseries, mostly cared for by groups of women, provide fruit trees, fast-growing species for building poles, and a variety of indigenous species. Methods of control and prevention of soil erosion, as well as farming methods most suitable for the degraded land, are demonstrated by groups of TACARE women. Conservation education has been introduced into all the schools in the area, including the Roots & Shoots program. Groups of the older students are taken on visits to Gombe so that they can experience the forest that should be their birthright. School projects include the planting of woodlots.

We place great emphasis on empowering women: teaching them skills that will enable them to acquire a small income and providing (in conjunction with the regional health authorities) primary healthcare, especially for women and children. At the same time we have introduced AIDS education and family planning. Most recently a number of micro-credit banks have been established, based on the Grameen system. Scholarships are provided to bright primary school girls so that they can attend secondary school. It has been shown in many parts of the world that, as women become better educated and gain in self-esteem, family size drops.

TACARE offers hope to thousands. The project manager is European, but the rest of the talented team is Tanzanian. None of our projects are simply taken to the village and imposed on them. Every step has been introduced after long discussions with the elders. Only if the village itself *asks* for help is any new project started. And the emphasis is on self-reliance — for example, the initial seeds in the tree nurseries are provided free, but the seedlings are sold and the next lot of seeds must be purchased. Because the project uses money wisely, because there are no huge expenditures on expatriate-level salaries, a number of the big donor agencies have begun channeling monies through TACARE so that a conservation education facility has been built in Kigoma with funds from

UNDP, and we are now building wells and hygienic latrines with funds from UNICEF.

TACARE has shown the local people, the regional authorities, and the central government that we understand that conservation of animals must go hand in hand with improving the lives of people. Human beings, whether we like it or not, are part of the environment. When you and your family are starving, you have no option but to cut down more and ever more trees to grow crops. You know that the cleared land will lead to desertification, but your problem is so immediate that you cannot afford to worry about the future. And so, all across Africa, the forests are gradually retreating before the tidal wave of the mushrooming human population. The great equatorial forest belt is vanishing, transformed into ever-shrinking patches of trees continually nibbled away from the outside in. Deforestation over hundreds of thousands of square miles has led to soil erosion and desertification, which in turn leads to droughts on the one hand, flooding on the other.

Timber companies, mostly from Europe and Asia, are devastating the forests of Central Africa. In West Africa they are almost gone. And it is the timber companies that are the cause of the greatest threat to the continued existence of chimpanzees in their last stronghold, the last great rain forests of Central Africa. Even when responsible timber companies from Europe practice sustainable logging, the animals are at risk. Roads are built into previously virgin forest. People begin to settle along the roads, cutting timber, setting snares, and introducing diseases to all of which the great apes — as well as the pygmies — are susceptible. Pygmy hunters, who have lived in harmony with their forest world for hundreds of years, are now paid to shoot animals not just to feed their families but to feed the two thousand to three thousand people living in the logging camps, the employees and their families. Hunting on this scale is simply not sustainable. When the logging camps have finally moved on, the pygmies will be left in a forest that is silent. No animals will be left.

Worst of all, hunting has become a vast commercial enterprise. Hunters from the towns are now riding the trucks to the end of the road where they shoot everything that can be eaten — chimpanzees, gorillas, bonobos, monkeys, elephants, antelopes, and everything else down to birds and bats. The meat is dried or even loaded fresh onto the trucks that carry the timber into the towns. There it fetches a higher price than that of domestic animals. There is no tradition of domesticating animals for food, and the meat of wild animals is preferred. Loads of bushmeat are being moved illegally across country boundaries. Bushmeat has been identified in exotic restaurants in capital cities around the world. So much money is being made through the bushmeat trade that only a huge and well-organized campaign, involving government officials in the African countries and from countries in the West, and organizations such as the World Bank and IMF, can hope to control it. And if this fails, it is estimated that there will be no great apes — and very little of anything else — remaining in the great Congo Basin in ten to fifteen years' time.

Other species of flora and fauna are becoming extinct before we can even record their existence. The incredible biodiversity of the planet is being destroyed in ecosystems everywhere. World climate is changing. The effects of El Niño and La Niña are becoming more devastating with tornadoes and hurricanes, floods and droughts. Water tables are dropping. The industrialized world — and more and more of the world is becoming industrialized — has poisoned and polluted the air, the water, and the land with chemical emissions and the unsustainable burning of fossil fuels. Our precious protective ozone layer is becoming increasingly damaged.

All of this, along with the human trait of cruelty, has led to massive human suffering. So many countries are ravaged by war and ethnic conflict. The refugee situation is horrendous. Everywhere we see evidence of suffering — poverty, starvation, and disease. In some developing countries the AIDS epidemic has reached epic proportions. A stark headline in the *Tanzania Daily News* in July 2000 announced, "Botswana Faces Extinction" — one in three of the population is HIV-infected. It is thought that the human AIDS epidemic originally stemmed from handling or eating chimpanzees infected with the chimpanzee equivalent of the HIV retrovirus.

So how is it that I can write a book entitled *Reason for Hope?* Do I really have hope for the future, even in the face of so much destruction and suffering? I think this is the question I am asked most often as I travel around the world. The statistics are grim. It is the *rate* of population growth, deforestation, desertification, and so on that is so alarming, and many environmentalists do not, in fact, have much hope for the future. My hope is based on an evolutionary perspective. I had the opportunity to work in Olduvai Gorge, where the Leakeys unearthed individuals representing some of our very early Stone Age ancestors. The first humans emerged into a harsh world, filled with all kinds of large predators with big claws and sharp teeth. Hominids were defenseless creatures, quite small and with no special abilities in the spheres of climbing or even running very fast. They survived by using their brains.

It is our brains that have enabled us to attain a position of domination in the world today. Simple stone and twig tools, like those used by the chimpanzees, have slowly evolved into the sophisticated technology that has taken us to the moon, built giant commercial airlines, and led to the present extraordinary excursions into cyberspace. One hundred years ago it would have been almost impossible to convince anyone that any of these things could possibly come to pass. They would have been written off as science fiction, along with most other modern technology.

By and large modern technology has resulted in much improvement in living conditions around the world. There have been great benefits resulting from sophisticated medical advances, from refrigeration, and so on. Of course, we have also bent our minds to developing weapons of mass destruction, and unfortunately the sheer number of humans, along with the greedy, materialistic, and selfish culture of the Western world, has taken, and wastes, far more than it needs to sustain a good quality of life. But it is not the technology itself that is the problem — it is the way we use it.

Nevertheless, I believe there is hope for the future. I have four main reasons for hope: (1) the sophisticated human brain; (2) the resilience of nature, given a chance and, perhaps, a helping hand; (3) the tremendous energy and commitment of young people around the world once they know the problems and are empowered to act; and finally (4) the indomitable nature of the human spirit.

The greatest hope is that finally, around the world, people in all walks of life have begun, or are beginning, to admit that there are serious environmental and social problems. Conferences on these subjects, often involving high-level government spokespeople, are proliferating. For example, the Earth Summit in Rio (UN Conference on Environment and Development) in 1992, and the climate conference in Kyoto (Third Conference of the Parties) five years later. These did not provide the level of commitment from governments that some of us hoped for, but they were, nevertheless, an encouraging sign that heads of state are actually beginning to think about the environment. This new concern, this admission of the problems, has already led to major advances in environmentally friendly technology that are beginning to replace older methods. Companies are being encouraged, or forced, to clean up the pollutants released into the environment. It is a beginning.

I vividly remember my first drive in an electric car. We zoomed along, silently, at sixty miles per hour, with no emissions. That car would last fifty years and was recyclable. Today there are new technologies that are even more environmentally friendly. Ways of harnessing the power of the sun, wind, and water are proliferating — we make use of solar energy at Gombe. There are hotels that encourage their patrons to refold their towels and to lay notices on their beds if they are prepared to use them a second day. One hotel even announced that, to prevent waste of water and energy and to minimize the release of detergents into the environment, they would only wash bathroom and bedroom linen if the guest called down to the reception desk. That is progress! Moreover, such schemes, so I was told by Disney Hotels, save thousands of dollars a year.

Gary Zeller, a chemist and inventor with a passion for the environment, creates "eco-bricks" out of industrial waste. They are lighter and cheaper than normal building bricks, they are being used to erect more cheaply schools, hospitals, housing complexes, and so on in various parts of the developing world, *and* they are helping to solve waste disposal problems at the same time.

Signs of changing attitudes are everywhere. A couple of years ago as I passed through the Bangkok airport, I saw newspaper headlines warning motorists of large fines if their engines were left idling more than a prescribed number of minutes — to cut down on air pollution. In the airplane, our "amenities bags" were made of organic cotton and all paper was recycled. A newspaper I bought when I arrived in Japan had an article about a big girls' school that was introducing uniforms made of recycled plastic bottles. Environmental problems, and steps being taken to address them, are sprinkled through all the Chinese newspapers.

The resilience of nature is amazing. A while back I visited Nagasaki, where the second atomic bomb was dropped that ended World War II. At the time scientists assumed that nothing would grow there for at least thirty years. In fact, greening took place many years sooner than had been predicted, just as it did after Mount St. Helens erupted. Many rivers that had become stinking channels for sewage and industrial waste have been cleaned up. The river Thames in England and the Potomac where it flows through Washington, D.C., are just two examples.

When I looked at twenty-year-old photographs of the area surrounding Sudbury, in Canada, I was horrified. The landscape was not unlike that which I had seen of Nagasaki after the bomb. In Sudbury the devastation had been caused by the emissions, which had contaminated the air and the groundwater, from two tin mines. The pollution was so bad that human health was seriously at risk, so the citizens decided to clean up their environment. A major operation, lasting more than ten years and involving the laying of tons of lime on the blackened ground as well as control of emissions from the factories, eventually resulted in a landscape where most of the scars have been at least partially healed. The peregrine falcon had been locally extinct for forty years when the cleanup began. It was symbolic of its success that falcons, reintroduced from a captive breeding program, are now flying and nesting in Sudbury again. There are so many, many other stories of a similar nature.

Despite these signs of hope, I encounter hundreds of young people who have lost hope and become discouraged. This leads to apathy. When I think of the damage that humans have inflicted on this planet during my sixty-six years of life, I feel deeply saddened. When I think of the nature of the world when I was a child and compare it with that into which my grandchildren have been born, I feel even worse. This is why I began the program for young people that is called Roots & Shoots. A symbolic name: roots make a firm foundation; shoots seem tiny, but to reach the light they can break open brick walls. The brick walls may be seen as all the horrors that we have inflicted on the planet. The symbolism is one of hope — hundreds and thousands of young people, of roots and shoots around the world, can break through, can make the world a better place.

Each group tackles three hands-on projects showing care and concern for the human community, for animals including domestic animals, for the environment we all share. The precise nature of the projects will depend on the age of the members (they range from preschool to university), their culture, religion, socioeconomic status, and whether they are inner city or rural, from America, Africa, Europe, or Asia. The program began in 1991 in Tanzania, where there are now more than one hundred schools involved from nine regions. Approximately seventy-five thousand children take part in the extracurricular programs. Roots & Shoots groups are now in more than forty countries around the world, with very many — about one thousand — in North America. And keen interest has been shown by the government in China, where we have recently started some fifteen groups in Chinese schools in Shanghai and Beijing.

People ask from where I derive the energy to keep up my crazy travel and speaking schedule (I have not spent longer than three weeks in any one place since 1986 except once, when my mother was very sick). The answer is that it comes to me from the people I meet. Wherever I go I meet truly amazing and wonderful people. One of my heroes is Dr. Muhammad Yunus, who began the Grameen Bank in Bangladesh. It all started when he gave a few coins to a Bangladeshi beggar girl, thirteen years old, who was trying to make a living on the street. He talked to her, and she said that if only she could get some capital, she could start her own business. She wanted the equivalent of 75 cents. So he made her a loan — and she paid him back. This led, eventually, to microcredit banking, which has helped thousands of the poorest of the poor to live in dignity. The Grameen Bank has now made loans in excess of $2 billion, and for the most part those were loans of less than $50.

There are people who tackle impossible tasks and never give up until they succeed. The late Margaret Owen heard about the danger faced by the Californian sea otters. She initiated a crusade that brought her into head-on confrontation with the abalone fishermen — but she was successful. The otters were saved from almost certain extinction. There are people around us who overcome terrible physical disabilities and lead lives of dignity that are inspiring to those around them. Like Gary Haun, who was left 100 percent blind after a helicopter accident while serving in the U.S. Marines. He worked hard to become independent despite his handicap. He became a magician, despite cautions that this would be virtually impossible. He is so good that the children do not realize he is blind. After the show he talks to them about never giving up, no matter what hand life deals you. And, on the side, he learned scuba diving, cross-country skiing, judo and karate, and sky diving.

One of my most precious possessions is the feather of a bald eagle, a sacred bird to the Native Americans. It was given to me by one of their spiritual leaders. It symbolizes the courage of so many of the indigenous people around the world, who, despite horrendous persecution, have hung onto their beliefs and their ancient cultural traditions. Their voice, now, is being heard again. And it is a voice that talks about our spiritual relationship with Earth, which nurtured us, Earth, which has given us everything that we have. It is the only Earth we have. There are signs everywhere that our hearts are awakening. The very morning of my talk to the EPA I read, in the *Washington Post,* that a major road into an industrial development area was moved because a pair of bald eagles had begun nesting nearby — just outside Washington, D.C.

My final point concerns individual action. We tend to sit back and point accusing fingers at the major industrial polluters of the world, at the developers, at all who are harming the environment, and at governments that fail to take a tough stand against them. We ourselves become overwhelmed by the magnitude of the task of restoring harmony once again between ourselves and the natural world. After all, there are six billion human beings on the planet. We are aware of all that we should and should not do with regard to the environment and society. But individually we cannot help but feel, "I am just one person. What I do and do not do cannot possibly make any difference." And so, as more and more people become aware of the problems that threaten our future, there are thousands, then millions of us all thinking, "It doesn't matter what I do. It's just me." Suppose we could turn this "just me-ism" around. Suppose all the millions of us who care realized that what we do each day does make a difference — because our actions will be magnified millions of times over.

In particular we, the affluent people of the world, have enormous power to effect change if we will make ethical choices in what we buy and what we do not buy. We are not forced to buy products from a company with a bad environmental record, or cosmetics tested on animals, or goods manufactured by child slave labor or in sweat-shops overseas. We can choose to buy organic food, free-range eggs, and so on. Of course it will — at least initially — cost a little more, and take time and effort to make these choices. Here the question is simple: are we, or are we not, prepared to pay a few extra dollars to buy the future for our children and grandchildren? We are the consumers, and in a consumer-driven society we have enormous power to effect change — if we act together.

So it comes down to the simple fact that the future lies in our own hands. It is up to us. That is my message. That is my hope for the future.

Appendix   THE EPA'S SEVEN CARDINAL
RULES OF EFFECTIVE RISK
COMMUNICATION

There are no easy prescriptions for successful risk communication. However, those who have studied and participated in recent debates about risk generally agree on seven cardinal rules. These rules apply equally well to the public and private sectors.

Although many of the rules may seem obvious, they are continually and consistently violated in practice. Thus, a useful way to read these rules is to focus on why they are frequently not followed.

RULE 1. ACCEPT AND INVOLVE THE PUBLIC AS A LEGITIMATE PARTNER.

Two basic tenets of risk communication in a democracy are generally understood and accepted. First, people and communities have a right to participate in decisions that affect their lives, their property, and the things they value. Second, the goal of risk communication should not be to diffuse public concerns or avoid action. The goal should be to produce an informed public that is involved, interested, reasonable, thoughtful, solution-oriented, and collaborative.

Guidelines: Demonstrate respect for the public by involving the community early, before important decisions are made. Make it clear that decisions about risks will be based not only on the magnitude and likelihood of occurrence of the physical hazard but also on factors of concern to the public. Involve all parties that have an interest or a stake in the particular risk in question. Adhere to the highest moral and ethical standards: recognize that people hold you accountable.

RULE 2. LISTEN TO THE AUDIENCE.

People are often more concerned about issues such as trust, credibility, control, benefits, competence, voluntariness, fairness, empathy, caring, courtesy, and compassion than about mortality statistics and the details of quantitative risk assessment. If people feel or perceive that they are not being heard, they cannot be expected to listen. Effective risk communication is a two-way activity.

Guidelines: Do not make assumptions about what people know, think, or want done about risks. Take the time to find out what people are thinking: use techniques such as interviews, facilitated discussion groups, advisory groups, toll-

This is a revision and updating of EPA Document OPA-87-020, authored by Vincent T. Covello and Frederick W. Allen.

free numbers, and surveys. Let all parties that have an interest or a stake in the issue be heard. Identify with your audience and try to put yourself in their place. Recognize people's emotions. Let people know that what they said has been understood, and address their concerns as well as yours. Recognize the "hidden agendas," symbolic meanings, and broader social, cultural, economic, or political considerations that often underlie and complicate the task of risk communication.

RULE 3. BE HONEST, FRANK, AND OPEN.

Before a risk message can be accepted, the messenger must be perceived as trustworthy and credible. Therefore, the first goal of risk communication is to establish trust and credibility. Trust and credibility judgments are resistant to change once made. Short-term judgments of trust and credibility are based largely on verbal and nonverbal communications. Long-term judgments of trust and credibility are based largely on actions and performance.

In communicating risk information, trust and credibility are a spokesperson's most precious assets. They are difficult to obtain, and, once lost, they are almost impossible to regain.

Guidelines: State your credentials, but do not ask or expect to be trusted by the public. If an answer is unknown or uncertain, express willingness to get back to the questioner with answers. Make corrections if errors are made. Disclose risk information as soon as possible (emphasizing appropriate reservations about reliability). Do not minimize or exaggerate the level of risk. Speculate only with great caution. If in doubt, lean toward sharing more information, not less—or people may think something significant is being hidden. Discuss data uncertainties, strengths, and weaknesses—including the ones identified by other credible sources. Identify worst-case estimates as such, and cite ranges of risk estimates when appropriate.

RULE 4. COORDINATE AND COLLABORATE WITH OTHER CREDIBLE SOURCES.

Allies can be effective in helping communicate risk information. Few things make risk communication more difficult than conflicts or public disagreements with other credible sources.

Guidelines: Take time to coordinate all interorganizational and intraorganizational communications. Devote effort and resources to the slow, hard work of building bridges, partnerships, and alliances with other organizations. Use credible and authoritative intermediaries. Consult with others to determine who is best able to answer questions about risk. Try to issue communications jointly with other trustworthy sources, such as highly regarded university scientists, physicians, citizen advisory groups, trusted local officials, and national or local opinion leaders.

RULE 5. MEET THE NEEDS OF THE MEDIA.

The media are prime transmitters of information on risks. They play a critical role in setting agendas and in determining outcomes. The media are generally more interested in politics than in risk; in simplicity than in complexity; and in wrongdoing, blame, and danger than in safety.

Guidelines: Be open with and accessible to reporters. Respect their deadlines. Provide information tailored to the needs of each type of media, such as sound bites, graphics, and other visual aids for television. Agree with the reporter in advance about the specific topic of the interview and stick to the topic during it. Prepare a limited number of positive key messages in advance and repeat the messages several times during the interview. Provide background material on complex risk issues. Do not speculate. Say only those things that you are willing to have repeated: everything you say in an interview is on the record. Keep interviews short. Follow up on stories with praise or criticism, as warranted. Try to establish long-term relationships of trust with specific editors and reporters.

RULE 6. SPEAK CLEARLY AND WITH COMPASSION.

Technical language and jargon are useful as professional shorthand, but they are barriers to successful communication with the public. In low-trust, high-concern situations, apparent empathy and caring often carry more weight than numbers and technical facts.

Guidelines: Use clear, nontechnical language. Be sensitive to local norms, such as speech and dress. Strive for brevity, but respect people's information needs and offer to provide more information. Use graphics and other pictorial material to clarify messages. Personalize risk data: use stories, examples, and anecdotes that make technical data come alive. Acknowledge, and say, that any illness, injury, or death is a tragedy and to be avoided. Avoid distant, abstract, unfeeling language about deaths, injuries, and illnesses. Acknowledge and respond (both in words and with actions) to emotions that people express, such as anxiety, fear, anger, outrage, and helplessness. Acknowledge and respond to the distinctions that the public views as important in evaluating risks. Use risk comparisons to help put risks in perspective; but avoid comparisons that ignore distinctions that people consider important. Always try to include a discussion of actions that are under way or can be taken. Promise only that which can be delivered, and follow through.

RULE 7. PLAN CAREFULLY AND EVALUATE PERFORMANCE.

Different goals, audiences, and media require different risk communication strategies. Risk communication will be successful only if it is carefully planned and evaluated.

Guidelines: Begin with clear, explicit objectives — such as providing information to the public, providing reassurance, encouraging protective action and behavior change, stimulating emergency response, or involving stakeholders in dialogue and joint problem solving. Evaluate technical information about risks and know its strengths and weaknesses. Identify important stakeholders and subgroups within the audience. Aim communications at specific stakeholders and subgroups in the audience. Recruit spokespersons with effective presentation and human interaction skills. Train staff — including technical staff — in communication skills: recognize and reward outstanding performance. Pretest messages. Carefully evaluate efforts and learn from mistakes.

CONTRIBUTORS

MAX BAUCUS, U.S. Senator from Montana, was born December 11, 1941, in Helena, Montana, and received his bachelor of arts and law degrees from Stanford University. After serving for a year in the Montana state legislature, he was elected to the U.S. House of Representatives in 1974, and again two years later. He was elected to the U.S. Senate in 1978 and was returned in 1984, 1990, and 1996. The principal Senate author of the landmark 1990 Clean Air Act, he is past chairman and ranking Democratic member on the Senate Environment and Public Works Committee, the ranking Democrat on the Senate Finance Committee, and a member of the Senate Agriculture Committee.

DAVID R. BROWER was born in Berkeley, California, in 1912, grew up in Berkeley, and lived there until his death at age 88. He joined the Sierra Club in 1933, becoming a member of its board in 1941, and served as the organization's first executive director from 1952 to 1969. In 1969 he founded Friends of the Earth, which now has branches in sixty-eight countries. In 1982, he founded the Earth Island Institute, which he served as chairman. John McPhee's book about him, *Encounters with the Archdruid*, has gone through more than twenty printings; he himself wrote three books, including two volumes of his autobiography, *For Earth's Sake: The Life and Times of David Brower*, and *Work in Progress*. He was awarded ten honorary degrees and received the National Parks Association Award in 1956, the Cary-Thomas Award for outstanding publishing in 1964, and the Sierra Club's John Muir Award in 1977. He was nominated for the Nobel Peace Prize in 1978, 1979, and 1998.

VINCENT T. COVELLO, a New Yorker born in 1946, received his Ph.D. in social psychology and sociology from Columbia University. After serving as director of the Risk Assessment Program at the National Science Foundation, he returned to Columbia as associate professor of public health and clinical medicine. Author or editor of more than twenty-five books and seventy-five articles in technical journals, he is former president of the Society for Risk Analysis, from which he also received the Distinguished Service Award. He is currently director of the Center for Risk Communication in New York City.

KATHRYN S. FULLER received her J.D. from the University of Texas and has carried out studies of wildebeest behavior in Tanzania and of coral reef crustacean ecology in the West Indies. She worked at the U.S. Department of Justice, first in the Office of Legal Counsel, then in the Land and Natural Resources Division, where she headed the Wildlife and Marine Resources Section. She joined the World Wildlife Fund in 1982, becoming president and chief executive officer in 1989. Over her years of leadership, World Wildlife Fund has doubled its membership, nearly tripled its revenue, and expanded its presence around the globe. She has received several honorary doctorates and such awards as the UN Environment Programme's Global 500 award, and serves on the board of trustees of Brown University and the board of the Ford Foundation.

JANE GOODALL has become a household name around the world for her pioneering studies of chimpanzees in the wild. At the time she developed it, her method of observing primates closely in their natural habitat without disrupting them was considered unorthodox — today, it is standard practice. She was born in 1934 in London and received her Ph.D. in ethology from Cambridge University in 1965. She has received numerous awards for her scientific work and also for her efforts in conservation and environmental education, and was made Commander, Order of the British Empire (CBE) by the queen in 1995. Her books include *In the Shadow of Man* and *The Chimpanzees of Gombe: Patterns of Behavior.* She is the scientific director of the Gombe Stream Research Center in Tanzania and the director of science and research for the Jane Goodall Institute for Wildlife Research, Education, and Conservation, based in Silver Spring, Maryland.

GARRETT HARDIN was born in Dallas, Texas, in 1915, and grew up in six cities in the Midwest. He received his doctorate from Stanford University in 1941. He was on the faculty of the University of California, Santa Barbara, from 1946 to 1978; since then, he has been emeritus professor of human ecology in the Department of Biological Sciences. He is especially well known for two essays, *The Tragedy of the Commons,* which has been reprinted in over a hundred anthologies in various fields, and *Living on a Lifeboat.* In 1993, his *Living Within Limits: Ecology, Economics and Population Taboos* was awarded that years' Phi Beta Kappa Prize for the best book in the sciences. His most recent volume, *The Ostrich Factor: Our Population Myopia,* appeared in 1999.

THOMAS E. LOVEJOY is a tropical and conservation biologist who received his Ph.D. from Yale University. He is generally credited with having brought the problem of tropical deforestation to the fore as a public issue. He introduced the term "biological diversity" into the environmental lexicon, made the first projections of global species extinction rates, and was the innovator of the concept of debt-for-nature swaps (which have by now exceeded one billion dollars), which is being adopted by a growing number of developing countries. He was elected president of the American Institute of Biological Sciences and of the Society for Conservation Biology, and is now a Smithsonian scientist serving as chief biodiversity adviser to the World Bank. In addition, he is founder of the public television program *Nature* and author or editor of four books, including *Global Warming and Biological Diversity* with R. L. Peters.

AMORY B. LOVINS, born in 1947, is cofounder and co-CEO of Rocky Mountain Institute (www.rmi.org), a fifty-person, independent, entrepreneurial, nonprofit applied research center in Old Snowmass, Colorado. A consultant physicist educated at Harvard and Oxford, he has received an Oxford M.A. (by virtue of being a don), six honorary doctorates, a MacArthur Fellowship, and numerous other awards; briefed fifteen heads of state; published twenty-seven books and several hundred papers; and consulted for scores of industries and governments worldwide. His latest book is *Natural Capitalism: Creating the Next Industrial Revolution*, with Paul Hawken and L. Hunter Lovins, 1999 (www.natcap.org). His next book, due in mid-2001, is *Small Is Profitable: The Hidden Economic Benefits of Making Electrical Resources the Right Size*.

JERRY D. MAHLMAN was born in 1940 and raised in Crawford, Nebraska. With a Ph.D. from Colorado State University, he joined NOAA's Geophysical Fluid Dynamics Laboratory (GFDL), in Princeton, N.J., in 1970, where for more than three decades he has carried out and overseen path-setting research on the physical and chemical behavior of the atmosphere. He was appointed professor of atmospheric and oceanic sciences at Princeton University in 1980 and director of GFDL in 1984. He has received the Presidential Distinguished Rank Award and the Rossby Medal of the American Meteorological Society. He has served as chair of the scientific Advisory Committee for NASA's Mission to Planet Earth and numerous other such groups and has played a leading role in the interpretation of human-caused climate warming for the nonscientific community.

WILLIAM H. MEADOWS has been president of the 200,000-member Wildlife Society since 1996. The only Southerner to lead a major national environmental organization, he was born in 1946 in Montgomery, Alabama, and grew up in Tupelo, Mississippi, and Memphis, Tennessee. After receiving an M.Ed. from Vanderbilt University, he stayed on at his alma mater for twenty years, becoming executive director of Alumni Relations and Development. He then served as vice president for college relations at Sweet Briar College and, from 1992 to 1996, as director of the Sierra Club's Centennial Campaign. In addition to working with church-based social service programs, he has been actively involved with Habitat for Humanity, Common Cause, and the League of Women Voters, for whom he has served on the board of directors.

GAYLORD A. NELSON was the father of Earth Day in 1970, and is the grandfather of all that grew out of that event, such as the National Environmental Protection Act, the Clean Air and Clean Water acts, and the Safe Drinking Water Act. A native of Clear Lake, Wisconsin, he received a law degree from the University of Wisconsin and served as an officer during the Okinawa campaign of World War II. After ten years in the Wisconsin Senate and two stints as governor, in 1962 he began an eighteen-year career in the U.S. Senate, where he authored legislation for preserving the two thousand-mile Appalachian Trail, mandating fuel efficiency in autos, controlling strip mining, and banning the use of DDT and Agent Orange. Since 1981, he has been counselor of the Wilderness Society. In 1995 he was awarded the Presidential Medal of Freedom, the nation's highest civilian award.

JON ROUSH was born in 1937 in Akron, Ohio, received a Ph.D. in medieval literature from the University of California at Berkeley. After teaching there and at Reed College, his interest in environmental issues led him to join the Nature Conservancy, starting as western regional director and eventually becoming chairman of the board of governors. After that, he served as president of the Wilderness Society. He is currently a senior fellow at the Conservation Fund, and he and his wife, Joyce Chinn, are consultants to environmental groups on organizational development and strategy. He has published extensively in the fields of conservation, organizational management, and the arts, and he has received numerous awards for his work in conservation.

WILLIAM D. RUCKELSHAUS was born in Indianapolis in 1932, and received his law degree from Harvard University in 1960. He practiced law in Indiana from 1960 to 1968, during which time he was deputy attorney general of the state and, from 1967 to 1969, majority leader of the Indiana House of Representatives. President Nixon created the U.S. Environmental Protection Agency in 1970 and named him to be its first administrator. In 1973, he became acting director of the Federal Bureau of Investigation and later was named deputy attorney general of the U.S. Department of Justice. When President Reagan reappointed him as the fifth administrator of the EPA, the Senate confirmed him with a 97-0 vote. After serving as chairman of the board of Browning-Ferris Industries, he is now a principal of the Madrona Investment Group, LLC.

PETER M. SANDMAN, born in 1945 in New York City and raised in nearby White Plains, holds a Ph.D. in communications from Stanford University. He was professor of environmental journalism at Rutgers University for fifteen years and director of the Environmental Communications Research Program. He also held an appointment in the Department of Environmental and Community Medicine at the Robert Wood Johnson Medical School. The author of numerous articles in the scholarly and popular presses, he is a specialist in the design of nonprofit information and education campaigns and is currently a self-employed risk communication consultant.

FRED L. SMITH, JR., was born in Mobile, Alabama, in 1940. He has undertaken graduate work in operations research at the University of Pennsylvania, is coeditor of the book *Environmental Politics: Public Costs, Private Rewards,* and has contributed chapters to various books, including the epilogue to *The True State of the Planet.* He has published in the *Wall Street Journal,* the *New York Times,* and numerous public policy journals and is a frequent guest on national talk shows such as *Crossfire.* After working as a senior policy analyst at the EPA, he founded and is president of the Competitive Enterprise Institute (www.cei.org), a free-market public interest group based in Washington, D.C., which the *Wall Street Journal* called "the best environmental think tank in the country."

R. E. (TED) TURNER was born in Cincinnati in 1938, and nine years later his family moved to Savannah. He graduated from Brown University. After several years with Turner Advertising, in 1970 he purchased Channel 17 in Atlanta, and in 1980 he began the Cable News Network (CNN). He is currently vice-chairman of Time Warner Inc., where, among other things, he oversees the company's sports teams — the Atlanta Braves, Hawks, and Thrashers. Serving on a number of environmental and philanthropic boards, he has focused much of his energy and influence on the important issues of our time — how we act toward one another, and how we treat our Earth. He created the Goodwill Games, was cofounder and first chairman of the board of the Better World Society, which produces and distributes television programming on critical global issues, and recently established the United Nations Foundation to support UN causes. He is also president of the Turner Foundation, a private, family foundation that has supported hundreds of environmental organizations.

BEN J. WATTENBERG is a 1955 graduate of Hobart College, from which he received an honorary doctor of laws degree in 1975. Before acting as a campaign adviser in Senator Hubert Humphrey's 1970 Senate race and in Senator Henry Jackson's 1972 and 1976 bids for the Democratic presidential nomination, he was an aide and speechwriter for President Lyndon Johnson from 1966 to 1968. He was appointed to the Presidential Advisory Board for Ambassadorial Appointments by President Carter in 1977, and by President Reagan in 1981 to the Board for International Broadcasting (which oversees the activities of Radio Free Europe and Radio Liberty), of which he became vice-chairman. He is currently a senior fellow at the American Enterprise Institute, in Washington, D.C., is the host of *Think Tank,* seen weekly on public television, and writes a weekly syndicated column that appears in two hundred newspapers. His most recent book is *Values Matter Most: How Democrats or Republicans Can Win, and Renew the American Way of Life* (1995).

ANTHONY B. WOLBARST received his Ph.D. in physics from Dartmouth in 1970. Formerly at Harvard Medical School and the National Cancer Institute, he is currently a senior scientific adviser at the U.S. Environmental Protection Agency and an adjunct associate professor at Georgetown University Medical School. He is the editor of *Environment in Peril* (Smithsonian Press, 1991) and the author of two texts: *Symmetry and Quantum Systems: An Introduction to Group Representations* and *Physics of Radiology.* His book for the general public, *Looking Within: How X-ray, CT, Nuclear Medicine, MRI, Ultrasound, and Other Medical Images Are Created, and How They Help Physicians Save Lives,* was published by the University of California Press in 1999.

INDEX

Praise for
Address: House of Corrections
and **Monice Mitchell Simms**

"Monice Mitchell Simms is a highly
gifted writer whose artistic voice and
literary style commands our attention
and praise."
- **Cornel West**

"Monice Mitchell Simms writes with
passion and authenticity in this
emotionally gripping story of family,
struggle and triumph."
- **Lyah Beth LeFlore,** NY
Times Bestselling Author
& Essence Bestseller

"Each of us has a gift. And for each
gift that we have, I believe, there's
corresponding need. When your gift
connects with its' need, then you are
walking in your purpose.

Monice Mitchell Simms has a gift. A
gift of writing. And there's a need for
that gift. Her gift has now met the
need and *Address: House of
Corrections* is the purpose.

It's a brilliant book. She's a
brilliant writer."
– **Tavis Smiley**

ABOUT THE AUTHOR

Monice Mitchell Simms is a talented writer, filmmaker and veteran journalist who penned *Stop the Great War* – a play she later rewrote and produced as a tele-drama for public television. She also brought to life *Carmin's Choice* – a Showtime showcase film about a female ex convict, and directed *Rain* - a Showtime showcase film about World War III – which she also wrote.

Producer of the award-winning television public service announcement, *Power*, Monice also recently ventured into the world of radio/television by producing *Prepare for Love*, an Internet relationship talk show hosted by her husband and relationship coach, Ryeal Simms. She also recently produced and edited the Internet trailer and bonus footage for the feature documentary, *Stand*; directed *Breaking the Silence*, public service announcement about teen dating violence sponsored by Verizon; and produced and edited a leadership documentary and public service announcement series for youth commissioned by the Tavis Smiley Foundation.

Currently, Monice is penning her second book of poetry, *Brighter This Time*. She is also producing and directing the audio digi-book series based on her debut novel, *Address: House of Corrections*, and writing *The Mailman's Daughter*, the second novel in the three book series inspired by the life of her mother.